Can the Catholic Church be reconciled with progress, liberalism, and modern civilization? An adequate response to such a question can only be given if we understand what modern civilization is, what the Church is, and what the results of various approaches of the later to the former have been. John Rao's wide ranging and profound writings are indispensable for coming to such an understanding.

—PATER EDMUND WALDSTEIN, O.Cist., lecturer in moral theology, Heiligenkreuz, Austria

Soon after I first met John Rao, a highly respected priest commented to me that Dr. Rao was a man completely emancipated from the assumptions of Modernism and Americanism. Over the past decade or so that I've come to know him, I have found this remark to be entirely true. As this excellent volume reveals, Dr. Rao possesses a profoundly Catholic mind, steeped in history—all the more important in an age of civilisational amnesia, when debates corrupt into competing abstractions, unanchored from the historical process by which God's salvation of mankind unfolds. In this work, Dr. Rao takes us on a journey through the dramas and controversies of Christendom's history, and by so doing he roots us in the history that is *ours*, for which reason we are profoundly indebted to him.

—SEBASTIAN MORELLO, author of *The World as God's Icon* and *Conservatism and Grace: The Conservative Case for Religion by Establishment*

Professor Rao's learning, devotion to history, love of the Faith, eye for telling incident, and vivid writing are all on display in his multifaceted presentation of the struggles of the Church in the modern world. Readers will deepen their understanding of the current state of the Church, how it came about, its deep background, and how it can be bettered.

—JAMES KALB, lawyer, writer, and Catholic convert

Dr. John Rao is an extraordinary figure within the contemporary traditionalist movement. This is due to the fact that he is someone who cultivates history philosophically. It is what allows him to evade the all too frequent errors of leniency, conservatism, and Americanism. Moreover, he is not only a profound intellectual but also an enthusiastic and effective systematizer of ideas.

—MIGUEL AYUSO, Ph.D., Professor of Political Science and Constitutional Law, Comillas Pontifical University in Madrid

Those who know him have long recognized that John Rao has an encyclopedic knowledge of European civilization and the history of Christendom, which he wears lightly. This new, welcome collection of essays, however, will finally introduce him to a new generation of readers. His intricate knowledge of episodes and events, people and places—which ranges from the Baroque spirit in Spain, to resistance to Garibaldi's revolutionary troops in Italy, to the challenges of the modern papacy—are sure to educate, enthrall, and inspire readers everywhere.

—ALVINO-MARIO FANTINI, editor-in-chief, *The European Conservative*, and director of the Centre Européen de Documentation et d'Information

THE MYSTICAL BODY
ON ITS MARCH THROUGH TIME

For the Whole Christ

THE COLLECTED WORKS
OF DR. JOHN RAO

VOLUME 2
The Mystical Body
on its
March Through Time

AROUCA
PRESS

ISBN: 978-1-990685-99-6 (pbk)
ISBN: 978-1-998492-00-8 (hc)

Arouca Press
PO Box 55003
Bridgeport PO
Waterloo, ON N2J 0A5
Canada
www.aroucapress.com
Send inquiries to info@aroucapress.com

CONTENTS

The Word Incarnate, "The Whole Christ," and the Drama of Truth

"When Christ was on earth he prayed in his human
nature, and prayed to the Father in the name of his
body, and when he prayed, drops of blood flowed
from his whole body. So it is written in the Gospel:
Jesus prayed with earnest prayer, and sweated blood
(Luke 22:44). What is this blood streaming from his
whole body but the martyrdom of the whole Church?"
—ST. AUGUSTINE, *Commentary on Psalm 141*

THERE IS NO DOUBT IN MY MIND THAT MY career was aimed in the direction that it actually took due to a reading of Fr. Emile Mersch, S.J.'s (1890–1940) *The Whole Christ*, a title coming from St. Augustine's commentary on the Psalms concerning the relationship between Our Lord and His Church. It was this study of the development of the doctrine of the Mystical Body that drove home to me both the unsurpassable dignity, as well as the day-to-day authority, of the institution that continues Christ's presence among us in a supernatural and natural manner until the end of time. But the growth and elaboration of that doctrine has, of course, entailed the necessity of clarifying the fact that the heads and ordinary members of the Mystical Body are themselves fallen human beings, struggling to gain their salvation and obliged *freely* to accept the infallible guidance and sacramental medicine offered to them by the Word Incarnate and the Holy Spirit in order to fulfill their specific tasks properly.

Sometimes Catholics have all fulfilled their various responsibilities smoothly, and with joy; sometimes they seem to have done their best to shirk their differing appointed roles, causing long-term damage to the Bride of Christ until their free will led them to do what the unfailing presence and promise of Our Lord had always given them the opportunity to accomplish; sometimes the clerical heads are to be praised for their steadfastness, and the laity chastised; sometimes it has worked strikingly the other way round. The Drama of Truth that is the story of the Mystical Body in history is therefore filled with the episodes of comic tragedy and tragic comedy that the Greek founders of the theater already somehow sensed it would be before this imperfect Seed of the Logos was itself offered to Christianity, also to be corrected and transformed in Christ for the edification of the faithful.

Allow me to mention one example of the Drama of Truth not covered by the articles in this volume, but akin to them: the confirmation of the Nicene dogmatic affirmation of the Son being consubstantial with the Father in the word *homoousios*. We do not know who suggested the use of this term at that First Ecumenical Council, but we are told that the overwhelming number of the Nicene Fathers enthusiastically accepted it. Nevertheless, the years between 325 and the First Council of Constantinople in 381 saw bitter struggles over that word, with St. Athanasius standing at the head of those defending it against a torturous succession of politically motivated maneuvers to alter it to serve the purposes of everyone from members of the Roman imperial bureaucracy to the time-serving "court bishops" adulating the emperors and "accompanying" the plans of their civil servants. Words, formulae, provincial councils, and forced adhesions to their contrived "truth" came and went, with arrests and exile becoming the fate of a good number of the remaining defenders of Nicaea.

The *homoousios* teaching—the true teaching—won the day, as it had to win it, but not without its being sharpened in the midst of the tragic turmoil. St. Athanasius himself realized that many of the supporters of the use of another term—*homoiousios*, or "similar in substance"—were led to accept this word because the Nicene formula had been used beforehand by some important churchmen in a heretical sense, so as to blur all distinction between the Father and the Son, making the latter seem to be nothing other than a different manifestation of the former. The great Bishop of Alexandria came to see the need to explain *homoousios* in a way that would definitively exclude such falsities.

And yet despite admitting that those insisting upon the other formula, with its extra *iota*, could actually do the same thing with their teaching, clarifying its meaning in an orthodox manner, he recognized that this word was now so hopelessly entwined with the whole wretched story of manifold mundane manipulations of the doctrine of the first council's Fathers as never to be "above suspicion" and free from further abuse. It was either the formula of Nicaea or exposure to further potential compliance with the powers that be. *Homoousios* was baptized in blood; another episode in the Drama of Truth.

Allow me to finish my introductory comments with reference to another example of that Drama in the life of the Word Incarnate in His Mystical Body, one with contemporary importance. Christ indeed came "to set men free", and Catholicism is the greatest friend of human liberty in world history. But the concepts of "freedom" and "liberty" have been so badly twisted in meaning by the dominant forces of an anti-Christian "modernity" that no matter how much they truly are at the center of the work of Our Lord, they cannot be written on our battle flag today. They can only retain their proper—and admittedly splendid—significance if the sinful heads and members of the Church first and foremost look for and accept the guidance of Our Lord, always present in her midst, but with Whom they must freely cooperate until the end of time. This is why Catholics in our revolutionary world, which refuses to put freedom and liberty in its proper context, must follow the magnificent example of the *Cristeros* in Mexico, which was also baptized in blood, in placing the contemporary Drama of Truth underneath the banner of the doctrine of the Social Kingship of Christ. For that, in effect, is exactly what those winning out in the other episodes of the Drama of Truth of the Whole Christ discussed in this volume also did, over and over again. It is only through focus on the Word Incarnate giving the Whole Christ its life and the Drama of Truth its happy ending that Church History has revealed to us how Christendom is effectively to be constructed to lead us to enjoyment eternally of the Music of the Spheres.

Viva Cristo Rey!

I

Christmas, 800[†]

CHRISTMASTIDE, 800, WAS THE SEASON
that Charles the Great, the King of the Franks, was crowned
Roman Emperor by Pope Leo III in the Eternal City. It was the
season in which the Triple Alliance of Christianity, Roman culture
and the Germans—whose most important tribe was the Franks—was
solemnly confirmed. Indeed, it was the season in which a stamp of
approval was placed upon the entire direction of medieval Catholic
civilization in the heart of the Christian camp itself. And because
of what it was, Christmastide, 800 still remains a beacon light for
Catholics in December of 1984.

True, the reader who investigates the events of Christmastide,
800, as they happened, may initially be disappointed. After all,
he will observe that these events hardly unfolded in any clear
and consistent fashion, and that their exact character has been
debated for the past 1184 years. Scholars have wondered whether
Charles the Great ever desired the bestowal of this honor in Rome.
They have asked if Pope Leo III planned it in order to forestall
a self-coronation by Charles that might have symbolized a rele-
gation of the Papacy to a subordinate role in western life. Many
have tried to determine whether Charles was ultimately flattered
or displeased by the gesture, and to imagine what it was that the
Romans thought about the revival of an Empire that a number of
them, still loyal to Constantinople, did not even consider to be dead.
In short, given the confused and potentially divisive character of
Christmastide, 800, the intelligent reader might understandably
accuse me of over-dramatizing its ultimate significance.

This understandable accusation would, I think, be false. It
would be false, first of all, because of the fact that the importance
of any given event is rarely clear, in all its facets, as it takes place.
How frequently do actions that seemed to have been crucial at
the moment in which they were undertaken appear, later, to have
been nothing other than groundless illusions with no meaning at

---

† First published in *The Wanderer*, December 25, 1984.

all? And how often, in contrast, does a decision made confusedly, under the pressure of circumstances and with a variety of motives in mind, seem, after a while, to have really been the logical conclusion of a series of previous steps; to have been firmly rooted in well-tilled soil? I would argue that the confusion of Christmastide, 800, masked a logic that was centuries-long in its development.

The events of Christmastide, 800, however bewildering in their initial appearance, were clearly the solemn confirmation of a Triple Alliance conceived in the 490s in the former Roman province of Gaul. Gaul had witnessed the settlement of Germanic allies of Rome within its borders during the Fourth Century and the invasion of a number of German enemies in the next. All these various tribes began battling among themselves for supremacy as the imperial government collapsed. Their conflicts were watched with a certain indifference by the Gallo-Roman population, which felt that it would lose, regardless of the group of barbarians that triumphed. None of the Germans were Catholics; they were all either pagans or Arian heretics. None had a real sense of the spirit that moved classical civilization, or a grasp of its laws, its art and its philosophy. War was their occupation, just as war was their sport. Classicism and Christianity were the inevitable victims in this reign of the gladiators.

Clovis, the King of the Franks, a tribe which had moved into Gaul as Roman allies, began to change the picture radically. He may or may not have had religious sentiments; he may or may not have appreciated Roman culture. Clovis definitely did want one thing, though. He wished to see the strength of his tribe increase. Moreover, he felt that he had found a key to this end in the acceptance of Catholicism. Catholic Baptism would signify association not simply with orthodoxy, but, because of Christian connection with the Empire, union with the Roman imperial ideal also. The result might well be to galvanize an indifferent local population for the support of his particular German tribe as its friend and protector. Clovis and the Franks did enter the Church; many Gallo-Romans did, thus, rally to their cause; a Triple Alliance had indeed been conceived.

Conception is not birth, however, and the Alliance conceived by Clovis caused western Europe a long and difficult pregnancy. Rome was not built in a day, and it proved to be impossible to construct either Rome or a Catholic sense of things in Frankish Gaul overnight. Neither Clovis nor his descendants were able to create a legal, cultural and religious order that might begin to please a serious Roman or a serious Catholic. Barbarous concepts began to corrupt Christian teachings and practices. There was no development of a state administration worthy of the Roman name. The Merovingian Dynasty, as Clovis' line was known, could not even sustain itself, and became more inbred and more incompetent as time went on.

Assistants to the king, called Mayors of the Palace, soon found themselves doing the job of the useless Merovingian monarchs. The task of Mayor gradually fell into the hands of another family, the Carolingian. One of the Carolingian Mayors, Pepin, was responsible for finally "delivering" the Alliance that was floundering in the medieval European womb. Pepin, by the 740s and 750s, wished to have the title of King of the Franks, since he was already doing the work that this entailed. He knew that the prestige of his father, Charles the Hammer, who had thrown back the Moslem invasion of Gaul in the 730s, had given his family great stature among the Frankish warriors. Yet something more than military prestige was needed to secure the title from an already reigning chieftain-king. That something else, he felt, was a more serious and explicit tie with the Church and with the mission of Rome.

Both the Church and Rome needed something from Pepin at the same time. St. Boniface, the Benedictine Apostle to the Germans, wished protection from the tribe of the Saxons, which was placing serious obstacles in the path of his work of conversion. He also wanted a chance for the Benedictines and the Benedictine spirit to reform the corrupted Church of the Frankish Kingdom, and give it a real Catholic sense. Such a reform would inevitably strengthen Roman influence among the Franks, since St. Benedict's Rule was a model of classical concepts of balance and law. Pepin had the ability to respond to both of Boniface's desires.

Moreover, Rome, now ruled by the Popes, was desperately in search of a shield and a buckler. The tribe of the Lombards was ravaging Italy and threatening the Eternal City. Rome's former protectors, the Eastern Roman Emperors, troubled by almost constant Moslem incursions, could no longer be called upon to perform this function. The Papacy was not even certain that it

3

wanted them to do so, given the fact that they had adopted the Iconoclast, or image-smashing heresy, and had begun to punish Rome in a variety of ways, economic as well as spiritual, for not following them down this unfortunate pathway. Perhaps, the popes reasoned, a German tribe seeking to bind itself to the Roman ideal might be trusted where New Rome, Constantinople, had failed.

Pepin, Boniface, and the Papacy seized their opportunity. The Benedictine Rule conquered the Frankish realm. Pepin offered the Benedictines assistance outside its borders. Rome gave him permission to replace his Merovingian predecessor on grounds of incompetence. Pepin promised to deal with the Lombards. St. Boniface, and then Pope Stephen II, made the long journey to the court of Pepin to give ceremonial form to the deposition and the Carolingian assumption of power. The new King of the Franks was anointed in the manner of David, who was marked out by Samuel as the replacement for Saul. Pepin swore an oath to defend the Faith, and, with it, therefore, the Roman order that Christianity had incorporated into its life and law. Frankish warriors expressed their approval when the ceremony was concluded. The Alliance conceived by Clovis, but left floundering in its womb by his descendants, had been brought into the light of day.

Charles the Great was Pepin's son. He took it upon himself to complete his father's work. This he did with a fury, and sometimes in unacceptable fashion. He defeated the Lombards and made himself their king. He devastated the Saxons and had them baptized. Benedictine monasteries were founded and funded by him throughout his domains. An attempt was made to provide serious education for the clergy, and to raise the moral and cultural level of the active population as a whole. Even Charles' failures, such as his inability to penetrate deeply into Moslem Spain, provided Western Christendom with some of its greatest chivalric legends for the future. It was thus only fitting that his work be rewarded by his coronation as Roman Emperor in Christmastide, 800. And it is thus only fitting that that coronation be seen as the confirmation of the Alliance conceived by Clovis and given birth by Pepin.

But there is a second and perhaps more profound reason for underlining the significance of the events of Christmastide, 800.

4

This is the fact that historical actions can have a symbolic meaning distinct from their literal sense. It can sometimes even be the symbolic meaning that has the greater influence upon the future of the world.

Western History is filled with illustrations of this truth. Rome, to take but one conspicuous example, conquered the Mediterranean world for a wide variety of less than elevated motives. The logic of its self-interested actions can be demonstrated through the confusion of events, just as the logic of the coronation of Charles the Great can be traced back to the decisions of Clovis and Pepin. How have the literal motives responsible for Rome's conquests actually influenced the movement of history? Little at all. One cannot say the same for the symbolic meaning of its victories. This was outlined by Greek historians like Polybius, who emphasized Rome's character as a place of law, order and justice, and her mission to conquer in order to spread these same goods to the rest of the world. The works written by such historians were used to educate the children of Roman notables. Subsequent generations thus publicly spoke as though this mission of law, order and justice were indeed the reason for the growth of the Empire. Rome became a concrete model for international organization and justice by no means warranted by its original intentions and activity. It is in this form that Rome continues to have meaning for us today.

It seems to me that there is an enormously important symbolic meaning in the events of Christmastide, 800 as well, indicated both by the way in which the Triple Alliance evolved and the season chosen for its solemn confirmation. The symbolic meaning of these events ought to be able to move us, in our own troubled day, to the same kind of creative ventures that it moved the Triple Alliance itself. What is it that distinguished Charles the Great, and, before him, Pepin, Clovis, and the Franks as a whole? What is it that set St. Boniface and the Benedictines apart? What is it that characterized the popes active in the work of the Alliance? What did they all symbolize? Courageous affirmation, commitment and action; courage in the midst of brutal realities that would have led others to despair.

The conditions for creating a new civilization, for giving life to a Holy Roman Empire of the German Nation were horrendous. They would have made a Mario Cuomo wring his hands in anguish.

The half-barbaric Franks still had little idea of the real significance of the Roman outlook at the time of Charles' coronation.
Greco-Roman conceptions of the state as an organized, administrative entity that provided for the common good and continued
beyond the lifetime of a given conquering chieftain remained quite
alien to them. St. Boniface, more than anyone, knew the crudity of
this people and the arbitrariness of its leaders. The papacy was all
too aware of the dangers that might result from Frankish domination and barbarization. No one need have done anything, given the
risks. Men often have preferred to go down to destruction rather
than alter one scene in a familiar picture. Germanic stupidities
could easily have been taken as an excuse to avoid contact with
the Franks entirely, and to yearn for some future Eastern Roman
aid. Men might have gathered in St. Peter's during a Lombard
invasion and waited for an angel to save them, as the population
of Constantinople gathered in Hagia Sophia during the Turkish
sack centuries later. The weakness of Rome and of the Christian
position could readily have been used by the Franks to justify
rejection of both. Men of strength have frequently crushed what
was fragile and difficult to understand. But Charles and Leo, Pepin,
Boniface and Stephen were men of courage, of affirmation and of
action. They did not deny the magnitude of their problems; they
simply chose to confront them rather than to run.

The courage of these people, their acceptance of opportunities and labors against appalling odds, can be seen in the work
of Charles the Great and Alcuin, the Benedictine scholar, with
regard to education. Charles himself, as his biographer notes, could
never master the alphabet, much less grasp the wisdom of the ages.
His Frankish subjects were, for the most part, infinitely more barbaric. Few places, with the possible exception of a contemporary
American university, could have offered a more dismal prospect
for intellectual development than the Kingdom of the Franks.

But Charles, nevertheless, wanted learning, and called Alcuin
from England to head a Benedictine school at Aix-la-Chapelle, the
Frankish capital. And Alcuin responded by presenting a breath-
taking vision of what might be achieved. He wrote to Charles of
the hope of establishing nothing less than a New Athens in the
Kingdom of the Franks. This New Athens, he explained, would be
infinitely greater than the Athens of old, because of the fact that

the modern center of learning would have more than the teachings of Plato and Aristotle to inspire it. It would be illumined, in addition, by the seven-fold gifts of the Holy Spirit. Alcuin envisaged an expanding intellectual universe in the center of what was, at the moment, nothing more than a Kingdom of Gladiators! The present realities of this world of warriors would have made other wise men tremble rather than act. But the "realists" were correct only in the short run; St. Thomas, the University of Paris, Chartres, Giotto and Dante show us who was actually right.

Christmastide was also the symbolically appropriate season in which to confirm the Triple Alliance. Why? Because the Christmas story demonstrates that courageous affirmation, commitment and action in the midst of brutal realities are built into the divine plan as a whole. There are innumerable fearless "leaps" indicated in the events surrounding Christ's birth and earliest days. They begin in the supernatural realm. God the Father courageously committed Himself to His own Creation, knowing that this dedication would lead to His Son's torture and death. He accepted the fact that the Divine Word would enter the world not in glory and power, as was His due, but through a poor and humble woman, and as a helpless child. Mary courageously allowed a pregnancy whose full consequences she did not understand, and Joseph stood by her in circumstances that must have been baffling to him. Both grasped perfectly only one thing: the misery that the apparent dishonor involved would entail them.

One example of courageous affirmation and commitment that forms part of the Christmas story stands out as most germane to my present argument. This is the fearless dedication to the Christ child of the Three Wise Men of the Orient, who represent both kingly power and learning. It is one of the great ironies of existence that those most interested in power often refuse to take the steps that can make their strength endure for generations. The military man and the statesman often reject contemptuously the serious wisdom that would root their work in a great mission and give it staying power. We are told that the Three Wise Men were kings. As kings, they had risen above the temptation to rely on brute force alone. They had allied their strength with learning.

Another of life's great ironies is the fact that those most interested in the search for truth are often the least willing to commit themselves to it when it is discovered. The life of learning is often accompanied by a paralysis of the will. This is partly due to the scholar's knowledge of the complexities of reaching definite conclusions, and partly the cause of a fear that his own importance will diminish should truth be actually attained. Paralysis frequently ends in ridicule of the whole concept of truth, especially if truths are presented from humble and non-academic sources.

All this makes the actions of the Three Wise Men the more brilliant. They came from the cradle of civilization, and carried with them the esoteric wisdom of ancient Mesopotamia, Egypt and Persia. It is also possible to take them as being symbols of ancient Greek wisdom and its problems, since the East had been partially Hellenized after Alexander the Great's conquests. Such men could have been expected to stay at home, continue their research and await workshop reports after noticing the Star of Bethlehem. Instead, the Three Wise Men took to the road. They may have had endless discussions over the meaning of it all on the way to Bethlehem. But when they arrived, the representatives of an often paralytic enterprise bent their knees. The emissaries of the cradle of civilization eagerly paid homage before the cradle of a new, higher and decisive civilizing force. The Wise Men, violating all of the best principles of academic objectivity, abandoning all the arrogance of political and military might, placed their wisdom and strength at the service of a helpless child; a helpless child cared for by poor, dishonored parents, who were away from home at the bidding of a distant emperor. Not even a scholar! Not even a conqueror! What of the ridicule of fellow kings and fellow wise men before their action? What of the possible conflicts of human knowledge and faith, of state and church? Later, the Wise Men, in a sense, answered. We will work them out later. The Truth is there before us in human form, and He has promised not to reject us, so long as we accept Him. Our future difficulties must not prevent our present abandonment to the Truth.

Sometimes one sees paintings in which the Three Wise Men are joined by others in their homage to the Christ child. I should like to think that their entourage consisted of men and women who had been tempted by life's risks and horrors to run, to hide and to despair. I should also like to think that these men and women were encouraged by the courageous commitment of the representatives of learning and power to embrace life's risks in the Truth. After all, three kings stood before them who had not been deterred from combining knowledge and power, despite the obvious problems involved. These same kings were now ready to unite such explosive forces with courageous affirmation of the helpless Christ child. If they were not afraid, either of the world or of God, why should anyone else be? Why flee from love, because of the dangers of loving properly, or from sex, because of its possible abuse, or marriage, because divorce and cynicism are everywhere to be feared? Why hide from song and dance, from art and beauty, from the table and the vineyard, simply due to the risk of their misuse? Bring them courageously into the sight of the living God, who will not reject them, so long as He is accepted. Embrace the world in Christ, and begin the adventure of life. The future difficulties will be worked out along the road.

I would paint an extremely crowded canvas of the visit of the Wise Men to Bethlehem. I would draw behind the Magi the joyous faces of representatives of all aspects and walks of life; the joyous faces of all those who had realized that courageous commitment to the Son of God gave them the chance—their only real chance—to embrace life, despite life's brutal realities. In the distance, I would draw the Coronation of Charles the Great, and, behind this scene, the fruits of the courageous affirmation that it symbolized, Christian civilization in all its glory. Finally, far away from the rest, I would sketch in the Heavenly Jerusalem. Because God's reward for courageous affirmation of life in the Truth is eternity.

The Christmas story need not have taken place at all. The Wise Men might have been frightened by the risks entailed for their reputation and power, and never set out on their journey. No crowd would have gathered to follow them. Joseph might have abandoned Mary: too much trouble and little happiness with that woman! Mary could have asked for some type of insurance policy from God. The Father might, with full justification, have admitted that His Creation was a cynic's delight, and left it on its own. There would have been no painting, no coronation, no Christian civilization, no Heavenly Jerusalem. For the prize for failure to affirm life in the Truth, with all its risks and hardships, is eternal death.

Christmas was, indeed, the perfect season in which to crown Charles the Great as Roman Emperor. Charles' coronation was, indeed, the symbol of a Triple Alliance of courageous commitment long in preparation. That courageous commitment remains the symbolic truth of the entire event. And what meaning does it have for us today? It has a meaning greater than perhaps ever before.

There is no more hopeless situation than the one that Christendom faces now. Everything that Christianity stands for is, for all intents and purposes, in ruins. Modern life is one enormous danger and risk. Even the simple things of life have become poisonous. It is enormously tempting for Catholics to run and hide from the world, as though the world and the world's wonders were our mortal enemies. Christmastide, 800, tells us something different. It tells us to rush in where "wise men" less sage than the eastern kings fear to tread. The work of our noble and courageous ancestors reminds us that the Christ child is still there, and that with orthodoxy and a little backbone, there is nothing in this entire universe that we need fear. What will our Christian commitment to this world produce? No one knows. I assure you that everyone, from St. Augustine to Charles the Great, would have been mightily surprised by the character of the High Middle Ages. Christmastide, 800, teaches us to march courageously into 1985, a full supply of weapons and handkerchiefs in hand (for evils and tears one will encounter therein), shouting the same acclamations sung by the Carolingians themselves: *Christus vincit, Christus regnat, Christus imperat!*

2

Cluny and the Reform of the Church in the Middle Ages[†]

I

CONTEMPORARY CATHOLICS OUGHT TO be more familiar with Church History in the West in the period extending from the death of Charlemagne in 814 until the Eleventh Century. Familiarity with this era would benefit them in three ways. An introduction to the nightmare faced by the Church in the Ninth and Tenth Centuries would, first of all, enable them to keep their balance in the midst of the current debacle. Secondly, such knowledge would give them a much-needed sense of pride in the accomplishments of those among their ancestors who, beginning in the 900s, gradually nursed the wounded Body of Christ back to health. Finally, it is permissible to entertain the hope that the example offered by a miraculous turnabout in the Church's fortunes may inspire them to a reconstruction of the shattered foundations of Christendom at the present time.

Although many works have been written on the horrors of the Church's position after Charlemagne's death, and on the major reform that eventually reduced them to manageable proportions, Christopher Dawson's *The Making of Europe* ought to be reserved a place of honor. Some historians lose themselves in a description of the endless variety of petty actions and banal thinking that accompany every human endeavor, the most wicked as well as the most sublime. They cannot see the forest for the trees. Dawson never allows the accumulation of "data" to clutter his vision of the true tragedy and glory that unfolds before him. It is that vision, above all, which guides this article.

II

One cannot begin to understand the deformation of the Ninth and Tenth Centuries without some grasp of the events of the final stages of Roman Imperial History in the 300s and 400s AD. The Empire, by

---

† First published in *The Wanderer*, February 2, 1984.

that time, was an officially Catholic entity, though it did not quite grasp exactly what this signified. It was especially confused with regard to the question of the relationship of the Church hierarchy to the State. Christian bishops, due to their influence upon the believing population, had assumed an importance and responsibility often exceeding that of the representatives of the Emperor. This frequently irritated those cultivated pagans and nominal Christians who, at best, had accepted the rise of the Church as a fait accompli. Such men had sought only to utilize Catholicism and its prestige for the propping up of that top-heavy, bureaucratic, uninspiring monster of a State that the Empire had become.

The various German tribes that ransacked Roman territories in the late Fourth and Fifth Centuries were, with rare exceptions, awed by the grandeur of the Empire. Nevertheless, their presence in large numbers was not welcome. Though impressed by the Roman State, the German tribes had no conception of its meaning. They thought of authority in terms of a personal relationship between a warrior and a chieftain. Loyalty, for them, was to flesh and blood, and not to an abstract institution. There was always the potential for a multiplicity of warrior-chieftain relationships to spring up within the structure of the same tribe, thus dividing its population and its lands. The idea that a unified domain and people had to be maintained, generation to generation, was alien to the German mentality. Moreover, German tribes were either pagan or Arian Christians, and this made their appearance on the scene a danger to the religious stability of the Roman world.

Organized imperial opposition to the German advance disappeared with the gradual dissolution of the seats of Roman power. Local state officials, who by the fifth century were left without direction or material support, often literally faded into the countryside. The only authorities remaining to defend the Roman population, Christian or not, and to maintain Latinity, baptized or pagan, tended to be the bishops. These prelates, many of whom came from the old senatorial aristocracy, found themselves expected to maintain essential services, defend their cities, and, ultimately, to act as intermediaries with the barbarian conquerors. In some places, such as Rome, which were never fully conquered, the bishop became the sole, permanent authority. In others, he was simply the recognized spokesman of the Latin peoples. A period of co-existence with the "enemy" began, protected by the German willingness to let the local population follow its own "chieftains," as well as by the curiosity and inferiority complex of the invading tribesmen. The two cultures vied for influence and control over one another, consciously and unconsciously, during this time.

Catholic bishops led the political struggle to resist barbarism, paganism, and heresy. Meanwhile, the internal spirit of resistance was being nurtured in the monasteries through the Rule of St. Benedict. Christian spirituality and Latin civilization, supernatural and terrestrial order, were cultivated here with the same vigor that later made these refuges centers of agricultural development. Christians could not help but sense in the monasteries the deepest expressions of their religion; many Germans could not help but wonder and demonstrate respect before this strange phenomenon.

One German barbarian kingdom, that of the Franks, was simultaneously respectful and ambitious. It recognized that its power might be immensely increased if it could find some means of overcoming the split between the two co-existing peoples. Hence, it became Catholic. When ruled, after 768, by that warrior genius, Charles the Great, it was able to conquer half of Europe. The Franks then solidified their position among both Germans and Latins by re-establishing the Crown of Imperial Rome. This gave the Christian Empire the chance to live again.

What more logical step was there to take than that of calling upon the services of those who most understood the meaning of "Rome," of "Empire," and "Christianity"—the bishops and the monks? What more sensible policy than that of employing bishops as political advisors, monks as teachers, and monasteries as centers of religious, civic, and social education? What could be more urgent than providing them the financial ability to carry out their new duties? This, Charlemagne did with a vengeance. He enriched the administrative and spiritual leaders of the Latin peoples and culture, uniting them more strongly to his cause than even his own warriors were. Charlemagne created the impression of a Europe on the move.

Alas! This impression of restored power proved simply to be the lull before the storm. While Charlemagne was conquering, the Vikings and Magyars were preparing a new wave of barbarian invasions; the Moslems were cutting off the seas and contributing to the drying up of old Roman towns; roads were falling into disrepair; trade ceased, and, with it, money disappeared from the European economy. That age of iron, which truly deserved to be called "Dark," fell upon Europe with a fury after Charles' death. His Empire was too big, too Roman, and too conscious of the meaning of the State to be understood by his own people. Only a man influenced by the classical tradition, only a bishop or a monk or a Latin would think that the unity of the State had to be preserved, unimpaired.

Charlemagne's son had three children. Why keep an Empire united, the Franks thought, when each of these potential chiefs had warriors willing to follow him and him alone? Hence, by 843, Charlemagne's domain was split into three parts. The chief, or King, of each of these zones found himself fighting as much with his other two Frankish counterparts as with outsiders. Armies and wars grew in number and in frequency.

A crucial question in the divided Empire became that of determining how to obtain soldiers, horsemen, chevaliers. Germanic warriors expected to be rewarded by their chiefs in exchange for their services, yet no money was available in this age of iron. Land was the only reward possible, and land was freely given. Enough land had to be given to each warrior to provide the wherewithal for at least one horse, weapons, and suit of armor. Sometimes, so much land was awarded to one man that he could subdivide it and obtain followers of his own. He could become a kind of "mini-chief." The land itself was tilled by peasants, fixed to the soil. That system known as feudalism, pregnant with internecine warfare, was begun: a necessary system, perhaps, considering the times, but one which, nevertheless, also disturbed the peace of Europe.

Where did the lands which were given to warriors come from? The bishops and the monasteries often provided the answer. Sometimes, heads of dioceses and abbots abandoned their religious duties, became warriors themselves, and hence directly solved the problem. Sometimes, they were cowed into accepting "protectors" who lived with them and utilized the fruits of their lands for warfare. Often, a king or powerful warrior appointed military henchmen as bishops and abbots. Occasionally, Church lands were simply stolen. All of these measures became commonplace in much of Europe in the 800s and 900s. The result was a thorough-going corruption of the Church. As the Council of the Diocese of Rheims argued in 909:

The cities are depopulated, the monasteries ruined and burned, the land is reduced to a solitude. As the first men lived without law or constraint, abandoned to their passions, so now every man does what pleases him, despising the laws of God and man and the ordinances of the Church. The powerful oppress the weak, and the land is full of violence against the poor and the plunder of the goods of the Church. Men devour one another like the fishes of the sea. In the case of the monasteries, some have been betrayed by the heathen, others have been deprived of their property and reduced to nothing. In those that remain, there is no longer any observance of the rule. They no longer have legitimate superiors, owing to the abuse of submitting to secular domination. We see in the monasteries lay abbots with their wives and their children, their soldiers and their dogs.

God's flock perishes through our charge. It has come about by our negligence, our ignorance, and that of our brethren, that there is in the Church an innumerable multitude of both sexes and every condition who reach old age without instruction, so that they are ignorant even of the words of the Creed and the Lord's Prayer.[1]

It seems clear that the Church in the 800s and 900s succumbed to the spirit of the times, which was a spirit of strength and war-making ability. This is not unusual. The Church in the United States, in this century, has succumbed to the spirit of our age, which is democratic, pluralistic, and materialistic. One could easily condemn the same abuse of submitting to secular domination noted in the passage above, although the type of secular domination concerned is different. It is no longer German warriors and Frankish kings and the military spirit that twist the Church to their secular ends. Instead, it is the manipulators of scientific data and sociological studies, the interpreters of Progress and the Will of the People. The fact is that the spirit of the age is always the death of the Church, and the Church always has a tendency to succumb to it.

Moments of despair in the history of the Church have repeatedly been the very period during which the seeds of revival were being sown. This was as true of the early 900s as it was to be true in the late 1400s and early 1500s, when the Protestant Reformation

---

1 Cited in Christopher Dawson, *Religion and the Rise of Western Culture* (New York: Doubleday, 1991), 120–121.

was about to break upon Europe. And just as unknown saints are today preparing the movements which, eventually, will restore the glory of the Body of Christ, the renewal of the 900s was beginning in the sanctification of individual men.

The 900s and 1000s witnessed a spiritual revival on what can only be described as a miraculous scale. While the sources of this revival were manifold, it is still safe to say that the most important of them stemmed from one monastery in the central part of Charlemagne's Empire, in Burgundy. Benedictine monasticism was fortunate to find in Duke William of Auvergne a man willing to sponsor a foundation which was intended to be free from secular manipulation. His creation was the Abbey of Cluny, which was established in 910. Cluny was destined to blossom forth and develop two vocations. The first of these, by far the more basic, was that of providing a new refuge for those concerned with their personal sanctification. Hence, it wished to restore the original purpose of St. Benedict. The second, flowing naturally from the first, was to so renew the spiritual fervor of the Universal Church as to wipe out the scandal of Christian acceptance of the spirit of the times. A remarkable succession of holy abbots kept Cluny true to its intended goals. These men reflected well the Gospel command to be innocent as lambs and wise as serpents. They guided what has commonly been known as the Cluniac Reform through the use of three effective means.

The first of these was the adoption of a new method of monastic organization: the federation. Cluniac abbots understood that one cause of the collapse of monastic life had been the isolation and weakness of each separate house. If Cluny could establish "colonial" houses, united with the mother abbey, a sense of power and singleness of purpose might be developed. Moreover, federation would facilitate the rooting out of corruption, firm houses being able to provide the corrective for those falling lax. Regular conferences and visitations, assured through the constant travels of the pilgrim abbots of Cluny, made federation a palpable reality. Hundreds upon hundreds of new foundations began to display the value of the system; hundred upon hundreds of houses stretching from one end of Charlemagne's old Empire to another.

A second means of achieving Cluniac ends was that of preaching. The peoples of western Europe, tired of constant warfare and weary of permanent exploitation, longed to see the holy men of Cluny and hear them speak. Their sermons emphasized a true "theology of liberation," one that aroused the peasantry and bourgeoisie not to rebellion, but to demands that the spoiled nobles of the age behave as Christian rulers. True, the language seems harsh, as in the words of St. Odo, Abbot of Cluny from 927–942:

> How are these robbers Christians, or what do they deserve who slay their brothers for whom they are commanded to lay down their lives?
>
> You have only to study the books of antiquity to see that the most powerful are always the worst. Worldly nobility is due not to nature but to pride and ambition. If we judged by realities, we should give honor not to the rich for the fine clothes that they wear but to the poor who are the makers of such things—for the banquets of the powerful are cooked in the sweat of the poor.[2]

But its effect was a salutary one. Some feudal lords were sincerely chastened in spirit. Some were merely frightened by the countenance of these holy preachers. All were terrified by the power that they could wield if they had wanted to unleash it. Whatever the means by which their submission was obtained, many of these ferocious men were tamed. Those pacific movements known as the Truce of God and the Peace of God, movements which limited the times, places, and objects of warfare, were launched. Noblemen were obliged to take oaths to uphold them. Secular influence in Church affairs was considerably lessened as a result.

A third method through which the men of Cluny pursued their ends was by placing their federation of monasteries underneath the special protection of Saints Peter and Paul. This, in effect, meant placing it under the guidance of the Papacy in Rome. The Roman Pontiff's prestige could still arouse an almost superstitious fear among the blood-stained nobles. His distant power could also be evoked as a healthy counterweight to the machinations of some local, corrupt, warlike bishop.

Herein, however, lay the difficulty. A movement of monastic reform that wished an end to all secular control of the Church saw the successors of St. Peter as its natural leaders. The problem

---

2   Cited in Dawson, *Religion and the Rise of Western Culture*, 123.

was that the successors of St. Peter themselves were corrupt, secularized, and in desperate need of reform. A powerful and wealthy institution, the Papacy invited abuse by various Roman families anxious to increase their influence and property holdings. Such families found it to be an easy matter to manipulate papal elections. These were confirmed in St. Peter's Square, where the Roman mob could approve or reprove a candidate through voice "vote."

A full range of colorful though vile characters were confirmed through the manipulation of this mob. One finds an adolescent pope, a pope who was strangled, dug from the grave, and tried for vicious crimes, a pope whose every action was later declared to be invalid. Buying and selling of important positions, in the interests of the chief Roman Families, abounded. Women began to exercise influence over the throne of St. Peter. So much power did Marozia—daughter, mistress, and mother of popes—have that some authors have referred to the Papacy of the Tenth Century as a "pornocracy." Its least interest appeared to be the world of religion.

The Cluniac reformers, once they became familiar with the condition of the Papacy, were aghast at what they saw. Indeed, they and their allies were tempted to revolt. Hence, the following statement at the Council of Saint Basle de Verzy in 991:

> Is it to such monsters . . . swollen with ignominy and devoid of all knowledge human or divine, that the innumerable priests of God throughout the world who are distinguished by their knowledge and virtues should lawfully be submitted?[3]

Reformers opposed to such rebellion clearly recognized that a renewal of the Church also required an urgent spiritual revival of the Papacy.

This revival, ironically, was accomplished precisely with the help of political interference in the affairs of the Church. It happens that the pacification of Europe during the Tenth and Eleventh Centuries was accompanied and directly aided by a renewed centralization of political power. The foundations of the French and English nations were very slowly being laid. Of more immediate importance, however, was a second "restoration" of the Roman Empire. This effort took place in the easternmost section

---

3   Cited in Christopher Dawson, *The Making of Europe: An Introduction to the History of European Unity* (New York: Meridian Books, 1956), 234–235.

of Charlemagne's domains, the area now called Germany. When accomplished, under Otto the Great in 962, the curious entity known as the Holy Roman Empire of the German Nation was born.

Pious Emperors, like Henry II (1002–1024), believed that a purified Church was a natural complement to a strengthened Empire. A purified Church was dependent upon better bishops and popes. Cluniac-influenced and Cluniac-like clergy were called upon to assist in cleansing the Body of Christ. Emperors like Henry, recognizing the depth of the problem, paid little or no attention to canonical rules in achieving their ends. Thus, they even usurped the right to name the successors of St. Peter. The Emperor Henry III (1034–1056) placed three men on the papal throne—Clement II, Damasus II, and St. Leo IX—with the almost unanimous approval of the reformers. St. Peter Damien called such actions manifestations of Divine Providence, and compared the Emperor's work to that of Christ driving the money-changers from the Temple. Reformers swelled the ranks of the German-Roman Emperors' clerical entourage during visits to Italy. They, therefore, entered the service of his papal appointments, and came to play a fruitful role at the center of Roman politics.

St. Leo IX (1049–1054) was, perhaps, the man most responsible for the revival of papal prestige and activity. It was due to his vigor, more than to that of any of his immediate predecessors, that the papacy really took charge of the reform movement. He was a pilgrim pope, traveling through much of western Europe, holding reform councils wherever he went, and encouraging the local population to express its discontent with secularized priests and bishops. He internationalized the Curia, enforced clerical celibacy, and sought a complete end to the buying and selling of Church appointments. So much did the Papacy become aware of itself again that it once more firmly demanded from the Patriarch of Constantinople the obedience due to the Supreme Head of the Church. In short, St. Leo IX gave the Papacy the sense of being responsible for a permanent movement of spiritual renewal.

A final step in the work of the Cluniac Reform took place during the reign of Emperor Henry IV (1054–1106), who came to the throne as a child. Holy Roman Emperors were elected by a small number of important feudal lords, who sometimes became frightened by the potential power that these Caesars could wield.

Such men, in one sense, were delighted to have a weak child on the imperial throne. The reformers in Rome were not. Holy Roman Emperors had been guiding the Papacy. Such guidance might now mean direction of the Church by German feudal lords. This is not what the Cluniac Reform intended. It had begun with an effort to curb the arrogance of just such nobles. The Holy Roman Emperors had been useful, temporarily, *per accidens*, in bringing the Papacy back to its senses. They might now become a new and more vicious means of secularization. The illegal interference of the Emperors had been a blessing for the Church in the extraordinary situation in which she had found herself, since that interference had been utilized to break an evil cycle of corruption. But it would be a mistake to institutionalize an extraordinary means of restoring a "child" to health, once it become a vigorous "adult."

The Roman Curia dealt with the problem in 1059. It abolished the usurped imperial right to choose the pope. The Curia did not restore the influence of the Roman mob, which had misused its powers so much. Instead, it created the College of Cardinals, which was dominated by reformers, and granted it the privilege of naming the successors to St. Peter. The election of the arch-reformer Hildebrand as Pope St. Gregory VII in 1073, and the publication of his *Dictatus Papae* several years later, demonstrated just how complete the papal declaration of independence announced by the creation of the College of Cardinals really was. The *Dictatus Papae*, which clearly stated papal prerogatives in the life of Christendom, did not apologize for escaping from imperial control. It even went in the opposite direction. St. Gregory VII claimed a papal right to dismiss political officials, from the Emperor on down, who did not fulfill their proper role as Christian rulers. One may question whether or not Pope Gregory VII's efforts to break secular control over bishops were realistic, given the fact that prelates now had a long history of political involvement. Could an Emperor or King claim no right to have some say in the appointment of those who would be his chief advisors? One cannot deny, however, that his actions illustrated the Church's "coming of age," the rebirth of its sense of dignity and purpose.

The movement of reform of the Tenth and Eleventh Centuries, a movement symbolized by the work of the Abbey of Cluny, was one of the most important in the history of the Church. It is also one of the most instructive. It demonstrates just how much Christian reform is built upon the drive towards personal sanctification. It indicates how deeply those who focus upon their personal sanctification meditate and act upon the problems of the world around them. It reveals how every movement of true Christian reform seeks to free the Church from the spirit of the times, and leads the Papacy to understand that it must direct the revival that began from below. And, finally, it shows that a reform concerned with sanctification, a reform that is firm, fearless, and unimpressed by the stupidities of the world, can end in the creation of a superior culture. For the Church that was cleansed through the medium of the Cluniac Reform went forward to preside, for two hundred years and more, over one of the most brilliant flowerings of the human spirit since the beginning of time.

3

The Theatines and the
Question of Catholic "Renewal"†

ONE OF POPE JOHN XXIII'S EXPRESSED PUR-
poses in calling the Second Vatican Council was to manifest
Catholic unity to a divided western world which seemed to him
to be grasping for the truth. Proponents of a "pastoral" council
argued that such an assembly would be instrumental in a "renewal"
of the spirit of the Church of Christ, a revival that, presumably,
would aid the epiphany desired by the Holy Father. Pious Catholics anxiously awaited the results.

Whatever the aims and hopes of popes, bishops and the faithful may have been, one thing ought to be patently clear today:
"renewal," during the last few decades, has been drowned in a tidal
wave of doubt, of cynicism, and, on the part of loyal Catholics, of
profound depression. It is afforded little encouragement from the
present generation of Catholic youth; a generation which has been
denied instruction in even basic teachings of the Magisterium, and
which, therefore, lacks all sense of that which needs to be renewed.
Secularized clerics, frantically attempting to combine a bourgeois
Marxism with a defense of moderate liberal hedonism, have silenced
the voice of religious heroes. Instead of seeing Christian unity, the
non-Catholic spectator is entertained by public squabbles over principles whose contestation only the boldest of radicals would have
proposed in 1962. The Body of Christ, like the world whose beacon
it was intended to be, seems temporarily to have lost its luster. One
need not suggest that Pope John and the Council caused the whole
disaster—it was much more deeply rooted than that—to admit
that it nevertheless exists throughout much of the western world.

What, then, can the serious defender of Catholic renewal do
to recoup the Church's losses? One inexhaustible source of hope
and instruction in the midst of the debacle is Catholic History.
Its effectiveness in this regard is two-fold, having both a "negative" and a "positive" sense. Catholic History first consoles by

---

† First published in *The Wanderer*, October 20, 1984.

providing a description of past ages affected by similarly impressive catastrophes. It then "positively" stimulates to action by offering the example of men and deeds which—insofar as this is humanly possible—were instrumental in Catholic renewal. A two-fold effect of such a kind may be obtained by examining one specific period of Catholic eclipse—the early sixteenth century—and the work of renewal encouraged by a network of small "brotherhoods," of which the Order of Clerks Regular or "Theatines" will be utilized as the central example.

The late fifteenth and early sixteenth centuries were rich in the creation of small, tightly-knit bands of laymen and clerics dedicated to the attainment of Christian holiness. The more the general situation of the Church declined, the more these Catholic cadres seem to have gained in popularity, particularly in the numerous cities dotting the Italian Peninsula. Franciscan and Dominican spirituality has been noted as being seminal in this context, and particularly the example given by Savonarola.[1] An early instrument for spreading such spirituality was the Compagnia del Divino Amore, established in Genova on December 26, 1497, with a membership of thirty-six laymen and four clerics.

The Compagnia was an elite group, secretive in character, in reaction to governmental suspicion of lay organizations as potential centers of subversive activity. Its chief aims were the stimulation of piety, the encouragement of frequent communion, spiritual aid for condemned criminals, and charitable work among the poor. Important among its functions was care for the incurably ill, especially for syphilitics, an office which ultimately resulted in its funding of the Genovese Ridotti degli'incurabili. A Rule provided for a prior elected for the brief term of six months.

Ettore Vernazza (1470–1524), a wealthy Genovese layman, appears to have been an animating force in the Compagnia. Vernazza was the spiritual pupil of St. Caterina Fieschi-Adorno (1447–1510), whose first biography he wrote, and a selfless apostle of the work of "divine love." He died in the plague of 1524, after having inspired charitable activities similar to those of Genova in Naples, and aided in the formation of a Roman Compagnia centered round the Church of SS Silvestro and Dorotea in Trastevere.

---

1   Alfred Bianconi, *L'opera delle compagnie del 'divino amore' nella riforma cattolica* (Città di Castello: Casa Editrice di S. Lapi, 1914), 14–59.

This Roman Compagnia del Divino Amore, established sometime between 1513 and 1517, was to prove to be of enormous influence. SS Silvestro and Dorotea is said to have been chosen due
to its proximity to the Genovese quarter of Rome, as well as to
the sympathy of its Rector, the Florentine Giuliano di Domenico
Dati, a penitentiary of the basilicas of St. Peter and St. John the
Lateran. Like its model in Genova, the Roman Compagnia founded
a hospital—that of St. Jacopo degl'incurabili at St. Giacomo in
Augusta. It was also responsible for the Monastery of the *convertiti*,
which aided former prostitutes, near Santa Maria Maddalena al
Corso. Associated with the Compagnia, or, later on, with one or
another of its various activities, were an entire generation and
more of Catholic proponents of renewal: among them, Gian Pietro
Carafa (1476–1559), Gaspare Contarini (1483–1542), Gian Matteo
Giberti (1495–1543), and San Gaetano da Thiene (1480–1547).
The regular gatherings of such men in Trastevere encouraged not
only a positive direction to their piety and charity, but also a sense
of working together for a common cause. Barnabites, Camilliani,
Oratorians, Scolopi, and Somaschi were all, to a large degree,
products of the Compagnia's influence.[2]

A direct offspring of the Roman "brotherhood" was also the
Order of Clerks Regular. This was first born in the mind of Gaetano da Thiene, and then put into effect with the aid of Carafa
and several others. A conviction of the possible impact of a union
of simple diocesan priests living a common life dedicated to prayer,
proper intellectual preparation for priestly functions, sound liturgical performance, good preaching, frequent communion, and
selfless works of charity motivated Thiene and reveals the lesson
learned in the school of "divine love."

Two practices of the Order of Clerks Regular seem to be particular developments of the lessons of the Compagnia. The first
of these, stemming from the recognition of the greater efficacy of
a solidly-knit organization, is the clear intention of being an elite
corps. The "Theatines," as they were commonly called, after the

---

2   Bianconi, *L'opera delle compagnie*, 14–59. See also Giuseppe Gabrieli,
"Memorie spirituali trasteverine (il Divino Amore)," *Roma* 12 (November
1934): 499–510 and Paul A. Kunkel, *The Theatines in the History of Catholic
Reform Before the Establishment of Lutheranism* (Washington: The Catholic
University of America Press, 1941), 15–16.

Latinized name of Carafa's See at Chieti, were designed to be exclusive. Not only did they keep from their ranks insufficiently rigorous members, but also those who might be useful elsewhere for the work of renewal. They respected an evangelical division of labor. Hence, in addition to establishing particularly strict rules for the entrance of novices, unconcerned with the limitations these clearly placed upon their expansion, the Clerks Regular blocked the efforts of men of the highest merit to join them. Giberti, the Bishop of Verona, whose reform constitutions for that city's clergy were later useful as models to Trent, was excluded, despite his entreaties. Joining the Theatines would have required his abandonment of his episcopal privileges, and, perhaps, an end to the good that he was doing in the Veneto. Indeed, if Thiene had had his way, Carafa himself would not have been admitted, since he, too, would thus be forced to retire from his work of reform in the diocese of Chieti. Only a passionate scene, during which Carafa apparently fell on his knees before Thiene, stating that he would hold the latter responsible for the state of his soul before God on Judgment Day were he not allowed to enter the envisaged Order, occasioned an exceptional bending of what was to be the rule.

A second development of the spirit of the Compagnia by the Theatines was the insistence upon an absolute evangelical poverty. Selfless expenditure of one's energies for the sake of the poor was the rule of "divine love"; total abandonment of one's means of survival as a priest became the guidelines for the Theatines. Even the mendicancy of Franciscans and Dominicans was rejected by them, partially due to a dismay over the corruption to which this had given birth. The Theatines simply "waited" for whatever aid came their way. Not only did such rigor complete the Theatine witness to the life of charitable self-abnegation; it also assisted their work for renewal, demonstrating the serious commitment of some priests in the midst of general clerical laxity. So sincere were they in this matter that they often lived in abysmal conditions, turning down any offer of regular contributions from regular donors, due to fears that these would compromise them and make them grow lax. Carafa, as required, retired from his diocese, retaining merely the title of bishop, and abandoned all of his revenues and his entire family inheritance. He vigorously rebuked every effort to accord him episcopal privileges, even after having been named a cardinal under Paul III. Fulfillment of the duties of this princely office, for which he held the greatest respect, often forced him to appeal to the pope for defense "from hunger."[3]

The early history of the Theatines was not without its drama. Many members of the Curia doubted the success of such a rigorous insistence upon evangelical poverty. It is said that only the intervention of Giberti, a man of great influence at the papal court and a constant friend, saved Thiene's idea. Whatever the truth of the matter may be, the Order of Clerks Regular was approved by the bull *Exponi Nobis* of June 24, 1524. It was given some brief guidelines by Carafa, who became its first head, in 1526, and a more formal structure on July 28, 1604. A certain initial ridicule on the part of the cynical Roman population did not trouble its life as much as did the devastating sack of the city by the troops of Charles V in 1527, forcing it to flee, along with other religious foundations, to the security of the Venetian Republic. The Church of San Niccolo da Tolentino in Venice, a Neapolitan center begun in 1533 by Thiene and Giovanni Marinonius (1490–1562), and San Andrea della Valle in Rome later in the century, became their main foci.[4]

It might be wise, at this point, to mention something about the two most important figures in early Theatine history, San Gaetano da Thiene and Gian Pietro Carafa. Although both came from noble families and were animated by extraordinary religious fervor, their resemblance ends there. Thiene was a northerner, from Vicenza; Carafa was a Neapolitan. The former led a somewhat irregular life before his ordination in 1516. Carafa, on the other hand, shared a childhood vocation with his sister, who became a religious, and with whom he remained in constant, affectionate contact. Thiene, the man of more harmonious virtues, the officially

---

3 Enrico Lucatello, *San Gaetano Thiene e gli inizi della riforma cattolica* (Milan: Istituto Propaganda Libraria, 1941), *passim*; Pio Paschini, *San Gaetano Thiene, Gian Pietro Carafa e le origini dei Chierici Regolari Teatini* (Rome: Storia e Letteratura, 1926), 42; Carafa to Giberti, March 1, 1533, and to Paul III, May 25, 1538, cited in Gennaro Maria Monti, ed., *Ricerche su Papa Paolo IV Carafa* (Benevento: Cooperativa Tipografi Chiostro S. Sofia, 1923), 157–168, 258; and Kunkel, *The Theatines*, 30–58, 112–140.

4 Bianconi, *L'opera delle compagnie*, 31–59; Paschini, *San Gaetano Thiene*, 43; Kunkel, 30–111, 148–163; and C. to Clement VII, October 9, 1531, cited in Monti, *Ricerche*, 138–139.

canonized saint, was the more tranquil of the pair. His writings are almost all letters on spiritual topics, none written to Carafa during the crucial period of his residence in Naples having been available to the author. Carafa, the passionate, extroverted, active foil to the almost invisible Thiene, has left a mass of historical evidence behind him. It would not be an exaggeration to argue that Thiene upheld the soul of the Theatine movement, but that Carafa was its driving force. Their combination was by no means an unfortunate one, as historians of the Order have contended.[5]

But it is indeed just to recognize that without the diplomatic ability of Carafa, and without his audacity, Gaetano would not have succeeded in giving life to and then maintaining his new institution. Providence paired the talents of the one with those of the other, and availed itself of the defects of Carafa, counterbalanced by the greater interior virtues of Gaetano, to give vigor to the new institution, which was to be then the model of many others.

The various Compagnie, and the Order of Clerks Regular following them, were outraged by the state of the Church in the early 1500s. So concerned for the cause of renewal was the latter that contemporaries are said to have applied the name Theatine indiscriminately to clerical reformers as a whole. "Renewal," in the minds of men like Thiene and Carafa, meant primarily internal revivification, the attainment of sanctity. Nevertheless, as far as one can determine from the historical record, the Theatines did not believe that they could fulfill their mission through prayer alone. Instead, they displayed a passionate interest in those admittedly secondary measures which might be taken to put the Body of Christ in better working order. This interest was founded upon the assumption that institutional order, like regularity in one's good habits, is the mundane basis for the flight of the spirit. I will identify four specific sources in detailing the Theatine program for institutional reform.

None of these sources involve Thiene, who, again, in this regard, proves to be a somewhat elusive historical figure. One is a document, undated and unsigned, entitled "Ricordi Richiesti da

---

5 Paschini, 40, 133; C. to Sorella Maria, cited in Monti, 179–244; Francesco Andreu, C. R., ed., *Le lettere di San Gaetano da Thiene* (Vatican City: Biblioteca Apostolica Vaticana, 1954); and Francesco Andreu, "Lettere Inedite di San Gaetano Thiene," *Regnum Dei* 2 (October–December 1946): 7–34.

Marcello II di Santa Memoria." This commentary on the initial phase of Church reform in the first half of the sixteenth century emanated from a Theatine pen in Naples, clearly sometime during or after the reign of Marcellus in 1555.[6]

The other three sources all concern Carafa. Carafa has left behind him as an indication of the Theatine attitude his actions upon being raised to the See of Peter as Paul IV (1555–1559), his letters, and a document destined for Pope Clement VII, dated 4 October, 1532. This memorial, occasioned by Carafa's dismay over the handling of the heterodox opinions and irregular behavior of several friars in the Venetian Republic—Bartolomeo Fonzio, Girolamo Galateo, and Alessandro da Pieve di Sacco—was given by the Theatine to Fra Bonaventura da Venetia to relate personally to the Holy Father. Fra Bonaventura, whose efforts were supported by those of Giberti, was, as he indicates in a letter to Carafa, accorded a polite but succinct audience by the pope. Clement was too preoccupied with an impending meeting with Charles V at Bologna to become involved with the Venetian issue. Carafa's memorial, though without immediate impact, was of sufficiently broad a nature to live on as a model for the Consilium de Emendanda Ecclesia under Paul III in 1537. This report was prepared by a commission, under the presidency of Cardinal Contarini, which included Carafa, Giberti, and a number of others, including several one-time members of the Roman Compagnia.[7]

Three deeply-rooted problems are brought to light by the written sources: the confused and corrupt behavior of clerics, particularly religious; the venality of the Roman Court; and, finally, the "moderate" approach towards dealing with heterodoxy and rebellion adopted by the Papacy.

One is given the impression of the greatest disruption in the clerical world. Religious life, especially that of friars, Carafa notes, "is already deformed and collapsed."[8] It was not unusual, he claims, to find lay friars hearing confessions, tempted by the prospect of monetary compensation for their absolutions. Worse still, priestly

---

6   Monti, 325–328.
7   Fra B. to C., November 2, 1532, and C. to Giberti, March 1, 1533, cited in Monti, 79, 157–168. See also instructions to Fra B., 57–77 and Kunkel, *The Theatines*, 112–140.
8   Cited in Monti, 70.

habits were being abandoned, and religious were apostatizing. An added difficulty was the fact that such men often continued their preaching in lay clothing. Indeed, some "wandering" religious and apostates had obtained positions as substitutes for absentee priests. Believers were being told that papal excommunications were of little importance, and that restrictions on their conduct were so few that many "excuse themselves by saying that their confessors gave them the license to do certain things which must not be done by good Christians."[9]

The Pope's conscience will surely allow him no rest, Carafa argues, when he grasps the fact that such confused and corrupted religious exercise great influence over the Christian population. Such "rogues" had long held the care of souls, been in charge of convent and signorial chaplaincies, and run schools for children, everywhere disseminating pastoral poison. Even now, even after clear abandonment of either habits or religious life as a whole, their preaching has an effect on all classes. Why? Due to the fact that such preachers still retain the aura and mannerisms of religious, because their arguments have the appeal of novelty, and since they give to everyone, high and low born, the chance to justify his own licentious behavior.[10]

It is interesting to note here a certain intellectual irritation with the spread of error and confusion. One ought to mention that many of the men connected with the various Compagnie and their offspring were themselves tied to Humanist or Christian Humanist circles. Big guns like Giacomo Sadoleto (1477–1547) were fellow-travelers. Vernazza had contacts with the humanist Cardinal Saulio. Even Dati produced works on the American discoveries, Scipio Africanus, and mathematical tables useful for calculating the times of eclipses. The Theatines applied scholarly rigor to the special task of revising the breviary entrusted to them by Rome, with Carafa brutally attacking what he called the "many foolish statements and dreams of apocryphal books" found in abundance in the older volumes.[11] Such Catholic reformers, therefore, often

---

9   Cited in Monti, 62.
10 Monti, 63–64, 68.
11 Bianconi, *L'opera delle Compagnie*, 33–43; Gabrieli, "Memorie," 499–510; Kunkel, *The Theatines*, 141–148; and C. to G., January 1, 1533, cited in Monti, 152.

depicted the struggle against their enemies as one of enlightenment versus ignorance, "considering that the heresies of these rogues are all old things already confuted and extinct from Holy Church for a long time."[12] The spread of error, as already indicated above, was thus frequently attributed not to any intellectual appeal of the concepts that were being propagated, but, rather, to the fact that friars and others "are badly disposed and immediately receive that doctrine which conforms to their customs and their life."[13]

The second enormous problem facing the Church was the venality of the Roman Court. This evil was said to be particularly blatant in the Datary and the Penitentiary. Both offices were potentially lucrative for those working within them, responsible as they were not only for confirmation of various propositions, but also for the granting of dispensations and the lifting of penalties, all of which involved payment of certain fees. Weak or vicious clerics succumbed all too readily to the many temptations around them. Carafa, in a letter to Giberti, bemoans the evil impression left by

> those most rapacious Cerberi that surround the poor prince, selling, at base price, the soul and the honor of His Holiness without his hearing one case out of a thousand. It is from this source that the immoderate favor comes which so many—not merely the most pernicious and criminal, but also those most heretical and hostile to Christ, His Holiness, and the whole of Holy Church—find and enjoy in that Court to the great dishonor and offense of God and His Church.[14]

This brings us to the third problem, that of the Holy See's "moderation" towards heterodoxy and rebellion. "Accidental" kindness, as a given method in a particular case, is one thing, Carafa explains, but leniency in principle is definitely another. The treatment accorded heretical and rebellious Venetian friars practically amounted to passionate embraces, so much so that dissidents were wandering about claiming that acceptance of heresy was just the tactic required in order to be "honored and named and rewarded by His Holiness."[15] It was a notorious fact, he insists, that

12 Cited in Monti, 69.
13 Cited in Monti, 69.
14 C. to Giberti, February 26, 1533, cited in Monti, 156–157. See also 157–158.
15 Cited in Monti, 59.

dispensations from sacred vows could easily be obtained in Rome, simply through payment of the requisite fees. When questioned regarding their status, laicized friars, for example, merely display the bulls that they have received, arguing that they were "forcibly placed in the monastery as a minor," or that they no longer had "the spirit to stay there," or that they have "contracted an incurable illness, and other lies."[16]

Friars refused to purge their own order, Carafa complains, arguing that the Pope had not yet shown any concern for heresy, and, hence, that they should not exceed his zeal. How could the rest of the Christian world be expected to move against error within the Church, the Theatines insisted, when the Eternal City was filled with heretics, and nothing was being done to dislodge them? The lack of movement, the "unnecessary marks of respect and pusillanimity" justified by the fear that a harsh stance would drive the restless into outright rebellion, depriving the Church of sufficient ministers, was the "greatest favor" that heresy could expect.[17] It made the heretic "more crafty and insidious," harmed the reputation of the papacy, and "saddened the souls of faithful Christians who see themselves offended by these scoundrels . . . under the title of the authority of the Apostolic See."[18] Is it not a scandal, the Neapolitan document asks, that the papal power, supreme in the Church, is frequently utilized to relax discipline, but never to enforce it?[19]

A two-fold approach to the institutional reform important to the cause of renewal is suggested in these sources. On the one hand, as the Consilium later openly indicates, it is necessary to admit the false attribution of certain privileges to the Holy See; to recognize that "the fundamental cause of the ills of the Church is the immense exaggeration of the pontifical power occasioned by the refined adulation of canonists without conscience."[20] Carafa begs that the Papacy not interfere in the day-to-day operations of sound religious families, such as those of Spain and Portugal, and, most importantly, that the traffic in apostolic dispensations be

---

16 Cited in Monti, 64.
17 Cited in Monti, 58.
18 Cited in Monti, 61, 65. See also C. to Giberti, March 1, 1533, cited in 163–164.
19 Monti, 327.
20 Cited in Monti, 42.

brought within some proper bounds. He writes in his instructions
to Fra Bonaventura:

> And for the love of God, entreat His Holiness to put a brake
> upon His Ministers, that such an abundance of Apostolic Bulls
> not be released for every most vile and alien thing.[21]

On the other hand, the Theatines, and particularly Carafa,
had the most exalted notions of that which the Papacy, acting in
its proper sphere, might be capable of accomplishing. The future
Paul IV writes that an active Holy Father would have the ability
to "make the giant mountains tremble down into the abyss."[22]
That which was required was simply vigorous, uncompromising
application of reform measures.

This insistence upon the futility of half-hearted reform was
apparently axiomatic in Theatine circles. The Neapolitan document, for example, notes that the decades-long commitment of
popes and council to the cause of reform had still, by the 1550s,
achieved practically nothing. Why? Because it had remained
within the realm of abstract discussion rather than leading directly
to action. An escape route was always left often by the Holy See
and Trent, in that great care was exercised in delineating the
conditions under which abuses might continue to flourish. These
"where licit" clauses of reform constitutions demonstrated that
problems were being treated not "according to what they are in
fact and in practice, but by way of theory and in abstract."[23] They
simply encouraged, or at least publicly tolerated, the practice of
obtaining dispensations. Moreover, given the nature of men, the
exception was inevitably elevated into the rule, and then despoiled
of its justifying conditions:

> Then, when they are put into practice, they are despoiled by
> men of those "legalizing" circumstances and dressed, most often,
> in a totally different fashion; thus, if one wishes to end usury, it
> is not enough to say "such a contract made with such a condition
> is licit," but it is necessary to see if it is made with that condi-
> tion, or true that the disease is inflicted by the law. Therefore,
> I believe that things similar in themselves, even under certain

---

21   Cited in Monti, 59, 65, 70–72.
22   C. to Giberti, March 1, 1533, cited in Monti, 163–164.
23   Cited in Monti, 326.

licit conditions, when it is discovered that in fact and in practice they have for a long time been badly used, must be reformed by means of total prohibition, because it is not enough to say: "I have written a good law"; but it is necessary to see if it is used as well as it is written, the prudence required being almost impossible given the quantity of evil that reigns in the world.[24]

No more councils were needed, no more decrees, no more pious sermons. Action alone could deal with the problem. Action was itself the best argument.

Carafa is himself filled with specific suggestions for how to act. Preachers and confessors, he explains, must be examined carefully with regard to their orthodoxy, an office which he himself performed for a time in Rome. Permission to read heretical books ought to be restricted, again, due to their appeal to the licentious, anxious to justify wicked behavior. A reformed, restructured, and strengthened Inquisition must be established in Italy, as eventually was done in 1542. It has been argued that Carafa was attracted to the idea of the Inquisition both by the fears expressed by Thiene regarding the spread of error in Naples, as well as by his own admiration for what had been accomplished with its aid in Spain, under the direction of a man like Cardinal Ximenez (1436–1517). Creation of a military-religious order, directly subject to the Holy See and founded upon a Venetian fragment of the secularized order of Teutonic Knights, is also mentioned as a possible tactic. It is only with regard to the religious orders that "half measures" are urged, "by reason of the great number of the worst types that are found therein, who so oppress the good that they can prevail in nothing."[25] Here, he claims, it would be best simply to set aside houses for observant religious, in order that they might possess some safe havens in which to fulfill their vows without hindrance. All useful steps, moreover, had first and foremost to be taken in Rome, in the pope's own garden. Only then, with a proper example given by the Vicar of Christ, could the movement for reform and renewal be expected to spread throughout Italy and the remainder of the Christian world.[26]

---

24 Cited in Monti, 326.
25 Cited in Monti, 72.
26 Monti, 54–55, 60–61, 72–77. See also C. to Giberti, February 26, 1533, cited in 156–157; and Kunkel, *The Theatines*, 59–76.

Carafa was certainly true to his word upon obtaining the tiara. Proponents of a new session of the Council of Trent were not surprised to see that it was not re-convoked during his reign. Instead, Paul IV sought to reform by means of unilateral actions, his ferocity in this regard becoming legendary. The Theatine Pope fell down upon the Datary with a sincerity that no man could question, cutting his own revenues in half when he could theoretically ill afford to do so, while engaged in a disastrous war with Spain. "Wandering monks," having failed to respond to his call to return to their monasteries, were rounded up and shipped off to the galleys. So certain was he of the importance of the work of the Inquisition that he attended its sessions even on the verge of his death. Paul's discovery, after years of blindness, of the corruption of the Carafa family members that he had placed in positions of authority, led to so swift and complete a punishment that the whole of Italy, reformers included, were stunned. Indeed, his greatest failure (of which there were several), the war with Spain, stemmed chiefly from his uncompromising desire to free the Church from secularizing influences. It is ironic, however, as Paul himself may have realized in the latter part of his reign, that he, of all men, should have been guilty of placing what many perceived to be a political issue above the cause of reform in more clearly Church-related matters.[27]

There are several important lessons that the contemporary Catholic can learn from the example of the Theatines, their work for institutional reform, and their interest in internal renewal. Perhaps all of these may be best noted by subsuming them under the general lesson of the need for freedom from the zeitgeist or "spirit of the times."

Attainment of this independence is not an easy task, for the zeitgeist always maintains certain advantages in its struggle with Christian Truth for control over man's mind and will. The spirit of the times is taken for granted; its erroneous axioms are one's daily bread. So strong is it, so omnipresent its guiding hand, that it uses the average Catholic to penetrate the Church herself. It bends the theologian to its will by attacking him on two fronts.

---

27 Ludwig von Pastor, "Paul IV (1555–1559)," in *History of the Popes, from the Close of the Middle Ages, vol. 14* (London: Keegan Paul, Trench, Trubner & Co., Ltd., 1924), 56–424.

His need to oppose secularism is satisfied by directing his wrath against the dead zeitgeist of yesteryear, while his acceptance of the present, living spirit is encouraged by convincing him that its embrace is dictated solely by intelligent reasoning. He, of course, could not be influenced by the purely atmospheric conditions around him! Once firmly ensconced in an ecclesiastical setting, it determines, to his own advantage, the battleground on which the Church may fight, the weapons that she may use, and the time that the conflict may begin. Counsel is given against taking the very measures most useful in freeing the Church from its grip, the work of the zeitgeist being praised as the movement of the spirit of God. That which is easy to correct is depicted as being difficult and even impossible; that which is wise is ridiculed as the handiwork of the foolish.

Independence of the zeitgeist is essential to the successful completion of the Church's supernatural mission, and such independence the Theatines, to a large degree, possessed. What did they do to attain this freedom? Little more than devote themselves to the proper goals of Catholic priests, and call things by their proper names. For, despite the difficulty of avoiding the influence of the spirit of the times, the means of effectively battling it are always immediately available at the believer's fingertips: honest devotion to the Christian life, and straightforwardness in one's dealings with society on the basis of Catholic teachings. The perspective won by the Theatines through their break with "accepted" clerical patterns of the day demonstrated to them the complete insignificance of and unwarranted importance granted to the cautions of time-serving prelates, the demands of well-entrenched bureaucrats, and the wishes of powerful laymen. No one is in a position to strike more boldly at the ways of the world and the petty illusions of daily existence than the single Catholic saint (or group of men struggling towards sanctity) plainly stating the simple Christian truths and the requirements of Christian morality.

Some have claimed that this freedom from the zeitgeist did the Clerks Regular little good; that the Theatines, and especially Carafa, as their most famous historical spokesman, were, like most reformers, too intense, and ultimately self-defeating. Was it really necessary, such critics ask, for the Order to go so far as to live in stables to demonstrate its embrace of apostolic poverty? Did Carafa

35

truly have to send monks to the galleys? Could not his reaction to his own family's corruption—for whose flowering his own blindness was chiefly responsible—have been a bit more balanced? And what, in the end, did his zeal for the independence and reform of the Church achieve? Defeated in a most unfortunate war with Spain, reviled by the Roman population, which entertained itself after his death by attacking symbols of his reign, treated by many subsequent historians as an obscurantist fanatic, Carafa's pontificate is said to have been a double proof of both exaggerated Theatine rigor as well as its ultimate uselessness.

One does gain the impression that the Theatine attitude towards institutional reform, as represented by Carafa and some of his colleagues, lacked the prudence required to govern the Church over a long period of time. It may, however, be the case that a symbolic bloodletting, in the form of rigorous and even brutal house-cleaning, was, given the corruption of the Church of the day and the cynicism of much of the Christian population, temporarily demanded to end Catholic torpor. It is certainly the case that once Carafa's scythe had cut through the Papal Court and Papal Rome, the props of the Renaissance Church were gone forever. Long-hallowed corruption was no longer sacrosanct. Old legends crumbled, as the Papal States did not collapse along with the powers of the Datary. Open abuses were obliged, to a certain degree, to go underground. Some have noted that the next papal nephew to hold a position of great authority in the Church after Carafa's reign was St. Charles Borromeo (1538–1584). If Paul IV and the Theatines were not necessarily the best instruments for directing a long-term reform of the universal Church, they were nevertheless crucial as vanguards destroying the age-old barriers blocking the pathway of surgeons carrying the medicine of Trent. And as travel guides indicating the route to that personal Christian renewal for which institutional reform was but a means to an end, their importance is lasting and unmatched.

The contemporary zeitgeist, anxious that the Church never recover lost ground, would react strongly against that which the Theatines have to say, and the example that they give. Their insistence upon the importance of small, committed, Catholic cadres utilizing the aid of "old school ties" from the Roman Compagnia would be depicted as an elitism unsuitable to an egalitarian and

democratic age. Their concern for social action and their definition of renewal would be shown to be so closely linked with
and subordinated to an interest in the life of the spirit as to be
theologically out of date. Their appeal to authority as a restorative
force would be attacked on the grounds of its self-evident offense
to modern understandings of human freedom and dignity; the fact
that it may have been efficacious would be an added outrage to it.

Much of the zeitgeist's energy must be expended in convincing
contemporary Catholics to ignore the list of sixteenth century
ecclesiastical abuses catalogued by Theatine writers. The spirit
of the times has generally sought to keep the Church away from
following historical examples in her attempt to climb out of the
pit into which she has fallen; it has insisted that the present age is
totally distinct from all other periods of human history, and, hence,
must forge totally different weapons to use against the enemies
of the Christian spirit. Alas! Theatine complaints have much too
current a ring to them to allow this argument to go unchallenged.
Anyone reading them sees little difference between the earlier
flight from discipline—mass desertion of religious, the desire for
an easier moral code, the disappearance of the concept of mortal
sin, the emotional excuses for inability to fulfill sacred vows—and
that of the 1960s and 1970s. Indeed, one can discern little distinction between the sixteenth-century Church's initial "intellectual"
and "moderate" efforts to deal with abuses and those developed
in the post-conciliar era. The same approach yielded the same
disastrous results: ineffective decrees and reform constitutions
instead of endless workshops and programs discussing the nature
of renewal; "where licit" clauses elevating abuses to the status
of accepted norms in place of gestures to the modern spirit that
transform extraordinary ministers of the eucharist into an everyday
reality; kindliness to heretics and to the rebellious, both then and
now, that makes loyal Catholics think that the rogues prey upon
them either with the approval or due to the laxity of the Holy See.
The zeitgeist must keep men away from the Theatine complaints,
since anyone carefully studying them will begin to question its
wisdom in all of its manifold aspects.

If the contemporary Catholic could only find his way to freedom
from this oppressive "wisdom," he would discover that the path to
recovery and to renewal is much simpler than the experts claim.

The experts are burdened with baggage unnecessary for the journey. Our age is not essentially different from any other; it is simply specific historical circumstances which differ, demanding modified uses of the same weapons which have always been available in the arsenal. Renewal needs no new definition; action and authority still demonstrate whether or not there is serious commitment to clean house; elite cadres, as the communists never have doubted, continue to be of immense importance in building the sense of purpose and understanding of one's mission essential to victory. Perhaps present-day "Theatines" should, in addition to developing their spiritual life, meet together regularly to rebuild their own weakened understanding of Catholic History and the glories of Catholic civilization. Mass effects may not be immediately possible, leaders of State may not respond to their enlightenment, but students and intellectuals who have been orphaned through their abandonment by representatives of official culture are anxious to hear what serious Catholics have to say. And but twelve good "Theatines" may be sufficient, in God's own time, to restore all things in Christ.

4

Dreaming the Dreams
of the Eldest Daughter†

"The nights are light in summer, so that at
midnight the beholders are often in doubt
whether the evening twilight still continues,
or that of the morning is coming on." [1]
—ST. BEDE THE VENERABLE

A PILGRIMAGE ALWAYS CREATES A PECU-
liar "time out of time" for its participants. It allows them to
pray and to nurture exalted Christian thoughts and dreams freed
from the distractions of so-called normal life. When the pilgrimage
in question happens to be the grand Pentecost weekend procession
of thousands of traditionalists from Paris to Chartres and Chartres
to Paris, the noble Christian thoughts and dreams accompanying
the prayers of the wanderers are suggested by the whole history
of the tribe of the Franks, the Eldest Daughter of the Church, the
first among the barbarian tribes to convert to Roman Catholicism,
the ancestor of contemporary France, the Low Countries, and
Germany. The present article is a meditation upon some of the
tales told by that history, inspired by the three days of last month's
Pilgrimage to Chartres, and, potentially useful, given recent events,
for the encouragement of dejected contemporary Catholics.

Frankish history passes on to its students much basic information
regarding the development of the idea of the pilgrimage as an essential theme in Christian life. More than that, however, it also offers
them vivid proof that the dreams which Catholics once dreamed
actually did once become the political and social pillars supporting a
brilliant civilization. Finally, and perhaps most importantly, it feeds
a substantive hope that such a progression from dream to reality
may be possible yet again—if, that is to say, we would really take
to heart the lessons that a truly Catholic history teaches.

---

† First published in *The Remnant*, June 30, 1995.

---

1   The Venerable Bede, *Ecclesiastical History of the English Nation*, ed.,
Lionel Cecil Jane (London: J. M. Dent, 1903), 6.

The Franks settled in the provinces of a deeply Romanized Gaul which had already grown fascinated with pilgrimages to the Holy Land in the latter fourth century. Two Gallic writings of the 300s, the *Peregrinatio ad loca sancta* and the *Itinerarum Burdigalense*, describe a well-trod pilgrimage circuit that involved not only sites in Palestine but visits to the pioneer monastic communities of Egypt and Syria as well. These works provide valuable information on everything from church discipline, liturgy, devotional life and architecture to the imperial transport system and the amenities available to the first pilgrims. They are also an introduction to a concept that many early medieval religious thinkers were eager to emphasize: the need for each of us to recognize that we are all wanderers through a fleeting earthly existence, and that even a brief moment on pilgrimage enables us to treat this basic but neglected truth seriously.

Unfortunately for the newly Catholic Franks of the late 400s, the shattering of the Pax Romana reduced their own pilgrimage goals to local destinations. Nevertheless, pilgrimages to the shrines of men like St. Martin of Tours and St. Julian of Brioude aided mightily in the development of popular understanding of Christian doctrine. Pilgrims often came to such sites to benefit from the miraculous powers of the bones of the saints which could be touched at them. They could not help but see in the wondrous cures effected in such humble locations and through such lowly means the broad consequences of an Incarnation transforming nature in Christ. All space and time appeared to have had been stirred by the fleshly entrance of the Almighty into history and His offer of supernatural grace. Pilgrim exaltation was so great on the feasts of the saints whose tombs were visited that these were days, as one Frankish source noted, on which the whole of the holy Catholic Church rejoiced and danced together.

Grand visions of a special, incarnational pilgrim mission entrusted to the tribe of the Franks emerged with the rise to kingship of the Carolingian Family of Pippin (751–768). The Carolingians managed not only to restore unity to much of the old western part of the Roman Empire and see Pippin's son, Charlemagne (768–814), crowned as its ruler, but also to mix the impossibly disparate elements now composing it into a new Catholic culture. This hard-won mélange reflected influences from Byzantium, Egypt,

Lombard Italy, Visigothic Spain, Ireland, and Britain. Alcuin (735–804), the great English Benedictine, responding to Charlemagne's call to head his so-called Palace School of Aix-la-Chapelle, well expressed the heady long-term hopes that such efforts amidst half-barbarian, illiterate, and often violent peoples encouraged in the educated Catholic elite:

> If your intentions are carried out, it may be that a new Athens will arise in France, and an Athens fairer than of old, for our Athens, ennobled by the teaching of Christ, will surpass the wisdom of the Academy. The old Athens had only the teachings of Plato to instruct it, yet even so it flourished by the seven liberal arts. But our Athens will be enriched by the sevenfold gift of the Holy Spirit and will, therefore, surpass all the dignity of earthly wisdom.[2]

Special Frankish Carolingian pilgrim responsibilities in a world in the process of transformation in Christ were deduced from four treatises popularized by the literary Renaissance noticeable in this New Athens: *The Celestial Hierarchy*, *The Ecclesiastical Hierarchy*, the *Divine Names*, and *The Mystical Theology*. These works were all written by a Sixth Century Syrian and had long been mistakenly associated with texts of Dionysius the Areopagite, the First Century Athenian convert of St. Paul. Now, by the 800s, the identity of that author was confused still further, this time through equation with the proto-martyr of Paris of the same name, the much beloved Saint Denis (i.e., Dionysius). New translations and studies of the so-called Pseudo-Dionysian corpus, doubly hallowed as the product of a hero both ancient and homely, then flourished in all major Carolingian centers, from western France to central Germany.

Pseudo-Dionysius expands upon certain aspects of Plato's famous allegory of the cave, developed in detail in the latter's dialogue, The Republic. This allegory spoke of the cave dweller who had escaped from unthinking fixation on the vague, shadowy images visible on the back wall of his dark abode, which up until this point had provided him all that he knew about the world at large. His liberation came from "turning round" (i.e., converting),

2 Alcuin of York, "Epistle 170," cited in Christopher Dawson, *Religion and the Rise of Western Culture* (New York: Doubleday, 1991), 65.

an action which revealed that the shadows he took for reality were actually cast by substantive figures outside the mouth of the cave. This revelation gave the convert the desire to, in effect, go on pilgrimage: to find and embrace the reality casting the shadows, something which could only be done by traveling upward and outside into the full light of day. A number of Church Fathers taken with Plato's arguments had shown that all one had to do to complete his message was to continue this pilgrim quest for light beyond nature, all the way to God, the Father of Lights, from whom every good and perfect gift flowed. A life of "turning around," or conversion, could thus be depicted as one, lengthy, vertical pilgrimage through nature to an eternal homeland with the supernatural God.

The writings of Pseudo-Dionysius emphasized the hierarchical, structured order essential to the successful completion of the majestic plan of God on the grand cosmic scale. Such hierarchy and structure could be seen operative everywhere in Creation, from the life of the angelic hosts downward. How could one not deduce from this omnipresence of hierarchical order the need to subject the earthly pilgrimage of individual Christian believers to a similar visible, communal, hierarchical organizing hand? God's Providence had entrusted that task not just to the Church, but to a Church protected by the Franks in general and the Carolingians in particular. If the Carolingian King-Emperors took their responsibilities as hierarchical organizers of the communal line of march through nature seriously, then all that men could humanly do to ensure the successful completion of the purifying pilgrimage to the Father of Lights would be done. God could ask no more of mankind.

But the Carolingians failed to perform their regal and imperial tasks efficiently and piously, and for a number of formidable reasons. The Franks, like other German barbarian tribes, really needed time to be able to digest the heady concepts of ordered hierarchical government and transforming spiritual mission being taught to them. Divisions within the Carolingian Family itself did not allow for this, the lands of Charlemagne soon being split into three and more warring parts. Frankish soldiers expected personal rewards for their efforts. A divided kingdom, competing for their labors, allowed warriors to play one Carolingian against another for ever higher stakes, and even to seek power illegitimately on their own behalf. Persistent Viking, Saracen, and Magyar onslaughts wreaked still further havoc with the established hierarchical order, encouraging parochial responses to unexpected local forays. This increased the need for hasty, haphazard recruitment and the rise to importance of self-interested castlekeepers and soldiers of fortune with no philosophical tie to celestial hierarchies. Even popes, bishops, and monks were seduced into this carnival of diffuse military activity, their lands robbed and given to others if they could not be lured away from their proper tasks to the work of blood and iron. The grand mission of the Franks under Carolingian rule lay in ruins. The organized Dionysian pilgrimage to the Father of Lights disintegrated, its participants shading their eyes from the glare of all too complicated Truths, and running for cover to the simple, brutal verities of the back of Plato's cave. All seemed lost. The late 800s and 900s present the picture of a totally disordered, violent, purposeless jungle that only a libertarian or neo-conservative warmonger could find appealing.

Still, Tenth Century Frankish lovers of the ordered pilgrimage to God did not give up a dream whose failure would evoke permanent cosmic consequences too dreadful to contemplate. Nevertheless, they were divided in their understanding of what needed to be done to relaunch the community and its individual pilgrims on the line of march. Three distinct approaches to this difficult enterprise gradually came to debate the shape of the project in question.

One of these was argued by influential northern prelates, among them Bishops Adalbero of Laon and Gerard of Cambrai. Very conservative in outlook, such men saw the task of reconstruction as one of simply getting the traditional political hierarchy firmly back into the saddle. They looked to the reordering of the wrecked pilgrimage of life under the direction of new King-Emperors emerging by the late 900s out of the leadership of the eastern part of the Frankish realm, that region which can now be called the Kingdom of Germany. These bishops held fast to the idea that the task of restoring and guiding the pilgrimage of Christian believers lay with the ruler and his advisors alone. It was up to them to support it politically, to do the prayer, fasting and penance which were its spiritual sustenance, and to designate the soldiers who were permitted to defend it. Every man's job was limited to physical labor and reproduction. His was not allowed to advise or fight, and his spiritual purification was to be achieved inertly and indirectly, with no effort on his part, through the sanctification of his political and spiritual superiors.

A second faction was composed of activists from the more disturbed areas of the southern Frankish lands, where the German or any other King's power was either unknown or totally meaningless. Men like the Bishop of Narbonne placed no faith in traditional rulers who could not control local renegade officials, or renegade officials whose usurped power itself then disappeared easily into the hands of castlekeepers and other militant riffraff. Instead of looking to an illusory hierarchical order guided by impotent kings to relaunch the proper procession to God, they turned to a total mobilization of their various flocks against the many disturbers of the peace around them. One sees in their thinking a kind of early liberation theology. They seemed to presume that a "diocese in arms," hurled into battle against the forces of evil behind the relics of its favorite saints, would automatically ensure the movement of men back towards God, as though the Christian People as a mass need not fear falling prey to its own temptations and its particular demagogic sins.

The third suggestion came from out of a variety of different Frankish monastic communities. Most important among these was the Burgundian abbey of Cluny, founded in 910 with the backing of a local count who allowed the monastery to go about its spiritual business without disturbance. A succession of powerful Cluniac abbots took sophisticated advantage of this initial grant of independence to construct a network of reformed Benedictine houses supported by an equally extensive and eclectic grid of friendly political authorities, from castlekeepers to counts to the new King-Emperors of Germany. Religious clout was added to their armory by adopting SS. Peter and Paul as patrons, and thereby linking the Cluniac network and its goals with Rome and the Holy See.

Central to the Cluniac plan for relaunching the pilgrimage to God was the awakening of all men to their need to work actively for its success. Each and every human person in the line of march was called upon by it to pray, fast, and do penance. Such tasks were not the province of King-Emperors and their advisors alone. All were called to the holiness symbolized by the Feast of All Saints, a Cluny favorite. The success or failure of any individual along the path to sanctity impacted upon the viability of the whole communal pilgrimage of the People of God. Carolingian inspired efforts to guide the procession failed precisely due to their insufficiency in this regard. They would fail again if resuscitated unaltered. Inchoate mobilizations of "dioceses-in-arms" were equally doomed. All men were sinful, and the recruitment of The People under the banner of their local saints for the violent overthrow of bad authorities was useless if unaccompanied by a painstaking, life-long dedication to attainment of the personal sanctification of each member of the Christian community.

Cluny had no quarrel with the Dionysian concept of the need for hierarchically-organized public guidance of the pilgrimage to God. Nevertheless, what counted most in its eyes was not who the hierarchs were but whether they wanted to carry out their tasks properly and had real power to do so. For Cluny, the transformation in Christ of whoever constituted the effective leadership of a given land was the primary key to success in aiming a population to the Father of Lights. This, ironically, was the same theme that the first Carolingians had themselves happily taken over from St. Isidore of Seville to justify their replacement of their incompetent Merovingian predecessors.

In any case, it was for this practical and spiritual reason that Cluny placed a premium upon the need, first and foremost, to arouse the wretched mass of renegade counts, castlekeepers and soldiers of fortune who had usurped authority in much of Western Europe to some sense of the responsibilities their de facto political role demanded of them. They had to be taught to pray, to fast, to do penance and to live the life of Christian saints in the realms under their control, where the writ of kings and emperors did not run. If they, the worst of the troublemakers, could be made to take up their Dionysian tasks of pilgrimage ordering in the full Cluniac understanding of them, the peace necessary for the rest of the population to make spiritual progress would be provided.

Cluny used two means to achieve its goal with the upstarts. The first, a *via negativa*, involved a mischievous illustration of the threat that could come from a mobilized "diocese-in-arms" if someone were revolutionary enough to evoke it. Abbots of the Burgundunian monastery traveled widely. Wherever they went, they celebrated solemn masses attended by the whole population of a given region. The abbots then delivered fire and brimstone sermons regarding the evils of warmongering and social injustice to arouse the mass of peace-loving men to fever pitch, aiming their ire at the troublemakers present. Some of the latter were sincerely moved to repentance by the preaching; most were alarmed by the violence that could be unleashed against them or the long-term consequences of being branded contumacious public sinners. The result, in both cases, was the agreement to take solemn open oaths to support what was called the Peace and Truce of God. Such oaths, in effect, defined combatants and non-combatants and led to a limitation of the effects of previously uncontrolled warfare.

Cluny's *via positiva* centered round a substantive teaching of these unruly, untraditional forces. It discovered an innovative means of doing so through use of a traditional tool, the pilgrimage, in this case the increasingly popular hike to the tomb of St. James the Greater at Compostella in western Spain. What better way of demonstrating the correct function of authority to men in love with physical coercion then by giving them a soldiering mission that was truly justifiable; that of defending unarmed pilgrims against bandits and marauding Moors? What better context for catechizing the brute, for transforming his "profession," for teaching him to pray, to fast, to do penance, and to see all of life as a wandering to God than the rather lengthy "time out of time" that the pilgrimage to Compostella offered?

Lessons taught through the two Cluniac paths ultimately had their effect. Renegade counts, castlekeepers, and other soldiers were shown the way to a Christian knighthood honed still further on those "armed pilgrimages" we call the Crusades. More traditional emperors and kings, already awakened to their cosmic responsibilities in earlier ages, were sharpened in their understanding of what these really entailed. The Roman Church, herself reformed and renewed through the inspiration of the Burgundian abbey, used the more peaceful atmosphere that its spirit engendered to apply what was learned to every other sphere of the life of Christendom. For the whole history of the High Middle Ages, from the 1000s through the 1200s, is, in effect, one enormous effort to transform the rest of the variegated pilgrim population of Christendom in the same manner that its rough and tumble soldiers had been won for the work of God. Its achievement was stunning. A New Athens was indeed created, and one characterized by a thoroughgoing hunt for communal and personal sanctification. Alcuin's dream had become a reality.

No Catholic can ever deny the fact that the omnipresent danger of sin makes even the most finely-honed pilgrimage a permanently threatened enterprise. The medieval pilgrimage to God failed partly by falling prey to its own special temptations and sinfulness. Nevertheless, that pilgrimage was also consciously fought by an alliance of heretics, money men, and unscrupulous power seekers who refused its incarnational dream and wished that no one had ever taken even a single step towards achieving it. Rather than attack a dream that had sunk too deeply into the consciousness of the West directly, however, this alliance coopted much of its language of hope, progress, and perfection, perverting it to serve its materialistic ends. The world that it created is the flat, spiritless universe that we in the United States and the European Union inhabit today; a world not on pilgrimage but on a dull and seemingly unstoppable sleepwalk to nowhere.

This brings me to a recent event, noted at the start of this article, one which ought to give even traditionalist Catholics all too familiar with political defeat a little glimmer of hope: the rejection by France of the soulless, technocratic European Constitution. Is it really a total accident that this rebuff came first from the most self-conscious of the heirs of the Kingdom of the Franks? I think not. Those of us on pilgrimage to Chartres saw the remnants of Frankish Catholicism, the modern standard bearers of the incarnational dream, still in vigorous action, against a false Europe as much as against falsity in every other revolutionary regard. Their voice played a powerful role in the anti-constitutional movement.

Admittedly, the rejection of the Constitution was by no means a completely Catholic and logical slight to the heretical and materialist forces dominating the revolutionary West for half a millennium. The coalition making for a negative vote was one built of many disparate groups, motivated by everything from racial fear to anarchistic dislike of all governmental interference, good as well as bad. Still, it revealed in the population responsible for it a continuing capacity for detecting a fraud, for thinking outside of the ideological perimeters which are set for us in every more insistent ways, for opening eyes and ears to a different message than the narrow one that we are ever more pervasively fed. It revealed that stubborn pride in the cultural achievement of the New Athens which appears in the French spirit of even the worst of anti-Catholic elements, a French spirit that cannot fully shake the glory of the vision that it once wholeheartedly loved and actually placed it on the road to somewhere.

Disparate and violent elements, seemingly impervious to cooperation and domestication, were already once painstakingly put together by Catholic Franks, Carolingians, and Cluniacs who understood how they could be purified of their sinful characteristics and transformed in Christ on the pilgrimage to God. Perhaps this vote is Providence's contemporary nudge to dejected Catholics to take heart, thwart the work of our materialist pilgrimage wreckers, and relaunch the line of march yet again. Perhaps the anti-incarnational European Union will be the first casualty of a militant Eldest Daughter of the Church back in the game once more, and till the final count this time round. And perhaps when she is done dismantling that Old World farce she has to face, she might stir up a little missionary fervor. Then the Eldest Daughter might get her Catholic American sibling to put down its freedom fries, and move to the Father of Lights humbly alongside her. *Procedamus in pace*. The morning may be coming on after all.

5
What's Past is Prologue[†]

A S CONFUSED AND HORRIFIED SPECTATORS
of the tragic collapse of the Church in the West in recent
decades, orthodox Catholics justifiably want to identify those
responsible for this disaster and punish them. We often look to
the decisions of this or that modern conclave, pope, or interest
group, or to any of a wide variety of conspiracy theories for what
are, indeed, often partial explanations of a seemingly inexplicable
nightmare. Nevertheless, our efforts to place the blame where it
belongs are often crippled from the outset by our lack of historical
knowledge. The Second Vatican Council and the post-conciliar era
have a complex historical background, one which begins with the
problems emerging from the Council of Trent (1545–1563). Once
this background is filled in, a good deal of the astonishment over
events of the recent past begins to disappear. What at first seems
incomprehensible can be shown to have been, in fact, predictable.
What seems uniformly deplorable may actually yield signs of hope.
The real role of conspiracies, individual decisions, or historical
accidents can be assessed with more accuracy than uninformed
speculation can afford, and that which is truly new or subversive
in the modern Church revealed in all its awful import.

Most educated Catholics do understand the significance of
Trent, doctrinally and pastorally. What needs to be emphasized
about that Council as an aid to calmer judgment and action in
the midst of the current debacle is four-fold. To begin with, one
must never lose sight of the fact that Trent deliberated under the
pressure of almost constant ecclesiastical, political, and military
crises, preventing it from discussing many matters as fully as a
number of Council Fathers would have liked, and forcing certain
"hot" topics to be dropped entirely. Secondly, Trent was bound,
both by tradition, as well as by prudential considerations of time
and energy, to a general policy of focusing only upon contested
issues which had led to a falling away from the Church. It sought

---

† First published in *Seattle Catholic*, August 16, 2004.

to avoid doctrinal disputes among different legitimate schools of theology happily flourishing inside the Catholic camp. Next, it follows from the first two points that much of what Trent said dogmatically and decreed pastorally was limited, incomplete, and open to further refinement and explanation under the pressure of future controversies. Finally, one has to underline the fact that Trent also experienced a "post-conciliar era" which involved inter-pretations of what its decrees did or did not mean, some of which interpretations were not authoritative, were tied to non-dogmatic personal or political considerations, and helped to engender a spirit of confusion and rancor in clergy and laity alike.

It is possible to give a sense of the problems bequeathed to us by Trent by subsuming all the manifold difficulties experienced by the Council under a discussion of two of the basic struggles coloring much of its history: the ecclesiological question of the relationship of the Universal Pontiff to the local bishops of distinct nations united in a Sacred Synod, and the broad issue of man's justification before God and the respective role of grace and free will therein.

Debate over the relationship of pope and bishops, bubbling under the surface and sometimes erupting violently since the first session of the Council, really reached its peak in the third sitting of 1562–1563. Discussion was three-sided. Pope Pius IV (1559–1565), papalist bishops (the so-called *zelanti*, mostly Italians), and certain theologians, among whom were a number of Jesuits who represented a reform-minded militancy in union with Rome, wished to have Trent confirm the decrees on papal primacy passed at the fifteenth-century Council of Florence. French delegates at Trent did not accept the validity of Florence, but looked instead to the contemporary teaching of the Councils of Constance and Basel, which affirmed the superiority of councils, weakened papal ability to guide individual churches, and thus gave support to the prerogatives of bishops and local concerns which in France were referred to as "Gallican liberties." A Church organized under such guidelines, they argued, followed the model of early Christianity, which was held out by the French as an object of imitation for all problems of teaching and reform. Meanwhile, Spanish bishops, as militant in their concern for the defense and spread of the Faith as any of the sons of St. Ignatius or St. Remigius, accepted papal primacy, rejected the French divinization of the early Church (whose actual character they felt to be still a subject more of speculation than of real knowledge), but did insist upon more precise definition of the dignity of the episcopal state as such. Thus, however much they might admit that the individual bishop owed his jurisdiction to Rome and obedience to her doctrinal leadership, they maintained that his role as successor to the apostles placed him under divine obligation to carry out his responsibilities in a way that required opposition to certain current curial practices. Hence, a conscientious bishop would have to oppose the widespread awarding of dioceses to people who worked in Rome and never actually administered their sees, and the granting of so many exemptions to individuals and religious orders that governance by a resident bishop became frustrating and almost impossible. As an episcopal college, in council, the Spanish bishops felt called upon to reform the papal court itself and eliminate such abuses. From the standpoint of the *zelanti*, this meant conciliarism in reality if not in theory.

Bishops gained support in their general quarrel with papal primacy or papal governing practices from the various existing and budding European nation-states. Their co-operation reflected a long-gestating national particularism which conflicted with the international vision represented by the papacy. Still, not all "episcopalists" should be tarred with this pronounced particularist brush. Many bishops simply wanted to emphasize the necessity of nuance in local applications of universal principles without in any sense wishing to reject those principles altogether. Some, like the French, were as eager to be as free from French royal control as they were from papal leadership, one expression of this desire being their concern to allow cathedral chapters to name bishops, again, it was thought, in imitation of ancient custom. State support was dangerous support, for it did contain a strong element of national, lay passion to dictate laws to universal Christendom, thereby swallowing up the religious whole in the secular-minded part. The fact that there were problems here that needed to be clarified led Council Fathers to press for discussion of a "reform of the princes" at Trent, and Cardinal Giovanni Morone (1509–1580), who presided, as papal legate, in the Council's last nine months, to use the threat of this discussion to convince the great powers to come to terms on the ecclesiological issue in general. In short,

Church awareness of the urgency of marking out the special needs and autonomy of the sacred sphere in the reform of Christendom was placed in vivid contrast to local state conviction that national concerns should dominate religious as well as secular discussion.

Before we examine the resolution of the ecclesiological battle at Trent, let us turn to the second major dilemma of the Council, that involving justification. Almost everyone at the Council was at one in rejecting Luther's concept of total depravity after Original Sin, and his consequent reliance on justification by faith alone. There was, however, significantly less agreement over exactly how to describe the nature of man's flaw after the Fall, and the relation of his free will to the grace that sanctifies him. Thomist, Scotist, and Augustinian schools, with their particular emphases and nuances, skirmished with one another in studying and reworking the original sketches of decrees written by men like Girolamo Seripando (1492–1563), General of the Augustinian Hermits at the time of the first sitting, and Cardinal-Legate at the last. Council Fathers lined up for or against efforts to keep the doors to reconciliation with the Protestants still open by building a decree on justification from the work of Cardinal Gasparo Contarini (1483–1542) at Regensburg in 1541, the last major bilateral attempt to heal the split in Western Christendom. "Double justification" had been the theme at that colloquy, a first reconciliation by faith being followed up by a second one that called attention to our personal contribution to our salvation. Accompanying all these controversies was another methodological battle. This saw theologians committed to doctrinal formulation in scholastic terminology crossing swords with others determined to work within a humanist framework, sticking as closely as possible to scriptural proof and language in conciliar decisions.

Ecclesiology proved to be so productive of division that Cardinal Morone and a group of leaders of the various nations at the Council concluded that the only way to deal with the matter was to drop it entirely. Still, with the outrightly conciliarist view somewhat muffled through the aid of the French leader, Cardinal Charles de Guise (1524–1574), bits and pieces of the other different ecclesiological positions made their appearance in one specific canon/decree or another in the months from July to December of 1563. Special prerogatives of the Holy See are alluded to, though the Council Fathers did, indeed, lay down certain reform guidelines

for the papal court itself. Detailed reform was deemed something that needed elaboration after the Council at the local level,
but the presence of papal legates at provincial synods seemed to
guarantee continued guidance from an internationally-minded
papacy. Religious orders were praised, but said to require changes,
and the regular clergy knew that it was being watched by local
bishops who did not like feeling hampered in the governance of
their dioceses by the independence that such orders cherished.
Anyone studying Trent in depth can see that the papal-episcopal
question had merely been calmed, but not satisfactorily clarified,
while State involvement in the whole matter, and, with it, the
broader issue of parochial lay interests in the life of a universal-
ist, clerical-guided and much more self-aware Church, remained
barely examined at all. The decision not to tread on State toes at
Trent meant, among many other things, that the whole question of
what was going on in the world-wide missions under Portuguese
and Spanish control, whether spiritual interests were being subordinated to secular ones in the evangelization of the indigenous
peoples, was left untouched. Trent thus dealt with the problems
of the Church in Europe and not those in the rest of the world.

The decrees passed at Trent related in one way or another to
justification did emphasize the work of both grace and free will,
though not in the context of a double justification, (criticized as
redundant), but as a single act of co-operation of man with God.
Traditional positions were reiterated as far as they could be co-opted
in the terms of a new debate, so much so that some of the Council
Fathers thought that the controversy of the relationship of free will
and grace had been left as unresolved as it was before Trent, or
that the need to strike at the specific Protestant denial of free will
had left the impression that freedom counted more than grace and
faith in the Catholic vision. Furthermore, some decrees were introduced by explanatory texts which canonists thought not to possess
the same weight as the precise canons and anathemas following
them. In short, just as with the ecclesiological issue and its related
problems of Church-State conflicts and the fate of non-European
Christendom, the post-conciliar era would also witness a hunt for
further clarity in matters concerning grace and free will.

One other obvious point helps to explain why the leftover
disputes of Trent must be taken into account in order to grasp the

current ecclesiastical nightmare: the fact that the sixteenth century Council was a pastoral as well as a doctrinal Council. Rooted in concerns that pre-dated the Protestant revolt, Trent was deeply committed, probably more committed in a practical way than any previous council, to a thorough evangelization of a Christian world which was believed to be still all too rooted in superstitious pagan practices. Evangelization was to be accomplished by a reinvigorated clergy, episcopacy, and papacy. But already from the beginning of the Council's first sitting, it recognized that any attempt to separate pastoral activity from zeal for doctrine was impossible. The minute one touched upon the first realm the second inexorably reared its head, the same being true when approached the other way around. The Christian evangelist had to accomplish his work with good doctrine behind him. He had to be able to teach.

Here lay the difficulty. There remained confusion regarding several key problems in ecclesiology, Church-State relations, missionary activity, and the grace-free will arena with crucial consequences for teaching. Hence, the warning of the great Jesuit papal theologian at the Council, Alfonso Salmerón (1515–1585) about the limitations one had to place upon the dogmatic claims of his own order's educational program:

> I think that we must not draw up lists of propositions that we might not be able to defend. This has been done, but it has not yielded good results. Still, if one would truly like to make a catalogue of this type, it would have to contain the smallest number of propositions possible, so that no one could claim that we desire to condemn before the fact opinions and theses that the Church has not absolutely banned.[1]

Identification of the supreme authority within the Church—pope or bishops-in-council—had still to be made more satisfactorily. Different weight was given to the canons and the explanatory texts coming from the Council itself. What was taught in seminaries and universities about disputed matters, and, *a fortiori*, about those topics on which the Council had not spoken at all, was, of necessity, more detailed than anything to be found in conciliar texts, nuanced according to the school of thought and preoccupations of

---

1   Cited in William V. Bangert, *Storia della Compagnia di Gesù*, ed. Mario Colpo (Genoa: Marietti, 1990), 201.

specific teachers, and potentially ground-breaking. But it was less authoritative than anything a Council might decree. Statements appearing in popular catechisms, devotional books and practices, preaching, and spiritual direction was subject to the same "school" mentality, and, given the highly personal nature of pastoral work, often justifiably tailored to a particular individual or group in the specific circumstances of their struggle to reach God. Here, one would be dealing with still less authoritative teachings than anything that might be found in the work of seminary and university theologians, themselves operating on a lower scale than Council Fathers and popes. Finally, the State, whose very justification in its work for social order was deeply intertwined with religion, saw the need for the spirit and the law to move in tandem. It worried about the assertiveness of the reform-minded clergy in defining the rules of the cooperation and taught its own version of the doctrines backing evangelization. Given its primarily secular focus, however, it was perhaps the least authoritative spiritual guide of all. Everyone believed that truly effective pastoral work needed to be done, but what was to be the most important force propelling it? Whatever the intrinsic theological merit of the particular force chosen, each had its committed cheering squad. Which authority was it to be? The teachings of popes? Of bishops in their local circumstances or in council? Of the canons of Trent? Of the canons elaborated on by their explanatory introductions? Of theologians trying to deal with unresolved disputes in answering the questions of seminarians and students? Of one's own spiritual director and guide to sacramental/devotional life? Of the laws of the Most Christian King? Couple the desire to transform the world with a confusion as to which authority should lead that transformation and the result had to be a new crisis in the life of what has always been a crisis-filled Church in pilgrimage to God.

Let us take but one example of the problems of Trent's post-conciliar era: that involving the Jesuits. The Society of Jesus, after Trent, was central to much of the work of Catholic evangelization in Protestant territories as well as in mission countries. It was associated in many people's minds with the Council and the Catholic Reform in themselves. But the Jesuits, who claimed to be followers of St. Thomas Aquinas, seemed to be opting for a clarification of the teaching of Trent which emphasized the importance of free will in a way that Dominican Thomists and Augustinians found to be excessive. This was tied together with devotional practices, spiritual direction and missionary practices emphasizing the same theme. Leaving the question uncontested might bring with it a branding of those underlining the significance of grace and, perhaps, promoting a different kind of spirituality, as crypto-Protestants. Hence the sense that the Jesuit position had to be assailed as being at least semi-Pelagian.

Battle was joined, the main lines being formed around the Jesuit Luis de Molina (1535–1600) and the moral theological doctrine of probabilism on the one hand, and a battery of diverse enemies on the other. These latter included the disciples of Michael Baius (1513–1638), the rector of the University of Louvain, Domingo Bañez (1592–1604), Dominican rector of the University of Salamanca, and, ultimately, the tidal wave of varied supporters of Cornelius Jansen (1585–1638), Bishop of Ypres, and author of the Augustinus, the initial "bible" of the Jansenist movement. The question of whether attrition and fear of punishment, or contrition and full love of God, were necessary for forgiveness of sins also played a major role in the conflict.

From inconclusive disputations under the presidency of Popes Clement VIII (1592–1605) and Paul V (1605–1621), through reiterated condemnations of rigorism and laxism, crypto-Protestantism and semi-Pelagianism, the debate continued to rage though the seventeenth and eighteenth centuries. It very quickly invaded the realm of spiritual direction, liturgical, sacramental, and devotional life, calling up the interest of nations, kings, and law courts, and all ranks of clergy and people, so that anybody who might stake any claim to teaching anything became involved. Since good doctrine was deemed essential to proper pastoral activity, the stakes were thought to be high. It is utterly impossible to give a complete description of the bitterness, rage, and venomous hatred unleashed by this struggle, especially against the Jesuits. From shaky victory to temporary defeat to renewed shaky victory, the free will camp fought to gain the upper hand, and appeared, indeed, to have done so by the time of Clement XI's (1700–1721) encyclical, Unigenitus, in 1713. Ironically, by this time, the issue had been complicated by so many other initially extraneous matters that it needs to be discussed as much as a part of the development of the

French Revolution as an example of post-Tridentine crises. But this is what serves as the link with our own time, illustrating the problems of the last council, the current post-conciliar era, and their continuity with the past.

It should be clear by now that the broad lines of what was discussed at Vatican II flow logically from what did not happen at Trent, what was disputed in the years after 1563, and also (something which lies beyond the scope of the present article) what was not fully thrashed out at Vatican I in 1870 either. It is hard to see how almost any issue that came up in the 1960s would have surprised the controversialists of the previous four hundred years. The papal-episcopal college question, Church-State relations, the advisability of the use of the vernacular and other changes in the liturgy, and, one should also add, the need for a clearer teaching on the sacrament of matrimony, were all issues familiar to them. The only way for much of this discussion to appear unusual is to think that Trent pronounced dogmatically on more matters than it actually did. And this, as I have noted, was a tendency that had its own history and did, in fact, enter, erroneously, into men's minds.

Hard as it may be to pick the wheat from the chaff amidst the rubble of contemporary Catholic life, hope can be entertained that the long-term effect of some of what we have experienced over four hundred and more years of controversies will be for the good. Knowledge of Scripture, the Church Fathers, and the Apostolic Tradition as a whole, deepened in the wake of the manifold post-Tridentine battles, clarifying and underlining the decisions of Trent and Vatican I in positive ways. How much more correct the rejection of "double justification" seems today, when a scripturally and patristically informed appreciation of the Mystical Body of Christ, lacking to the Council Fathers of the 1540s, teaches us that everything good which we freely accomplish is done in unity with Christ; the very Christ who simultaneously offers us the grace we need for reconciliation with God.

What is disturbing about developments in our own day is the way in which lessons which were learned at Trent and in its post-conciliar era have been abandoned, wreaking inevitable havoc in consequence. This is especially true with respect to the erroneous presumption that it is possible to deal with pastoral problems separately from doctrinal issues. Again, this attempt to downplay the importance of doctrine in favor of a pastoral approach to Christian life also has a long history behind it. Erasmus (1467–1536), whose ideas commanded the attention of large numbers of Catholics and Protestants, was one of its chief proponents. States troubled by religious disputes already before Trent tried, unsuccessfully, to keep that Council focused on purely pastoral matters to avoid further rancor. Those that continued to be so disturbed after Trent grew in their conviction of the need to avoid emphasizing doctrine. Society, some of their spokesmen argued, needed the moral framework provided by the Decalogue to carry out its business in orderly fashion, and the Decalogue was accepted by all the main parties to religious dispute. Why dwell on more detailed theological matters insignificant to the peace of the commonwealth? Moreover, Trent itself placed such a value upon practical questions of evangelization and the positive social results accruing from them that one line of Tridentine-inspired reformers did, in fact, end by giving support to the "salvation by pastoral work alone" thesis. Such a tendency became especially pronounced at the end of the 1600s, when the moral aberrations connected with the mystic Quietism of Miguel de Molinos (1628–1696) were given a bad press. A pastoral focus seemed more peaceful, productive, and likely to win favor from God than anything too demanding intellectually, and subject to perversion mystically.

Still, Trent, as we have seen, rejected the idea that pastoral matters could be treated without reference to doctrinal ones as an impossibility. And the history of pastoral concerns in the seventeenth and eighteenth centuries in general has yielded more than ample evidence of the way in which the "practical approach" actually involves its own doctrine, which sometimes conflicts radically with the orthodox position.

One would do well to look briefly at certain aspects of the Jansenist movement with this in mind. Many Jansenists, eager to divert attention from their doctrinal deviation, turned instead to "pastoral" work. They denied the existence of a Jansenist faction, claiming simply to be going about the business of Christian evangelization in line with the perennial tradition of the Church. Enemies who continued to harass them on doctrinal grounds were accused of private vendetta and perversity, and of being "schismatic" in their desire to stir up trouble where, Jansenists claimed, no grounds for it existed. Through spiritual direction, the publication of catechisms and devotional works, translations of the liturgy, and other activities, they sought to build individual men and women of conscience ready to live and defend their faith.

But since Jansenists forming such conscientious Catholics de-emphasized the role of free will in the relationship of man to God, they necessarily had to clash with the pastoral activities shaped by those, like the Jesuits, operating with a different doctrine. Jansenists had to strike at the concept of men working in union with grace to raise themselves and everything around them to the greater glory of God in a natural world already beautifully structured by the ancient Greeks and Romans. This they did, launching an assault on all the "arrogant," "pompous" forms of "Jesuitical" Baroque practice in the name of noble simplicity, ancient Christian humility, and individual, self-abasing sincerity. Everything elaborate, everything indicative to them of man's and nature's pride had to go. So did all that emphasized God's closeness to man. Thus, as the 1700s progressed, one heard Jansenists thundering more and more, on the "pastoral level," against Latin, music, art, processions, eucharistic devotions, feast days, the rosary, the way of the Cross, and adoration of the Sacred Heart. The spirit and substance of Jansenist pastoral concepts, as well as their inevitable tie-in with a doctrinal system of their own, can be found in the pages of the long-lived clandestine eighteenth-century French periodical, Nouvelles ecclésiastiques (Church News), in the reforms undertaken in Austria under Maria Theresa (1740–1780) and Joseph II (1780–1790), and in the decrees of the Synod of Pistoia (1786) in the Grand Duchy of Tuscany. Still, the fact that pragmatic pastoral activity seemed to be their chief concern confused those who did not share Jansenist ideas, making them into unwitting aids of a belief system not their own.

The focus on pastoral activity alone has grown together historically with a demand for the abandonment of the use of authority in the service of spiritual matters, whether by a doctrinally-minded papacy or a State conscious of its responsibilities towards religion. Jansenists also worked to weaken the influence of popes and monarchs who stood in the way of "true" Christian practice. Interestingly enough, in the three cases noted above, they did so in union with other authorities—the French parliaments and desacralizing rulers—the imposition of whose will was deemed essential to the creation of a more inward-looking, pastorally-minded Church. The political theory used by these forces defined the word "spiritual" in such a way as to give to religion control over nothing except the inner conscience of an individual, everything else being subject to arbitrary twisting on the basis of changeable interpretations of what was required to establish public order. The ecclesiastical theory developed by the Jansenists gave each "sincere" conscience the certainty that it could and must guide the Church as it determined, even if pope, bishops and the vast concourse of the faithful were against it. In both cases, the pastorally- and spiritually-minded Church became the plaything of arbitrary forces making the supposed concern to eliminate the appeal to power in religious matters from religion laughable. Again, fellow travelers equally preoccupied with pastoral improvement often did not see the doctrinal deviation and practical consequences to which they were giving unintended support.

If one is truly interested in the role of conspiracy in history, the almost unknown but fully documented conspiracy of Jansenists and their sympathizers against Jesuits, Jesuit pastoral activity, and the post-Tridentine Church that they were said to corrupt is a fine place to begin. It had its centers in Rome, Paris, and practically all of the Catholic courts of Europe, as numerous modern secular historians have identified. Every tool useful in imposing the will of a minority upon a majority and masquerading it as a just and democratic act played its part in this plot: the creation of the cause célèbre, the manufacturing of an outraged public opinion demanding satisfaction, the commission of brutal deeds fueled by a hatred of which only the opposing, orthodox side is said to be capable. Moreover, it was a successful conspiracy, albeit only temporarily so. For the realities of the French Revolution and the fight against it awakened the "Baroque" Church to what was eternally essential in her character, long enough to recognize and deconstruct the trick being played on her, and to open the eyes of many purely "pastoral-minded" reformers as well.

None of these problems of a purely pastoral approach towards dealing with ecclesiastical questions have disappeared since the eighteenth century. If anything, it ought to be much clearer now than two centuries ago that a "pragmatic" policy which is also said to secure protection for "conscience" entails the triumph of hidden doctrines and the victory of determined minorities. The same tactic has been used to telling effect again and again in the intervening period, the very social doctrine of the Church having to a large degree been developed to underline this fact. Why, then, has the lesson been lost?

Three reasons may be noted briefly here. There have never ceased to be Catholics arguing for a focus on pragmatic pastoral work in a way that both denigrates the role of authoritative Church teaching of doctrine and yet opens wide the door to *ex cathedra* pronouncements by the spirit of the times. Nineteenth-century Liberal Catholicism, Americanism, and one strain of twentieth-century Modernism have worked powerfully to this end. Contingencies (chance, if you will) have also played their role. There is no denying that the growth of industrialism and the popular press, the impact of deadly ideological warfare and the sympathies of specific prelates and pontiffs have all contributed to a desire to retreat from the realm of divisive intellect to one unified on the basis of what is immediately and universally appealing. And, finally, there have always continued to be those men honestly dedicated to evangelizing the world and in no way eager to allow false doctrines to subvert the direction of their action, who, nevertheless, saw the pastoral gaps after Trent still looming large before them; saw them, and fell prey to the temptation to relax doctrinal preoccupations under the "new" conditions of the enlightened 1960s.

Unfortunately, our recent pastoral experiment was not worth the proven risk. As ought to have been expected, the children of darkness were savvier than the children of light. Every positive word of every constitution of Vatican II has come to mean, in the minds of most Catholics, whatever the most willful pragmatic group in a given parish, diocese, or society has wanted them to mean, which is generally something which they ought not to mean. Hence, the validity of what Dietrich von Hildebrand prescribed as the necessary prologue to a truly Catholic pastoral renaissance built from the lessons of the past: the appeal to sound doctrine, the precise pinpointing of error, and the reiteration of the glorious words, *anathema sit*.

Holy Fathers of the Council of Trent, pray for us.

6

The Venetian Interdict of 1606–1607[†]

THE DIVINE RIGHT OF REPUBLICS, AND THE TRIUMPH OF THE WILL

One of the most important events of the Catholic Reformation era was the Venetian Interdict of April, 1606 to April, 1607. It involved practical economic matters and power-political relationships which the Church may not have judged correctly. Nevertheless, it also represented a cause célèbre engaging much of the European continent in a debate on the relationship of mankind to a changing environment and the unchanging God, in which the Church was indeed on the side of the angels. Examination of the entire episode yields interesting insights into the development of the Church-State framework of twenty-first century America.

THE DISPUTE AND THE INTERDICT

A basic outline of the history of the Venetian Interdict can be sketched quickly. Venice and the Papacy, which often quarreled over jurisdictional questions, clashed especially harshly over a number of such matters in the years 1602–1605. Laws which, in effect, legitimized lay confiscation of lands which had been leased from the Church (1602), prohibited the construction of church buildings without state permission (1603), and ended transfers of property from secular to ecclesiastical hands (1605), followed one upon the other. Meanwhile, two clerics, Scipione Saraceno, a canon of Vicenza, and Abbot Brandolino of Nervesa, accused of crimes ranging from mockery of the symbols of state authority to sorcery and murder, were arrested by the Republic to be tried in secular—rather than ecclesiastical—courts.

Pope Paul V (1605–1621), excoriating all these measures, put Venice on warning that failure to change her behavior would lead to excommunication of her leaders and the laying upon the entire commonwealth of an interdict, a prohibition of all sacramental life save in life or death emergencies. Warnings came to naught. By

---

† First published in *Seattle Catholic*, September 21, 2004.

April 1606, therefore, the Papal threat became a reality.

There then took place a battle of great bitterness for the obedience of the clergy and the laity within the Republic, in the midst of which the bulk of the churches were kept functioning by the government, and especially pro-papal forces like the Jesuits were expelled. A Venetian protest of the interdict tried to interest all secular authority throughout Europe in the Republic's plight, citing it as an example of unjust Church interference in the life of the State with general repercussions for everyone. Protestants, especially English and Dutch Protestants, became excited over the possibilities for penetrating the Italian peninsula. French Gallicans were called into the fray. Rome weighed the prospects for a military solution. Finally, after a year of turmoil, the French Cardinal Francois de Joyeuse, building upon the mutual (and anti-Spanish) friendship of Venice and his own kingdom, negotiated a settlement (April 21, 1607). Rome let the censures drop, Venice abandoned her protest, and the Republic promised to hand the clerical criminals whose immunity it had violated over to the King of France, who might, if he so wished, give them up to the Pope for judgment.

Already, beforehand, Cardinals Cesare Baronius (1538–1607) and Robert Bellarmine (1542–1621), two of the greatest contemporary defenders of the Church, had their objections to the suggestion of an interdict against Venice. Almost everyone since them has agreed that it was a mistake and a failure on the practical level. Not only did Paul V underestimate the extent to which seventeenth-century clergy and laity might cavalierly disdain commands which would have made even hostile medieval peoples tremble, but he also could be accused of a dreamer's indifference to Venice's serious economic concerns about land usage, and political fears for her survival in a Hapsburg-dominated Italy. Not only did he pick a weapon, the interdict, which seemed to strike at the innocent as well as the guilty, but he also used it against Venice while sparing the Hapsburg Spain that terrified her: a land which men like Baronius considered to be much more guilty in these jurisdictional matters. Other states were aroused to sympathy for Venice in a fashion that hurt papal prestige. Even the settlement of the issue proved to be an embarrassment for the Papacy. The Republic forbade celebration of the reconciliation and the seeking of absolution for canonical penalties incurred by violating the interdict, insisting that it was apologizing for nothing and changing nothing in its behavior. Venice made it clear that its compromise in the matter of the criminal clerics was a one-time event, in no way prejudicial to its future jurisdictional demands. In short, the good sense and effectiveness of Rome were seriously called into question by the Venetian Interdict, and some of the greatest minds in the Catholic world could have said, "I told you so."

But does that mean that nothing that was spoken or done against Venice over the issues inspiring the interdict was for the good, or that no battle with the Republic ought to have been waged at all? Here the answer must be a decisive "no." For the long-term correctness of papal concern over the Venetian actions—and with it the overall correctness of the Catholic vision in and of itself—comes out when one examines the spirit behind Venice's struggle with Rome. Even a superficial glance at much of the Venetian writing in defense of the Republic reveals an outlook that the Church needed to combat and can be proud to have resisted. And, in fact, men like Bellarmine and Baronius, who were uncomfortable with some of the specific political and legal aspects of the interdict, were in the forefront of the battle against certain monstrous intellectual errors at play alongside them.

THE GIOVANI

Who were the spokesmen for this unacceptable Venetian spirit? One cannot aspire here to a complete listing of every name of significance. Let it suffice to say that the main figures of importance were men appreciated by or directly connected in one way or another with a political faction called the Giovani—the "Young Turks" we would say—which managed to gain control of the Republic in 1582. The Giovani were men with deep intellectual roots, highly conscious of the distinct historical position of Venice in the life of the West, and very eager for their city to overcome her commercial, agricultural, and strategic problems and survive.

Reference should be made specifically to the names of Paolo Paruta (1540–1598), author of Political Discourses and a work On the Perfection of the Political Life; Enrico Davila (1576–1631), known for his History of the Civil Wars in France; Leonardo Donà (1536–1612), Doge from 1606 onwards, for whom service to the State was an act of religious commitment evoking from him a vow of celibacy; Giovanni Marsilio (d. 1612), ex-Jesuit and bridge between the realms of politics and theology; and Fulgenzio Micanzio (1570–1654), a Franciscan who served as spiritual consultant to the Republic after the death of the most famous of all those involved in the battle: Paolo Sarpi (1553–1623). Sarpi, a Servite friar who came to epitomize the revolt in the eyes of Rome, and was excommunicated along with Marsilio and Micanzio, was counselor to the government from 1606 onwards. His Treatise on Benefices, History of the Interdict, History of the Council of Trent and Thoughts cannot be overlooked by the student either of the Venetian Interdict or of the development of modern secular culture as a whole. This is witnessed by no less an enemy of Christianity than Edward Gibbon (1737–1794), who considered Sarpi, along with Davila, Machiavelli, and Guicciardini as bright lights in the recent development of historiography.

A full treatment of the arguments of the Venetian spokesmen can be found (and presented, I might add, in a more favorable light than I will do in this article) in Bouwsma's work on Venice and the Defense of Republican Liberty. Briefly stated, without untangling the specific positions of each of the different thinkers mentioned above, what one finds therein is a high-minded appeal to spiritual principles and the State's role in defending them, combined together both with a view of the universe as the realm of irrationality, sin, and lust for power, as well as a haughty indifference to the contradictions and consequences of this confusion of ideas all too reminiscent of our own zeitgeist. The entire vision is seasoned with an equally familiar disdain for everything Roman. Let us explore this vision and its dangers beginning with the anti-Roman bias.

Venice had had a different history from much of the rest of Latin Europe. Proving the extent of this distinction was one of the main stimuli to Venetian historiography in the first place. History had indeed kept the Republic out of the Carolingian-Western Roman imperial sphere of influence. Its historians fantasized that Venice surely must have remained somewhat separate from the original Imperium as well. Nothing Roman, the Giovani felt, should therefore be allowed to exercise an "unhistorical" control over Venice. This included the Roman Church, many of whose medieval demands had, in fact, effectively been kept at bay over the course of the past five hundred years.

Here is where the problem lay. Since the time of the Council of Trent, the Roman Church had been awakened from her dogmatic slumber and had dedicated herself to a reform that deeply threatened the unique historical position of the Venetian Republic. Rome, the Giovani believed, wanted to drag Venice into an ecclesiastical Imperium that broke with her whole tradition, and claimed to be acting in the name of God in doing so. This was an aggression that offended them for three reasons.

THE STATE IS THE ONE, PROPER VICAR OF GOD IN THE SECULAR SPHERE. IT RULES BY DIVINE RIGHT.

For one thing, the Giovani were convinced that the State was the sole instrument created by God to act in the secular realm in the name of things spiritual. It ruled by Divine Right. Rome, by emphasizing the rights of the supernatural order in the natural sphere, was sacrilegiously invading the space of God's State. In reality, Rome was merely reiterating what had been stressed since the days of Pope Gregory VII (1073–1085), and Gregory argued at that time that he himself was only reviving the ancient canonical tradition which had been suppressed by bad political customs over the course of what we call the Early Middle Ages. Hence, the Giovani had not only a pre-Tridentine, but a pre-Gregorian understanding of the State's spiritual role in the life of Christendom. Constantine might have understood their practical desires, though not necessarily their deeper explanation of their position, which involved a more contemporary development of an admittedly age-old intellectual battle.

THE SECULAR WORLD IS THE REALM OF FLUX AND CANNOT BE GUIDED BY UNIVERSAL OR ARCHITECTONIC PRINCIPLES.

This brings me to the second objection of the Giovani and their supporters, a twist on the ancient complaint of the rhetoricians against philosophy. The earthly realm, they insisted, is the sphere of constant flux and change, the sort of condition described by history (the discipline held to be most suited to demonstrating Venice's unique position in the West). God wants His spiritual agent, the State, to examine the changing reality around it, different for different societies, and use all the tools necessary to move

66

people to do what is required to survive in its midst. He is with the State in all that it demands.

Now, however, the Giovani protested, the Church, descending from its proper field of action into another, unsuitable one, was claiming that the realm of flux had to be guided by theological and metaphysical constructs (ideological principles, we would say, if we wished to indicate the same negative judgment). For example, she wanted individual states' foreign policies to be conducted with an eye to the overall interest of Christianity and Christendom, a demand which could embroil Venice in wars against the Turks. For Venice, however, a foreign policy which aimed strictly at practical issues concerning her survival and growth might lead to commerce with the Moslems rather than crusades.

Moreover, the Church wanted such practical economic interests to be guided by broad Catholic moral aims, rather than the laws of agricultural and industrial advantage alone. This was a mistake. Great truths were beyond human definition and application to the natural world, the Giovani concluded, and any institution that sought to intervene in the secular realm in their name was acting absurdly. For Sarpi, this critique even extended to the dogmatic activity of the Church, since such activity required the use of natural, human language, itself inappropriate for expressing divine truths accurately. It is difficult to see how Christianity could be anything for him in the long run but the observable spiritual life of distinct, changeable local "churches," incapable of any serious advancement down the path of doctrinal formulation. Indeed, it is hard to see how anyone could be permitted by Sarpi's view and that of some other Giovani even to use history as a model for their action, since to do so would be to turn an historical argument into an intellectual guideline attempting to explain and shape pure "flux." The State, the agent of God, must merely act, commanded by nothing rational or architectonic. Discrete moments of life and reaction to them are the stuff of its existence. On the other hand, consistent obedience to State decisions is the will of God.

THE WORLD IS THE REALM OF SIN AND THE STRUGGLE FOR
POWER AND CANNOT BE TRANSFORMED TO THE GREATER
HONOR AND GLORY OF GOD.

Thirdly, Rome offended the Giovani by acting as though the
earth could be transformed *ad majorem Dei gloriam*. Such a transformation was, for them, an utter impossibility. The world was the
realm of sin, with the lust for power being the specific sin that lay
behind all human endeavor. Lust for power was the special distin-
guishing mark of Rome throughout her history, the Popes devoting
themselves to the continuation of the old imperial aggression. In
fact, the Giovani claimed, the whole Tridentine reform effort,
the entire enterprise of transformation of the world in Christ,
the thrust of the growing interest in dogma and its application to
daily life was one enormous mask for building Roman power. It
was therefore the duty of the intelligent man to uncover the lust
for power behind every action, to "deconstruct" these seemingly
principled moves to reveal the omnipresence of sin. It is this that
Sarpi did particularly cleverly, after the interdict was lifted, in his
History of the Council of Trent.

Of course, such an idea means that the State, serving as
lion-tamer in a jungle of irrational conflict which may change
form but never end, must then itself logically exhibit that same
sinful, mindless lust for power that it is supposed to identify and
manage in its subjects. Still, if the State insists upon its Divine
Right to obedience, cuts off all discussion of higher principles, and,
to enforce its will, relies on the kind of terror that Sarpi has no
qualms about encouraging, it can easily prevent "deconstruction"
of its own role as God's agent in the world.

THE PRINCIPLE OF PRAGMATISM BECOMES A DOGMA

This brings us to a final underlying contradiction. According
to the Giovani, no universal ideas were to be allowed a role in
shaping the life of states with their different histories and varying
problems. Politics was to be the realm of the "pragmatic." But it
is clear that the pragmatically-minded Giovani were religiously
devoted to their political conclusions. Many of them spoke of their
Republic as though she had sprung fully formed out of the almost
supernatural wisdom of her Founding Fathers, with universally
applicable practical lessons for a world desperately in need of

enlightenment. Hence, they were teaching pragmatism as dogma. A contradiction, indeed, but it should be clear by this time that we have entered an era in which consistency is dismissed as the "hobgoblin of little minds."

THE GIOVANI AND AMERICA

Paolo Sarpi's book on the Council of Trent was taken to the Plymouth Bay Colony by William Brewster (1567–1644), the spiritual leader of the migrants. John Locke was deeply interested in the Venetian Question. Holland was looked to by the Giovani for support at the time of the Interdict, and offered inspiration to Sarpi, among others. All the above have had their influence on America, and the dominant forces in American life have continued to emphasize much of what the Giovani had to say. America, too, demands belief in the Divine Right of her Republic. She, too, has tried to keep the Church out of secular affairs, insisting on the importance of her political institutions as the real agent for injecting spiritual, liberating influences into human life. Our system also works with an understanding of mankind as a herd of self-interested, warring animals whose factiousness can only be observed and managed, but never cured by obedience to a higher truth and a call to the practice of virtue. It, too, jumbles spiritual and practical claims together in contradictory ways, prohibiting dogmatic guidance of the natural world if this guidance is based on ideas of truth, goodness, and beauty, but requiring it if the dogma being taught is one that underlines the purely "pragmatic" actions of power-driven men. Religious dogma, for America as it was for the Giovani, has been seen as something unreal and, ultimately even "unspiritual," while the dogma of man's sinful, irrational life of flux is recognized as truly realistic and, quite bizarrely, somehow spiritually uplifting. To say that this involves a deep cynicism or confusion about the essence of things spiritual is but to touch the tip of the iceberg. Catholicism could not be reconciled with this vision in 1606–1607 and it cannot be reconciled with it today.

We live in a time when practically every element in the traditional life of the Church has been challenged or destroyed. In order for us to fight properly and fight well for the restoration of everything that ought to be restored, we would do well to try to distinguish what is essentially important to the life of the Church from what is secondary and ephemeral. The real glory of the Church and a number of her apologists in the Venetian Interdict issue was their recognition of the essential error lying behind the vision of the Giovani: the recipe for the triumph of the will, the glorification of the will to power—the "right to choose"—of the strong over the weak without having to be called to account for their action; a triumph of the will and a glorification of the will to power brilliantly argued for the benefit not of a monarchy or a dictatorship, but of a republic. They had the acuity to "deconstruct the deconstructors," to show where true cynicism had taken root.

Not every prelate and apologist in the seventeenth century was so perceptive. It was difficult for them to understand that the spiritual role which they all admitted the State to possess was being given so radically different a definition by their opponents. Indeed, their opponents themselves may not have seen all the consequences of their thought either. Whatever the case may be, the bulk of the Catholic attacks on Venice were centered on the particular facts of the jurisdictional battle, which involved issues that did touch upon legitimate Venetian political and economic fears, and on which the Church might in fairness have compromised but did not wish to in 1606–1607.

It is the insistence of our own age and land on the Divine Right of its Republic to do what it chooses to do based upon the will of its Founders, regardless of the demands of reason and Christ's Church, which is the essential dogma requiring the labor of Catholic apologists, now as with the Venetians in the seventeenth century. It is to the confused and often cynical claim of a "godly" and "spiritual" foundation for this invitation to the willful use of power that attention must be turned. The failure to recognize the essential, and the direction of attention to specific issues of ephemeral importance alone, such as the accidental benefits or detriments of a particular article of the Constitution or piece of legislation, is an enormous diversion of effort to uprooting a tree while a thick forest is left to cover everything in utter darkness.

7
Lose the Past, Lose the Present†

IT IS DOUBTFUL THAT MANY TRADI-
tion-minded Catholics would question the argument that he
who controls the depiction of the past also has a powerful means
for controlling the present. After all, it seems quite clear that once
the picture of historical events has been painted by those who
have the will and the power to place their canvas before the whole
population's eyes, it will be virtually certain that few people will
critique the scene it offers. Indeed, it will be virtually certain that
almost everyone will interpret current issues in the context of the
sketch of history that has been made familiar to them.

Although they may not know this to be the case, believing
Catholics are nevertheless often among the worst offenders in
the neglect of history. And in neglecting it, they contribute to
allowing their enemies uncontested opportunities for poisoning
the attitude of millions of our contemporaries towards a religion
whose true history might actually appeal to them.

Catholics began to lose control over the depiction of the past
already at the time of the Renaissance. This was certainly not
because of Humanism and Humanist methodology in and of themselves. Humanist love for language, literature and antiquity in general was valuable in the development of what is called "positive theology," a theology dedicated to exploration of the primary historical
sources of Christian life: the Scriptures, the Fathers, liturgical texts,
early canonical legislation, conciliar decrees, and references to the
behavior of the faithful through the ages. It also became a powerful
stimulus to the publication of broad texts in Church History, which
sought to coordinate the information pouring in from those varied
sources. The problem was that certain Humanists constructed out
of their love for ancient rhetoric and antiquity an historical vendetta against what they saw to be a stylistically barren and barbaric
medieval culture. "Systematic" or "speculative" theology, a theology
that leaned heavily upon logic and other philosophical tools to

---

† First published in *Seattle Catholic*, November 1, 2004.

build the grand cathedrals of Christian thought characteristic of medieval scholasticism, was among the prime targets of their barbs. The theme of the corrupted medieval world, guided by overblown and drably expressed dogmatic visions lacking contact with real life, had been created. Such a theme could not help but stain the reputation of the Catholic Church, which had reached such high pinnacles over the centuries since late antiquity.

It was, however, the Reformation which really put the Catholics on the run, due to the persistent, enthusiastic, and often quite talented efforts of Protestants conversant with Humanist methodology to use this literary tool as a weapon in the anti-papist arsenal. Labeled innovators by their Catholic opponents, and yet convinced, as they were, that the Church had introduced changes of disastrous proportions into the life of Christians, such Protestants hammered at arguments drawn from positive theology to drive home their apologetic points. They knew how to uncover scriptural, patristic, legal and liturgical problems embarrassing to the Church. They knew how to weave these into broad historical assaults calling her whole mission into question. Their feel for language, now extended to the vernacular in addition to the ancient tongues, enabled them to present their accusations in gripping, often rude, but always crystal-clear ways to wide audiences. Hence, with a sense of purpose, science, and style, they fixed the theme of medieval Catholic corruption even more firmly in the minds of both the intellectual elite and the masses.

Martyrology was one field of study of Christian behavior that Protestants used to build an anti-Catholic world view from a very early date. What they did was to link up the suffering of Christian heroes from the past with those of "Gospel Christians" of their own day, so as to show that the persecution of true believers was a specialty of the Roman Church from time immemorial. Martyrologies of this type appeared in many languages. Prominent among them were Martin Luther's *The Burning of Brother Henry in Dithmarschen* (1525), William Tyndale's *Examination of Thorpe and Oldcastle* (1535), Ludwig Rabus' *Stories of God's Martyrs* (1552), Jean Crespin's *The History of Martyrs* (1554), Matthias Flacius Illyricus' *Catalogue of Witnesses to the Truth* (1556), Adriaen van Haemstede's *History and Death of the Pious Martyrs* (1559), both the Latin and English editions of John Foxe's *Acts and Monuments* (1559/1563), Agrippa d`Aubigne's poem, *Les Tragiques* (1580), and Simon Goulard's more ambitious *History of the Reformed Churches of the Kingdom of France* (1580).

A sub-category of this literature involved a specific attack on the Inquisition, especially useful in places where it was at first difficult outrightly to condemn the Roman Church, and where one might also tap into anti-Hapsburg and anti-Spanish sentiment. In this line were the anonymous *On the Unchristian Tyrannical Inquisition that Persecutes Belief,* Written from the Netherlands (1548), Francesco de'Enzinas' *History of the State of the Low Countries and the Religion of Spain* (1558), and *A Discovery and Plaine Declaration of Sundry Subtell Practices of the Holy Inquisition* (1567) by "Montanus" (Antonio del Correo), translated into English by Thomas Skinner (1568). Though not Protestant, the Venetian Servite Paolo Sarpi's *On the Office of the Inquisition* (1615/1638) was a further addition to the genre. It was out of these and related attacks that the famous "Black Legend" was born, through which figures like Philip II could be dehumanized, and people spared the (by definition) impossible task of finding serious reasons behind Catholic action in this realm.

Again, as some of the titles noted above demonstrate, Protestant efforts went beyond using and drawing conclusions from merely one field of study of Christian behavior in the assault on Catholicism. A complete anti-Catholic history had to be written, with respect to individual nations as well as with regard to the life of Christendom as a whole. Martin Luther and Jean Calvin were both involved in this sketching-out of the broad Romaphobic landscape, the former tracing the roots of Catholic error to an earlier date, the latter adding the Carolingian Family and its insatiable ambition to the list of villains responsible for the deviation of the Church from its proper constitution. But the most impressive Reformation-inspired Church history, because of the universal vision it offers, is the "orthodox" Lutheran work produced by Matthias Flacius Illyricus and his associates at the city of Magdeburg. This text is referred to as *The Centuries* (8 Vols., 1559–1574), its name clearly following its manner of dividing up the material presented. Here one finds many of those spicy but erroneous stories, like that of Pope Joan, which still figure into the average "educated" man's anti-Catholic repertoire.

The painters of the anti-Catholic historical picture never slackened their efforts. Enlightenment thinkers of the eighteenth century entered into the studio following the Reformation Era to sharpen the image. By the 1800s, the "Whig Interpretation of History" (to borrow the title of Herbert Butterfield's famous book on the subject), which continues to batter Catholic self-esteem on the popular level, was complete in all its particulars. The world was given a black-and-white standard by means of which to judge all events, past and present, one which condemned anything Catholic in argument and culture as being by definition fantastic, alien to real life, retrograde, and drab to boot. Meanwhile, the same measure was used to show that everything that tore at the heart of Catholic Christendom (and, given the increasing role of Anglo-Saxon influence in undertaking this mission, all that aided the process of Anglicizing the globe) was progressive, intelligent, and good.

Some of the Council Fathers at Trent deeply felt the sting of attack from Protestants using positive theology against the Church. Time and time again, they had to admit that while they firmly believed Catholic doctrines to be true, and Catholic canonical norms and liturgical practices to be justified, they were frequently ignorant of where these came from and upon what they were based. Hence they felt themselves to be at a disadvantage in dealing with Protestant critiques of indulgences, communion under one kind, private confession and clerical celibacy as unjustifiable innovations, and explaining why people rejecting them should come under ecclesiastical censure. Repeatedly, help had to be sought from Catholic experts in positive theology outside the Council to save it from confusion and potential ridicule.

And fortunately, such Catholics there were, skilled in the use of the same tools as their Protestant opponents, but ready to turn them to the defense of the beleaguered Church. In the 1500s and 1600s, Catholics engaged in research on the primary sources of Christian teaching and life were legion. Scripture was being probed by men such as Sixtus of Siena (d. 1569) and Cornelius à Lapide (d. 1637); patrology by Cardinal Guglielmo Sirleto (d. 1585), Marguerin de la Bigne (d. 1589), Fronton du Duc (d. 1624), and Luc D'Achery (d. 1685); dogmatic history by Dionysius Petavius (d. 1652), archeology and martyrology by Onofrio Panvinio (d. 1564) and Antonio Bosio (d. 1629), author of *Roma Sotterranea.*

Guides to Christian literature in general, following in the line of St. Jerome's early work, were provided by Suffridius Peti (d. 1597), Antonio Possevino (d. 1611), Angelus Rocca (d. 1620), Cardinal Robert Bellarmine (d. 1621), and Miraeus (d. 1640). The lives of the saints were studied by Laurentius Surius (d. 1578), Heribert Rosweyde (d. 1629), John van Bolland (d. 1665), and the Bollandists, as well as (among their manifold pioneering endeavors) by the Benedictine Congregation of St. Maur, or Maurists, and its perhaps most famous representative, Jean Mabillon (d. 1707). Cardinal Pietro Sforza Pallavicino (d. 1667) dedicated his labors to analysis of the recent contributions to positive theology from the documents and events of the Council of Trent.

More than this, broad historical texts constructed from primary source materials and capable of answering the Magdeburg Centuries were also being produced. The name that immediately rises in this context is that of Cardinal Cesare Baronius (d. 1607), author of the *Annales Ecclesiastici* (12 Vols., 1588–1607).

Baronius' story is linked with that of St. Philip Neri (d. 1595), founder of the Roman Oratory. Neri was fascinated by the direct approach to the ancient martyrs and the various sites of Christian antiquity which was possible in a city like Rome; hence, his popularization of pilgrimages to the catacombs and early basilicas and stational churches. Aware as he was of the *Magdeburg Centuries*, and the way in which Protestants were trying to claim for themselves the role of representatives of a Christian antiquity subverted by Catholic Rome, Neri promoted an historical response to their threat. He urged—indeed, commanded—Baronius, who had moved in his orbit from a very early age, to prepare lectures on history for the meeting of his Oratory from 1558 onwards. From such modest beginnings, his work expanded, continuing even after he became a cardinal in 1596. He eventually completed twelve volumes on Church history, carrying the *Annales* down to the eve of Innocent III's reign in 1198. Baronius, in consequence, made the Catholic view something that had to be answered rather than just an inviting target for any hostile scholar's sharpshooting practice.

A number of nations offered men who sought to follow in Baronius' footsteps in the 1600s, including the Italian Oratorian, Odorico Raynaldi (d. 1671). Still, it was France, so important to Catholic thought and life in every regard throughout the seventeenth century, that perhaps did the most in this realm. French scholars laboring in varied fields of positive theology in the 1600s turned their attention at one time or another towards the publication of broad ecclesiastical histories. Perhaps not surprisingly, it was a member of the French Oratory, Charles Lecointe (1611–1681), who is most noted for such work. Eight volumes of his *Annales Ecclesiastici Francorum* appeared between 1665 and 1683.

In short, a bright future for Catholic historical studies, drawing from original research in positive theology, might have seemed secured. The chance for Catholics to shape the world's attitude toward the past, and thereby gain the edge for interpreting the present, might have been judged very good indeed. Unfortunately, despite the massive efforts of still later heirs of Baronius, including the rather recent figures of Ludwig von Pastor and Hubert Jedin, this desirable Catholic shaping of historical attitudes never materialized. It was the Humanist-Protestant-Enlightenment-Anglo-Saxon-Whig presentation of the past that was to tighten an iron grip on the western mind, putting the Catholic perpetually on the defensive, incapable of organizing the framework of scholarly debate, fighting merely to be heard, much less hearkened to.

The explanation of what went wrong is a subject worthy of an entire volume, and not just a paragraph or two in a short essay. Nevertheless, certain Catholic contributions to this debacle should be noted here.

On the one hand, although intensive work in positive theology continued throughout the eighteenth century, some of the Catholics engaged in it fell prey to that contempt of traditional systematic and speculative theology originally inspired by certain Humanists. Indeed, this tendency was already noticeable in the 1600s as well. Yet without a systematic Catholic theology to complement it, positive theology yielded nothing but raw data which still had to be guided by an organizing principle to make it fruitful. The organizing principle came from the zeitgeist, the "spirit of the times," a power that is difficult to resist at any moment and in any land. And the zeitgeist, by the 1700s, had its own systematic cosmology, a hodge-podge of contradictory literary, heretical, mathematical, and scientific dogmas, hammered at by an enthusiastic army of writers who promoted it as the latest progressive element in the historical picture described above. Hence, the results of specific

Catholic research were often fit into the system of the enemy, by now taken as a given, as the obvious diktat of "common sense." Creation of a distinct general Catholic vision of history was rendered superfluous and downright unthinkable. Catholics could work, but their enemies would tell them how their work could be used and what it meant.

On the other hand, Catholics concerned for the presentation of a general picture of history from an orthodox viewpoint, simultaneously drawing from positive theology and yet aware of the need to operate under the guidance of systematic theology, were not given the full support that the importance of their work deserved. It is not surprising that even in the seventeenth century, the fifth Jesuit General, Claudio Aquaviva, found it impossible to carry to completion plans for a Catholic Academy of History. The Church was in the commanding position at the beginning of the growth of the anti-Catholic historical theme. She was all too frequently as indifferent to making massive new intellectual efforts to oppose those whom she considered to be simple rebels as she had been to undertake serious purgation of the scandals that helped to feed the Protestant Reformation. Having built up a systematic theology which, together with the ancient philosophical heritage, worked impressively to defend belief both in an ordered universe and its need for redemption, Catholics did not necessarily see why one had to undertake a complementary study of the roots and development of the Christian message. Moreover, historical research could cause painful political conflict, as Baronius discovered in his battles with Spain over Hapsburg claims to special, age-old rights to control Church affairs in Sicily and Naples. Finally, digesting the fact that the victorious historical picture has been drawn to their disadvantage, and that much of positive theology's raw data has been dragged into a systematic attack upon the Church, many Catholics have drawn the conclusion that history, its sources, and its tools must be rejected as innately suspect.

This brings us back to the initial premise of the article: the neglect of history by believing Catholics. In their love for the Church's Magisterium and just estimation of the superiority of systematic theology and philosophy in the teaching of Catholic truth, the faithful have indeed all too often exiled history from their midst as either unnecessary or misleading. Again, in their recognition of the faithless way in which the raw data of positive theology is frequently treated, they are tempted to avert their eyes from all primary sources and the historian's efforts to evaluate them. Why bother to study the "grammar" of the history of dogma in the work of the Fathers, they have, in effect, argued, when superior dogmatic treatises are available in the great systems of the medieval scholastics? Why look at eucharistic worship throughout the ages, they seem to say, when it might create the impression that the doctrine of the Real Presence emerged from history rather than having been taught outrightly by Christ?

These are not unreasonable questions, but they are queries which ought to be answered with a still firmer affirmation of the importance of historical work and all the disciplines of positive theology that feed it. The Catholic needs to know his roots if for pastoral reasons alone. Why? Because his abandonment of history does not free him from the personal problem of escaping the modern zeitgeist. In fact, it merely delivers him over to its control more fully. For in ignoring history himself, he allows the anti-Catholic picture of the past to reign unimpeded and shape all of his understanding of the environment in which he lives. Thus, one frequently sees conservative Catholics using anti-intellectual arguments, and basing a defense of their positions on eighteenth century "Common Sense" principles, or, barring that, on nineteenth century notions regarding the respect owed to the will of the "Silent Majority." A deeper historical knowledge would demonstrate that these concepts have been produced by opponents of Catholicism, and accord badly with basic Catholic beliefs.

Ironically, neglect of history hands one over more fully to the control of precisely that view of the past that condemns the meaningfulness of systematic, speculative theology itself! Moreover, rejection of positive theology and its raw data demonstrating the development of doctrine is not a sure barricade against disbelief. It buries a fount of evidence that the perceptive believer steeped in the practices of his religion can readily see to be of central value to apologetics. It then often replaces this solid testimony either with "proofs" from pious legends that strangely merge together with millenarian, apocalyptic or Americanist presuppositions, or with arguments which really amount to nothing more than stronger assertions of belief; the latter, as telling in their effect as the efforts of a passport controller speaking English louder and more deliberately to a foreigner who does not have a clue as to what he is saying, whether uttered in a whisper or a screech. In both cases, it is easy for opponents to demonstrate the same point with telling effect: that we do not know the historical foundations of what we claim to be an historical religion.

The mind of man was created by God to give us the means by which to try to understand nature and aid us in our approach to Him. Catholics do not have to fear it. That is why systematic, speculative theology which uses the mind to understand and explain the teachings of the Catholic Faith is a necessity and a blessing. But Catholics have nothing to fear from enriching their knowledge of the scriptural, patristic, archeological, exegetical, and general historical realm—of positive theology—either. For it is from such a realm that the food for speculation began. It is through regular contact with this realm that the systematic theologian reconfirms his conviction that he is not merely speculating in thin air, and gains a better understanding of how to become a great apologist.

How glorious it would be for the contemporary Traditionalist Movement to deepen its own knowledge of positive theology, and of broader Church History in particular. In doing so, it would see that there is very fine work being done in this sphere by many non-Catholic writers who might be won for the Faith by traditionalist efforts. And by deepening its knowledge in conjunction with a more profound practice of Catholicism, it would be in a position to forge a union of positive theology with the higher science of systematic, speculative theology more solid than that existing before the current crisis. Through this more perfect union, the Traditionalist Movement might begin the process of regaining control of the depiction of the past and the strength necessary, in consequence, to conquer the present.

8

Can Anything Good Come from France?[†]

ONE OF THE FEW REMAINING ACCEPTABLE
public prejudices in the United States today is disdain for
France. Contemporary Iraqi issues aside, this disdain most often
appears in contemptuous criticism of ever-weakening French efforts
to defend what is left of that nation's heritage. Part of the explanation for the anti-French prejudice lies with a residue of English
animosity towards a traditional enemy still alive in what was once
a basically Anglo-Saxon America. More important in forming this
bias in the early twenty-first century pluralist American environment, however, is France's possession of a distinct culture. That
culture, at its peak in the seventeenth century, was very much
concerned with educating and perfecting itself and its people.
Much of what it sought to do is still alive in the traditionalist
mentality. Nothing could be more destructive to pluralism, built
as it is upon the vision of a world where toleration alone can
stave off evil, than the kind of educated alternative to formless
openness that France represented. The breeze wafting in from
tradition-soaked Gaul nudged—and still in many ways nudges—
people into a pilgrimage towards a distinct, splendid, and, hence,
"divisive" goal that pluralist America cannot help but recognize
as dangerously alien.

What is it that shaped this distinct goal and the passion for
an education to reach it in traditional French culture? Catholicism played an enormous role in the enterprise, and perhaps
never more fervently and consciously than in the seventeenth
century, when the Church, in the aftermath of Trent, was urging the re-evangelization of Christendom. Still, Catholicism had
competition in its efforts to shape the education and character of
French culture, some of which worked back on Catholics themselves, weakened their control over France's ultimate destiny and
helped to bring on the hostile educational policy of the Revolution. In other words, France experienced a pedagogical battle in

---

† First published in *The Remnant*, December 31, 2004.

the seventeenth century with manifold consequences, only some of which will be addressed here, but which must be examined by anyone eager to grasp the nature of our own contemporary pedagogical and political battles.

In order to understand the character of the French conflict clearly, one must always keep in mind the spiritual and material nightmare France endured between 1559 and 1598. In the course of those years, France saw the growth of the Calvinist Huguenot power, backed by many illustrious aristocrats; a Catholic reaction centered around cities like Paris and various leagues guided by orthodox noblemen, academics, magistrates, and bourgeois keen on purifying France of a strange and often violently iconoclastic menace; revulsion on the part of both groups with a monarchy that did not seem to rule consistently in line with God's laws; religious wars and regicide; foreign exploitation and even threats of absorption into the Spanish Hapsburg power bloc. The mounting confusion only ended with the victory of the Huguenot leader, Henry Bourbon, Henry IV (1589–1610), who defused the Catholic opposition by obtaining absolution from the pope for his abjuration of the Faith and then committing himself to aiding many aspects of the cause of Catholic reform. Protestant resistance to peace was cut off first by Henry's abandonment of the leadership of that resistance, and then by his promising his erstwhile co-religionists, in the Edict of Nantes (1598), various guarantees for the practice of their faith. The nightmare seemed to end once peace with Spain was concluded in 1598, and the country then prepared to devote its energies to its own recovery and development.

A battery of diverse and enthusiastic Catholics thought that they knew what the country needed. What came to be called the dévot party in seventeenth-century France included bishops like Cardinal François de la Rochefoucauld (1558–1645) of Clermont/Senlis and priests such as Adrien Bourdoise (1584–1665), active at the Parisian Church of Saint Nicolas du Chardonnet. Religious from reformed Benedictine, Carmelite, Cistercian and Dominican houses, especially in or near Paris, added their fervor to the cause. Members of the new Capuchin, Discalced Carmelite, Fatebenefratelli, and Ursuline orders originating in Italy and Spain were also active, not to speak of the fathers of the Society of Jesus, who provided such dévot leaders as Nicolas Caussin

(1583–1651), confessor to Louis XIII (1610–1643). Orders founded by French-speakers, including St. Vincent de Paul's (1581–1662) Congregation of the Mission and the Visitandines of St. Francis de Sales (1567–1622) and St. Jeanne de Chantal (1572–1641), played a significant role as well. Moreover, organizations of secular priests, ranging from the network of Aa (Association d'amis) to Cardinal Pierre de Bérulle's (1575–1629) French Oratory, Jean-Jacques Olier's (1608–1657) Company of Saint Sulpice, and St. Jean Eudes' (1601–1680) Congregation of Jesus and Mary offered many zealous foot soldiers for the movement.

All of these prelates, priests, and religious were aided immeasurably in making their influence felt by an army of laywomen, among them Madame Barbara Acarie (1566–1618), who eventually entered religious life as the Carmelite Marie de l'Incarnation, and Louise de Marillac (1591–1660), whose work with St. Vincent de Paul led to the creation of the Daughters of Charity. Louise's uncle, Michel de Marillac (1563–1632), was one of the most important political figures from the large pool of laymen in the dévot camp. While Jesuit Marian congregations, and sodalities sponsored by other priests and religious, were often the locus for lay involvement, private homes also became dévot foyers. Nobles such as Henri de Lévis (1596–1680), Duke of Ventadour, created and fueled the lay Company of the Blessed Sacrament, which operated in France almost as a kind of Catholic Freemasonry.

If one thing could be said to unite all these diverse elements, that cement, as indicated above, would have to be found in their joint concern for education: education of the clergy, the average man, and society at large. Education of the clergy to a sense of its dignity and its lofty responsibilities was the theme set by de la Rouchefoucauld in his *De la Perfection de L'état Ecclésiastique* (1597). From 1612 onwards, Bourdoise used his church to provide unofficial seminary training in a Paris still lacking clerical preparatory institutions. Creation of a new secular clergy, almost *da capo*, was the special mission of de Bérulle's Oratory, and this spirit lay behind the work of Olier and Eudes as well. St. Vincent de Paul sought to instruct Parisian priests by means of a continuing series of Wednesday conferences.

Meanwhile, colleges of Jesuits and Oratorians, the circles around the Cistercians of Port Royal, and, a bit later, the Brothers of the

Christian Schools of St. Jean Baptiste de la Salle (1651–1719), sought the elevation of laymen. Laywomen, whose education was more and more considered to be crucial to the improvement of family life, were formed, to begin with, by Ursulines and Visitandines, and later, with the encouragement of Louis XIV's (1643–1715) second wife, Madam de Maintenon (1635–1719), and the great François de Salignac Le Mothe Fénelon (1651–1715), Bishop of Cambrai. General education was continued through the development of the episcopal pastoral letter and the perfection of the preaching art, which reached its apex by the end of the century with Fénelon, Bishop Jacques-Bénigne Bossuet of Meaux (1627–1704), and the Jesuit Louis Bourdaloue (1632–1704). The Jesuits made use of the theater as a teaching tool, while the period also saw the widespread dissemination of devotional and catechetical works. The Jesuits, Eudes, and the Congregation of the Mission, convinced that France itself was a mission country in need of evangelization, organized highly sophisticated sweeps of the countryside to teach, preach, and firm up commitment to practice of the faith. Each sortie was repeated at regular intervals to make sure the good seed had not fallen by the wayside.

In the long run, of course, this was education of the soul in its approach to union with God, and mystical in its flavor. The mystical character of the movement was aided by stimuli from Italy and Spain, and by the rediscovery or republication of works of the early Christian centuries, such as those of the Pseudo-Dionysius. A rich French strain of mystical writing soon emerged, including the Capuchin Benoit de Canfield's (1562–1660) *Règle de Perfection* (1609), Pierre de Bérulle's *Discours de L'état et des Grandeurs de Jesus* (1623), Olier's *Journée Chrétienne* (1670), and the posthumous (1694) compilation of the teachings of the Jesuit Louis Lallemont (1588–1635), the *Doctrine Spirituelle*. Marie Guyard (1599–1672), an Ursuline active in Canada under the name Marie de l'Incarnation, and many others, taught mystical concerns by example. Different in their specific approaches, all urged some form of meditation on Christ's Sacred Heart and His love for mankind, self-abasement before His majesty, grace and goodness, imitation of the Holy Family, friendship with Mary, and specific penitential and eucharistic practices. One type of devotion to the Sacred Heart received especially powerful support from the revelations to Margaret Mary Alacoque (1647–1690) and the writings of her Jesuit confessor, Charles de la Colombière (1641–1682).

But were personal and corporate prayer life alone sufficient for education and elevation of the soul to union with God? A resounding "no" came from different *dévot* circles. What was referred to as "devout Humanism," as found in the Jesuit Pierre Coton's (1564–1626) *Interieure Occupation d'une âme Dévote* (1608), or the spirituality of Saint Francis de Sales' *Introduction à la Vie Dévote* (1609) and *Traite de L'amour de Dieu* (1616), spoke volumes about the need for active individuals to raise themselves to God through their particular vocations in the world. All Christians, St. Vincent de Paul, Louise de Marillac, and their friends argued, had charitable responsibilities to perform for the sick and the poor. Social sins like dueling, the neglect of agriculture and the peasantry, and the disturbance of the peace of Europe in general, were problems that *dévots*—from the time of St. Vincent and the Company of the Blessed Sacrament to Fénelon in his great work, *Télémaque* (1699)—believed that the Christian on pilgrimage to God had to tackle. And then there was the scandal caused by the continued dead weight of Protestantism in French society, which the *dévots*, by a combination of evangelization and State action, wanted to see removed entirely.

Many of these *dévot* concerns obviously entailed political activity. No Tridentine reforms could be made fully effective until the decrees of the Council were given force of law and the backing of the king. This was due to the fact that some of the decadent practices of the late medieval church, as well as the quite different reform measures stemming from the fifteenth-century Councils of Constance and Basel, were legally binding before the French courts, the parliaments. For example, someone opposed to a Tridentine-inspired action could make what was referred to as an *appel comme d'abus* from Church to State authorities on that basis. French kings had the right, vouchsafed by Francis I's Concordat with Leo X in 1516, to name practically every bishop in the country, the pope retaining only the subsequent power of confirmation of royal choices. Consequently, influence over the monarch was essential to bringing individual dioceses into the Tridentine reform camp. None of the specific desires of the various *dévot* groups—reintroducing sound diocesan and monastic discipline, establishing colleges and seminaries, improving the plight of the peasant, and assuring a Catholic-friendly European harmony—could be achieved without backing from parliaments and king. Hence, the effort of pro-Tridentine bishops, culminating in the petition of the clerical representatives at the Estates-General of 1614, to accept the decrees of the Council officially, once and for all.

But the problem was that there were a variety of groups that did not like the political agenda of the *dévot* party. There were still certain Huguenots whose voices were heard in court and parliamentary circles. A myriad of self-interested groups, such as monks receiving support for a life of prayer which they did not carry out, could be counted on to assure endless litigation and anti-Tridentine agitation. Many ordinary people opposed reform because it struck against what were actually long-entrenched superstitious practices masquerading as religious activity, one prime example being the sacrificing of bulls to the Virgin in times of trouble. A skeptical faction, whose great intellectual mentor was Michel de Montaigne (1533–1592), and a so-called libertine party, with support from Louis XIII's brother, Gaston d'Orleans (1608–1660), were opposed to a France committed to pious causes. Dramatists like Molière (1622–1673) satirized the *dévot* movement, depicting the religious-minded layman as a pretentious hypocrite in *Tartuffe* (1664) and other works.

It was the apparent Ultramontanism of many of the late sixteenth- and early seventeenth-century *dévots* and the Roman-backed Tridentine reforms they supported that brought out most of the effective French opposition to their victory. This opposition was expressed in the name of Gallicanism and the special liberties of the Church in France, which were ultimately thought to be the ancient prerogatives of all local churches vis-à-vis Rome. It was in the name of Gallicanism that the parliaments criticized as agents of a foreign court the nuncios whom the *dévot* saw to be crucial links with the Holy See. It was in the name of Gallicanism that the Jesuits were often bitterly opposed, their doctrine of indirect papal power over law (justified by Cardinal Bellarmine as a consequence of the possible corruption of law caused by error and sin) being understood as an assault on French sovereignty leading even to regicide. This latter argument was particularly powerful in France, given the murder of Henry IV in 1610 by François

Ravaillac (1578–1610), who feared a long-term protestantizing effect stemming from the king's policies. The conviction, real or alleged, that the dévot cause was dangerous to the State, which must, at all costs, be left to its own devices in establishing policy, is well captured in the petition of the Third Estate at the Estates-General of 1614. This successfully criticized legal sanction for Trent and demanded official assertion of the independence of French politics from outside spiritual control.

Perhaps the most effective of the opponents of the *dévot* camp were those partial to the use of the term *bon Français* to describe their position. Emerging from what had been called the *politique* vision at the time of the Religious Wars, a *bon Français* no longer claimed to try to stand above the Catholic-Huguenot battle, as a *politique* might have done. Catholicism had re-asserted itself much too strongly for such an approach by the early 1600s. Instead, he argued that while seeking to do the right Catholic thing, he wished to do it without detriment to France. The problem was that this could, and did, expand to encompass the idea that the right Catholic thing to do, and the benefit of France itself, must be guided not by the pope, nor even by the Gallican bishops, but by "Reason of State," understood by a divine right monarch mystically protected by God. In other words, in making a powerful appeal to patriotism, the *bon Français* implicitly criticized a Catholic who did not accept his claims as being a *mauvais Français*. He then confused the issue by making it unclear whether his opponent's lack of patriotism was ascribed merely to political miscalculation or to the very desire to submit the State to the higher law of morality, as interpreted by the Papacy and *dévot* prelates. Whatever the case, a heavy dose of Gallican disdain for external papal involvement in the affairs of France was part and parcel of the whole *bon Français* position, as was a dislike of independent internal Catholic influence as well.

Battle was joined between the *dévot* and *bon Français* parties over the issue of France and religious war in the period from 1618–1648. The dévots believed that France should dedicate whatever military energy it possessed to the elimination of Protestant fortified places still existing within the country by the terms of the Edict of Nantes, move to suppress public Huguenot worship entirely, and turn its attention to needed internal reforms, especially in agriculture. They believed that France should be at least neutral, if not positively friendly towards the Spanish and Austrian Hapsburgs in the Thirty Years War, since the result of their victory would mean the definitive international triumph of Catholicism over Protestant heresy.

For the *bon Français*, internal reform was of little interest, and the Huguenots concerned them only insofar as they did continue to pose a threat to domestic security. The real question was whether or not the power and glory of the Hapsburg Family might surpass and eclipse that of Bourbon France. The *bon Français* supported war with Spain and Austria, and, in consequence, alliance with the very Protestant powers whom the *dévots* wished to see crushed. A pamphlet war in the 1620s saw the *dévot* "True or Friendly Word of Messieurs the Princes" and the "Admonitio ad Regem" pitted against tracts such as the "Discourse of the Princes and States of Christendom," "On the Progress and Conquests of the King of Spain and House of Austria" and the "Parallel of St. Louis and Louis XIII." It flared up again in the mid-1630s with the appearance of Bishop Cornelius Jansenius' (1585–1638) "Mars Gallicus," which attacked French aggression and was challenged in works like "How the Piety of the French Differs from that of the Spaniards within a Profession of the Same Religion and Gallican Vindications."

After taming the internal Huguenot military threat in the 1620s, France experienced a complete *bon Français* victory. This was symbolized by the triumph of Cardinal Armand-Jean de Plessis de Richelieu (1585–1642) over Michel de Marillac and his allies on what has come to be known as the Day of Dupes (November 10, 1630). France entered the war against Spain and Austria. She won the power and glory that "Reason of State" demanded. She also found herself, by the end of that conflict, racked by the internal revolt of the Frondes, suffering from agricultural and industrial turmoil, and prey to the kind of sufferings poignantly described by the circles around St. Vincent de Paul.

Moreover, the *dévot* camp, by the latter part of the century, had lost whatever unity its diverse elements had once possessed, with baleful results for a coherent education of Frenchmen and French society. For one thing, the *bon Français* argument had had an impact on many of its followers who wished to be both good Catholics and good patriots. De Bérulle contributed to a *bon Français* pamphlet. Many Jesuits, much to the scandal of other members of the Society outside the country, toned down their Ultramontanism in favor of Gallicanism, making France, as one modern writer puts it, the graveyard of internationally-minded Jesuit Catholicism. Even Cardinal Richelieu himself illustrates this point. Always supportive of Tridentine reform on a diocesan level, and tied in his early career with de Bérulle, he, nevertheless, was willing to ally France with Moslems against fellow Catholics and press for the creation of a French patriarchate with quasi-papal powers, so long as dynastic glory and Reason of State required it. It is no surprise that the French *dévots* were bewildered. After all, Pope Urban VIII (1623–1644), while condemning the principle of Reason of State in theory, himself frequently acted in practice during the Thirty Years War as though Protestant defeat were indeed secondary in importance to humbling Hapsburg power. A *dévot* might be forgiven for wondering if politics and patriotism did perhaps have special mystical rules for operating which were different from those of private individuals. And, besides, the personal piety of the French monarchs seemed assurance enough that a Catholic spirit would somehow triumph through the confusion anyway.

On the other hand, the budding Jansenist movement, itself emerging from a segment of the *dévot* party, and taking its political cue from "Mars Gallicus," continued its resistance to the demands of a king basing his actions upon Reason of State. The penitential practices of the Jansenists involved an "opting-out" of the world which was alien to the Richelieu vision of a dynastic France, majestic and mighty among the nations. Their episcopal leaders sometimes challenged French regalism in a way that earned them the gratitude of popes, especially Blessed Innocent XI (1676–1689).

But the Jansenist rump of the *dévot* party was troublesome as educator even more than the *dévot*-turned-*bon Français*. It did win glory for defending things spiritual against the incursions of the temporal realm, but in a faulty way. Jansenist theology led to condemnation by the papacy and the vast bulk of the French episcopacy alike. This, in turn inspired a Jansenist appeal to the individual conscience, shaped by a self-conscious sincerity, as the ultimate teaching authority in the Church. With the papacy and the French bishops against them, the Jansenists obviously could not rest secure in Ultramontanism or in a Gallicanism looking to native prelates for protection against the pretensions of Rome. A Gallicanism based on the support of the King was equally impossible, since the monarchy saw Jansenists as being really or potentially rebellious, and puritanically opposed to the attainment of glory to boot. The only escape route available to them was to appeal to the law courts, the parliaments, as more suitable defenders of Gallican freedom and individual conscience. Parliamentarians did, indeed, take up the cudgels on the Jansenists' behalf, both because many of their members were sympathetic to the movement in and of itself, and because they had always contested the right of bishops and/or king to be the sole spokesmen for Gallicanism and the French State.

Hence, out of the debris of the *dévot* party, dedicated to the education and the elevation of Frenchmen and France, two basic tendencies, shot through with contradictions, had appeared. One, Ultramontanist at heart, had sufficiently sold itself out to the principle of Reason of State to help to baptize this un-Catholic principle. Ironically, the royal *bon Français* needed the support of Rome in opposing the Jansenists, so that the nation found itself exposed to the spectacle of a monarchy appealing for final judgment to a papacy that was supposed to bow to the regal will. Which, then, was the court of last instance? Papacy or Monarchy? Spirit or Strength? The second tendency had no doubt that the spiritual authority was the superior guide, but reduced this spiritual authority to infallible "sincere" individual wills (in effect, as many little "kings" operating by their own reasons of State as there were different persons appealing to it) and then compounded the recourse to force that this entails by surrendering itself to the often brutally anti-royal political program of the parliaments. It is hardly surprising in such a situation that the eighteenth-century *philosophes* saw the quarrels of Catholics as proof positive of their inability to teach anything cohesively to anyone.

Can, therefore, anything good be said to have come out of seventeenth-century France? Yes. Three goods, to be specific. One was positive: the example of Catholic thinkers and spiritual leaders seriously trying to educate their world in the best sense of

Greek *paideia*, by using all the tools available to them, from the State to the theater, to aid the passage of souls to God. The second two were negative: a powerful warning about the way in which respect for the State and the sentiment of patriotism could be used to override the message of Christ's Church in favor of that of the spirit of the times; and a poignant reminder that wrong-headed zeal, in the manner of the Jansenists, could degenerate into heresy, creating believers whom one French prelate called "pure as angels and proud as demons."

Historians often lament the fact that France did not devote its attention in the seventeenth century to dealing with its internal problems. Yet France, as we have seen, was not lacking in influential people who shared this judgment-after-the-fact, at the moment when it might have actually meant something for national policy. Why, then, not admit that the *dévots* were on the right track? Because to do so is not permissible in our global, pluralist world. It would mean admitting that one form of teaching might be preferable to another, and that Catholicism might be that preferred truth. It would mean rejection of the purely "pragmatic" guide to life that pluralism cherishes, precisely that kind of guide which uncritically spews forth whatever the spirit of the times defines as being practical, including the drive for power and glory lying responsible for the mistakes of seventeenth-century Reason of State. It would mean recognizing that the answer to assaults on freedom is not the pluralist canonization of as many despotic wills as there are individuals and groups in society—the practical consequence of Jansenist deification of sincerity as well—but the submission of will and conscience to solid truth, both rational and supernatural. In sum, it would involve a realization that the present age is headed toward the same cul-de-sac that marked an end to France's golden century, and that the mistakes guaranteeing its progress to nowhere are not orthodox Catholic ones, but errors central to modernity's own heart.

9
Great Western Schism
(1378–1417/1429)†

I. LESSONS FOR THE TROUBLED CATHOLIC PRESENT FROM ITS CHAOTIC PAST

"Every age has its afflictions, but you have not seen, and no one has seen a time so troubled as the present." [1] —ST. CATHERINE OF SIENA

WHY STUDY THE GREAT WESTERN SCHISM?

A detailed review of the chaotic years of the Great Western Schism is extremely helpful in coming to terms with the troubled Catholic present. It is useful, in this context, for three reasons. First of all, it shows us—as do all historical studies—that crises do not pop up out of nowhere, and that a given generation's miseries generally have been prepared in a previous age suffering from perhaps even more fundamental woes. Secondly, it demonstrates that resolution of the specifics of any given ecclesiastical disaster may not proceed precisely "by the book," especially if the problems involved are basically new ones and have not been adequately confronted by theologians and canonists before.

Finally, it points to the fact that the Church's full awakening from a nightmare which has diverted her energies away from her real mission is a very difficult enterprise indeed; that it cannot be accomplished "on the cheap"; that if it is to take place at all, it must be built not only upon a humble digestion of the lessons taught by recent adversity, but also on a deeper inspection of all of the wisdom that the book and jewel box of her Tradition contain. Only thus can she truly arouse herself from her doctrinal and pastoral slumber and be better armed for the next inevitable battle with her outer and inner demons.

---

† First published in *Seattle Catholic*, February 2006.

---

1 Cited in Ludwig von Pastor, *History of the Popes, from the Close of the Middle Ages, vol. 1* (London: Keegan Paul, Trench, Trubner & Co., Ltd., 1938), 143.

THE ATTACK ON THE INCARNATION AND CO-OPTION BY THE LOW ROAD

Allow me to begin by noting the fact that life in later medieval Europe was made miserable by a deep disillusionment with the dramatic monastic and papal reform movement promoting a political and social "transformation of all things in Christ" since the middle of the Tenth Century. Such disenchantment was encouraged by a variety of Manicheans, Millenarians, Nominalists, Legalists, and Money Grubbers, all of whom had been peddling their depressing wares in tense alliance with one another for almost as long as the ecclesiastical reformers had themselves been active. Some of these outspoken critics were simply overwhelmed by the practical failures of a powerful visible Church in living up to the public demands of her noble mission. Others jumped upon the critical bandwagon with the hidden, cynical aim of discrediting all exalted visions placing obstacles in the path of satisfaction of their own base self-interests. Still others rejected the very possibility of a political and social transformation in Christ out of honest conviction. Such an enterprise they understood to be, at best, a hopeless waste of time, and, at worst, a blasphemous attempt to baptize the inevitably satanic earthly realm, a horrifying dance with the devil. In rejecting the vision of the great reform movement of the High Middle Ages, however, such honest critics were turning their backs on the most profound discussion of the deepest consequences of the Incarnation and how human beings could use their free will to "give flesh" to the fullness of Christ's teachings.

A broad intellectual and spiritual disillusionment was driven home and given further clout by a seemingly endless succession of temporal calamities beginning in the mid-1200s and lasting throughout the whole of the Fourteenth Century. These catastrophes included the collapse of the central authority of the Holy Roman Empire, the destruction and internal dislocation caused by the Hundred Years' War between France and England, the loss of the Holy Land, the appearance of the Ottoman Turks in Europe, and an ever more open economic and social class war. All such problems were worsened by the successive waves of plague breaking upon Europe from 1348 onwards and the self-preoccupation perhaps inevitably accompanying them. Surely now, critics of "giving flesh" to the consequences of the Incarnation might argue, anyone who thought that nature was meant to serve the greater glory of God had to see that he was battering his head against a brick wall. Surely now he had to realize that actively working to achieve such a goal made him either a fool or a conscious cooperator with malevolent materialist forces.

Catholics are probably best acquainted with the contemporary misfortunes flowing from the humiliation of Pope Boniface VIII (1294–1303) at the hands of King Philip the Fair (1285–1314) and his anticlerical legal advisors: enemies of "transformation in Christ" if ever there were ones. Consistent statist attacks on ecclesiastical rights during that monarch's reign forced a Church preoccupation with conditions in his troublesome kingdom. This fixation in turn seemed to dictate a temporary papal presence in or near France, as well as the selection of a line of Gallic popes suitable for handling French affairs.

Pontifical absence from Rome contributed to the chaotic conditions disturbing much of Italy in the 1300s, where the breakdown of imperial authority had further promoted the growth of autonomous, quarreling city-states. Increasing Italian instability then, in turn, confirmed the papal resolve to stay at its "temporary" residence in the city of Avignon, the entirety of which was finally purchased during the reign of Clement VI (1342–1352). Here, directly adjacent to the Kingdom of France, but on the road that led to Rome, anyone could make the best of an ever-longer Gallic vacation.

Most Catholics familiar with these problems think of the post-Boniface VIII era as one of papal captivity and weakness. In many respects, it really was not. French kings had too many life-and-death problems over the course of the next century to pursue a consistent policy of papal humiliation. The popes came to and left France and Avignon on their own steam. Moreover, they developed therein the most centralized and refined administrative apparatus that the Church had ever possessed; one that both imitated and yet often surpassed in efficiency the bureaucracies of any of the troubled secular governments of the day. Popes, Cardinals and officials of the Chancery and Apostolic Camera appointed bishops, collected taxes, and imposed disreputable political interdicts and excommunications throughout much of Christendom with greater abandon than ever before. They did so in tight association with countless princes and other representatives of the late medieval Establishment. Bankers were particularly welcome in their entourage. As Alvaro Pelayo, himself a fervent supporter of the Holy See, noted in *De planctu ecclesiae*, "Whenever I entered the chambers of the ecclesiastics of the Papal Court, I found brokers and clergy, engaged in weighing and reckoning the money which lay in heaps before them."[2]

A myriad of astonishing abuses, many of them the product of exceedingly pro-papal canonists influenced heavily by Roman Law and purely utilitarian power considerations, became associated with the Avignon administration. Charitable covers for raking in illicit funds were multiplied. Sees were left vacant or filled in ways that furthered the increase of gross curial muscle and wealth. Legal cases were painfully delayed so as to milk more loot from long-suffering plaintiffs and defendants. And, once again, all this was done in dangerous cahoots with locally important political and banker hacks.

Even more destructive was the treatment of diocesan matters as property rather than pastoral questions. Bishoprics were assigned either to curial officials—to provide, from their endowments, salaries the Papacy could not otherwise pay—or to friends of political allies whose cooperative behavior needed to be rewarded. Since it was impossible for papal employees to leave their governmental positions in Avignon to tend to even one diocese—much less the two or more often entrusted to their misuse—episcopal charges inevitably entailed the same absenteeism already practiced by the pope himself. Perhaps the most bizarre long-term development from such unfortunate policies was to be the creation of nominal "bishops" who were often not even priests. Lay "bishops" got the revenues from their "property," and then employed some hireling to do the episcopal tasks they themselves could not legitimately perform.

All this indicated a diversion from the Church's understanding of her main mission and what she most needed in order to fulfill it. It revealed a "preferential option for the low road," a massive placing of her faith in purely earthly tools and gimmicks, a bow to the cynical preoccupations of those who did not really, in practice, believe in the greater strength coming from spiritual transformation in Christ. Avignon's abuses merely confirmed the convictions of those who already thought of the Church and her mission as a blasphemous work of Satan. This was the major reason why her

2   Cited in Pastor, *History of the Popes*, vol. 1, 72.

scandals were so detested by orthodox believers. Their reactions ranged from the harsh, prophetic, and well-known attacks of St. Bridget to the practical adoption by various cities and countries of complicated political measures limiting or even prohibiting papal misrule entirely. In Germany, for instance:

> In October 1372, the monasteries and abbeys in Cologne entered into a compact to resist Pope Gregory XI. in his proposed levy of a tithe on their revenues. The wording of their document manifests the depth of the feeling which prevailed in Germany against the Court of Avignon. "In consequence," it says, "of the exactions with which the Papal Court burdens the clergy, the Apostolic See has fallen into such contempt, that the Catholic Faith in these parts seems to be seriously imperiled. The laity speak slightingly of the Church, because, departing from the custom of former days, she hardly ever sends forth preachers or reformers, but rather ostentatious men, cunning, selfish and greedy. Things have come to such a pass that few are Christians more than in name." The example of Cologne was soon followed.[3]

Chaotic conditions in a France crippled by the Hundred Years' War eventually threatened the security, both physical and financial, of Avignon. Still, before a return to Rome could be contemplated, the Eternal City had itself to be pacified. Pacification required a calming not only of the power of a large number of local notables and their mercenary bands, but also of many others from central Italy, Naples, and as far afield as Milan. Different popes tried diverse tactics. Innocent VI (1352–1362) relied upon the military-backed mission of Cardinal Albornoz (1353–1363), while his Benedictine successor, Urban V (1362–1370), bet on a personal sojourn in Italy and peaceful persuasion. Gregory XI (1370–1378) returned permanently to Rome in early 1377 before the work of pacification was in any way complete. He died on March 27, 1378, as the situation hung between negotiations and a potentially very expensive papal war with the neighboring Republic of Florence.

THE GREAT WESTERN SCHISM

The conclave that met at Rome in April of 1378 was ill-prepared and heated. Two Gallic factions, both of which disliked Italy, nevertheless felt compelled to promise the threatening inhabitants of

---

3 Cited in Pastor, vol. 1, 91.

the Eternal City that they would once again be given a pope who was at least Italian. So fearful were some of the electors of the possible reaction of the parochial-minded mob to their choice of the Archbishop of Bari, Bartolomeo Prignani, as Pope Urban VI (1378–1389), that they temporarily passed off the half-dead Roman Cardinal Tebaldeschi as the new pontiff, and then fled for their lives. But the well-known Urban actually proved to be acceptable to the local citizenry, his coronation was performed without incident, and the frightened Princes of the Church returned. Unfortunately for them, however, this pure, austere and learned man quickly alienated his electors and their corrupt entourage through reform measures reflecting a "naturally arbitrary and extremely violent and imprudent" character.[4]

> But instead of proceeding with the prudence and moderation demanded by a task of such peculiar difficulty, he suffered himself from the first to be carried away by the passionate impetuosity of his temper... The very next day after his coronation he gave offence to many Bishops and Prelates who were sojourning in Rome, some of them for business, and some without any such reason. When, after Vespers, they paid him their respects in the great Chapel of the Vatican he called them perjurers, because they had left their churches. A fortnight later, preaching in open consistory, he condemned the morals of the Cardinals and Prelates in such harsh and unmeasured terms, that all were deeply wounded. . . Urban also issued ordinances against the luxury of the Cardinals, and these measures were no doubt most excellent. Would only that the Pope had proceeded in a less violent and uncompromising manner! He certainly did not take the best way of reforming the worldly-minded Cardinals, when, in the Consistory, he sharply bade one of them be silent, and called out to the others "Cease your foolish chattering!" Nor again, when he told Cardinal Orsini that he was a blockhead. . .. St. Catherine of Siena was aware of the severity with which Urban VI was endeavouring to carry out his reforms, and immediately exhorted and warned him. "Justice without mercy," she wrote to the Pope, "will be injustice rather than justice." "Do what you have to do with moderation," she said in another letter, "and with good-will and a peaceful heart, for excess destroys rather than builds up. For the sake

4   Pastor, vol. 1, 122.

of your Crucified Lord, keep these hasty movements of your nature a little in check."[5]

Urban remained intransigent, convincing many of the men around him, worldly or not, that he had gone stark raving mad. By August 9, the thirteen Gallic cardinals had had enough, and condemned his election as coerced and correspondingly illicit. Then, on September 20, at Fondi, south of Rome, with the quiet support of their three Italian counterparts, they elected Robert of Geneva as Pope Clement VII (1378–1394) in his place. The Great Western Schism had begun.

Rome had undergone a "mystic invasion"[6] due to the return of the Papacy to the Eternal City. Saints like Catherine of Siena, one of the generals leading that holy assault, were scandalized by the action of the renegade cardinals, and begged for their peaceful return to the allegiance of Urban VI. But the "Roman" pope thought that he could solve his woes through military force alone. He called a Crusade against Queen Joanna of Naples, who had offered sanctuary to Clement, and succeeded in forcing his competitor out of Italy after the Battle of Marino. This initial victory did not, however, prevent Clement from returning triumphantly to Avignon (June 29, 1379). Here, he was able to make immediate good use of the bulk of the papal administrative apparatus, which had never followed Gregory XI to Italy in the first place.

By 1379, both sides, their bases established, began a fervent competition for political and financial support. Tax collectors from Rome and Avignon appeared almost everywhere. Bankers, with their usual concern for even-handedness, often served both pontiffs simultaneously. In many dioceses, two bishops and two cathedral chapters emerged, with the very validity of the masses offered by the opposing sides coming under theoretical and actual physical attack. Pro-Urban bishops were barred entry to certain Sees and pro-Clement prelates to others. Serious Catholics looked upon the spectacle with an equal mixture of confusion and horror. Archbishop Peter Tenorio of Toledo prayed simply, in the Canon of the Mass, for the man who was truly pope, since he

---

5 Pastor, vol. 1, 123–124.
6 Jean-Marie Mayeur et al., *Histoire du Christianisme, vol. 6, Un temps D'épreuves (1274–1449)* (Desclée/Fayard, 1990), 93.

himself could not determine who that might be. Still, at least he continued to offer supplication. In some places, public worship ceased altogether.[7]

Supporters of Urban included most of the States of the Church, the Emperor, Flanders, England, and Portugal. Clement gained the backing of important sections of the hopelessly splintered Empire, such as Speyer and Mainz, along with Savoy, Scotland, and—after much soul searching and delay—Aragon, Castile, and Navarre. Many French prelates and the University of Paris were terribly troubled by the split. Nevertheless, the Kingdom of France accepted Clement in 1379 after an orchestrated public assembly of the sort perfected by the legalists of Philip the Fair to give that monarch's crimes a broad respectability. The university's coerced public stamp of arrival in 1383 led faculty and students who disagreed with the decision to leave for new centers of higher learning like Heidelberg and Lerida. Many cities and some states, like Naples, really could not make up their minds concerning whom they wished to support, or switched their allegiance due to dynastic changes. The mystic front eventually divided in two along with the rest of Christendom, Catherine of Siena remaining firmly with Urban, Vincent Ferrer and Peter of Luxembourg with Clement.

The Roman line of popes suffered due to its lack of administrative structures. It has a badly documented history. We know that Urban's situation remained forever troubled. He had miserable relations with his twenty-nine newly created Cardinals, some of whom he imprisoned, tortured, and put to death under atrocious conditions. Difficulties with Naples pursued him throughout his reign, while he continued the very abuses that he had so vigorously condemned when they were perpetrated by others. Prignani was followed onto the throne of Peter by a sick, badly cultivated, and impossibly simoniac Boniface IX (Pietro Tomacelli, November 2, 1389–October 1, 1404). Boniface was perpetually destitute and lived by dubious expedients, offering enough examples of sales of benefices and plenary indulgences, Jubilee corruption, and outright robbery to give credence to Nicholas de Clémangis' claim, in his book *On the Ruin of the Church* (1401), that "money was the origin of the Schism, and the root of all the confusion."[8]

7 Pastor, *History of the Popes*, vol. 1, 141–146.
8 Cited in Pastor, vol. 1, 146.

He was succeeded by Innocent VII (Cosimo Megliorati, October 17, 1404–November 6, 1406), and Gregory XII (Angelo Corrario, November 30, 1406–July 4, 1415).

Avignon's line is much better known. It is also simpler to memorize. Clement VII, who died on September 16, 1394, was followed only by the Aragonese Benedict XIII (Pedro de Luna, September 28, 1394–either November 29, 1422 or May 23, 1423). Nevertheless, this one superhumanly wily figure, ordained a priest only after his election, gave the Roman popes more than a run for their money for the prize of greatest irritant to prostrate Christendom.

As the original protagonists of the Schism died, more and more contemporaries began to echo Archbishop Tenorio's fear that there might not be any definitive way to know who the true pope really was. Perplexity was accompanied by an expansion of local and national efforts to ensure self-protection. Aragon had very speedily organized its own Apostolic Camera to collect Church taxes. England soon re-enacted laws to fill the kingdom's bishoprics promulgated during earlier tiffs with the pre-1378 Avignon Papacy. Others then followed suit, with certain rulers beginning to enjoy the benefits of the game so much as to argue that there should be as many popes as there were political jurisdictions. Peter Suchenwirt related popular reactions to the situation in simple poetic form:

> In Rome itself we have a Pope,
> In Avignon another;
> And each one claims to be alone
> The true and lawful ruler.
> The world is troubled and perplext,
> 'Twere better we had none,
> 'Than two to rule o'er Christendom,
> Where God would have but one.
> He chose St. Peter, who his fault
> With bitter tears bewail'd;
> As you may read the story told
> Upon the sacred page.
> Christ gave St. Peter pow'r to bind,
> And also pow'r to loose;
> Now men are binding here and there,
> Lord loose our bonds we pray.[9]

---

9   Cited in Pastor, vol. 1, 140.

Meanwhile, the number of apocalyptic-minded lamentations and expressions of heretical contempt grew ever higher:

> The preaching of a Saint Vincent Ferrer responded to the expectations of the crowds to whom he announced the arrival of the Antichrist. The whole labor of Gerson displays his horror before the peril that the schism caused the Church to run. It is to the people which the preaching of Wycliffe and Huss were addressed. The numerous prophecies of the epoch, Hildegarde, Saint Briget, Ermine, Telesphorus well illustrate the popular inquietude. The recluse, Marie Robine . . . saw appear before Christ all the curates of the world, the priors, the abbés, the bishops, the pope and twelve cardinals; they were simply dressed, but their words were lying. . . . Against them was raised the cry of vengeance of all those who died, through their fault, without being succored.[10]

Once again, the greatest undeserving loser in the entire pathetic experience was the magnificent medieval movement for giving flesh to all the consequences of the Incarnation; for transforming all things in Christ. "They say that the world must be renewed," the pious Giovanni dalle Celle cried out, indicating the enormous temptation of even the most orthodox thinkers to abandon the long-term goals of so many holy monastic and papal reformers; "I say, it must be destroyed."[11]

II: NO SOLUTION "BY THE BOOK"

Three suggestions were offered, and played with by both the Roman and the Avignon Courts, as means of exiting from the Schism: the *via facti*, or reliance on military support; the *via concessionis*, which sought a solution to the problem through joint resignation; and, finally, the *via conventionis*, or resolution of the division through the meeting either of representative cardinals of both papal courts or a General Church Council. Despite the early appeal to the *via facti*, employed both by Urban and Clement—the Avignon pope in alliance with France and its claims to the Kingdom of Naples—the future really lay with the latter two suggestions.

---

10 Mayeur et al., *Histoire du Christianisme*, vol. 6, 107–108.
11 Cited in Pastor, vol. 1, 145.

Jean Gerson, the great theologian and later Chancellor of the University of Paris, in both a discourse of 1391 and a treatise *Super Materiam Unionis Ecclesiae*, saw the path to sanity in a joint resignation of both men for the common good of Christendom. The ten thousand graduates of the University of Paris who placed their comments regarding possible means for ending the confusion in a chest at the Church of St. Marthurin in January of 1393 thought the same. They urged the calling of a commission or a General Council only should mutual abdication fail. Others, however, were already mapping out the precise route that the *via conventionis* would have to take. These even included firm supporters of Urban VI like Henry of Langenstein, Professor of Philosophy and Theology at Paris, who addressed the subject in his *Proposition of Peace for the Union and Reformation of the Church by a General Council* of 1381.

Political pressure of some sort would be required to get either of these two approaches involving resignation or conciliar negotiation moving. Gerson and Philippe de Mèzières, a prolific, devout, crusading and spiritual author of the day, argued that such pressure must inevitably come from the King of France. Charles VI (1380–1422) was certainly willing to play the role of royal nudge, though his increasing insanity ensured that any French activity would be sifted more and more through the conflicting influences of his brother Louis, the Duke of Orleans, his cousin John, the Duke of Burgundy, and his uncle, the Duke of Berry.

Although Clement VII had enough influence with the French Court to deflect such growing pressures, and the good sense to die before they became overwhelming, his successor, Benedict, was under the gun from the very outset of his reign. The new Avignon pontiff had, after all, hesitantly taken an oath, along with the other *papabili* during the Conclave, to resign if his Roman counterpart did the same. He repeated this solemn promise, voluntarily, after his election. When it instead became clear that he had repudiated his pledge and showed some preference for the *via facti*, the French government turned against him. A Council of Paris, in early 1395, presided over by Simon de Cramaud, Bishop of Poitiers and a notable representative of that legalist Gallican spirit which was again very much active in its push for vigorous state interference in Church affairs, publicly called for the joint abdication of the two popes. The king's relatives, accompanied by university experts, went to Avignon from May 22 to July 9 in a frustrating mission to get Benedict to agree to the *via cessionis*. Negotiators were dispatched to other countries, like England, to obtain their backing for the proposal as well.

Benedict adamantly rejected requests for his early retirement. When his stubbornness became clear, the University of Paris radicalized its utilitarian-minded canonists above all others. Anti-papal writings multiplied. A new Council, attended by three hundred archbishops, bishops, abbots of monasteries, and delegates from each cathedral chapter and university, once again presided over by de Cramaud, met in May 1398 to tackle the problem. Thoughtful, careful theologians like Gerson and his great teacher and friend, the future Cardinal Pierre d'Ailly, urged tremendous moderation in dealing with Benedict. If for no other reason, they argued, moderation was dictated by the need to avoid giving scandal to ordinary believers. Nevertheless, the Council, stirred by the preaching of two Gallicans, the Abbé Pierre Leroy of Mount St. Michel and Bishop Gilles Deschamps of Coutances, withdrew its support from the Avignon pope and established a new Church order for the Kingdom of France. A number of Benedict's cardinals eventually joined in the action. Withdrawal of obedience was followed, in September, by an outright assault on Avignon and a lengthy siege of the Apostolic Palace by a royal army under the command of a French Marshal.

But not all worked out well with this 1398 settlement. The anti-Benedict *Blitzkrieg* shocked even many of those people who were not disposed to be friendly to him. English policy changed with the death of the pro-French King Richard II. A Gallican Church in a semi-chaotic France proved easily controlled by ambitious noblemen and the women whom they wished to please. Further disputes among the king's close relatives, opposition from a clergy which discovered that corrupt and hateful Church taxes were being more efficiently collected by royal officials, and growth of precisely that scandal among the common faithful feared by Gerson and d'Ailly condemned the Gallican scheme to a swift death. The *coup de grace* came with the pope's dramatic escape from his besieged palace on May 11, 1403, to freedom in Provence. On May 28 of that same year, an assembly of bishops gave up the rebellion and restored French obedience to Benedict and the Avignon line.

Still, restoration of obedience did not mean surrender to Benedict's obstinacy and perceived perjury. Jean Gerson, in a sermon preached before the pope in Tarascon, on New Year's Day, 1404, continued to urge pursuit of every lawful means to end the schism. The radicalized University of Paris remained exceedingly hostile to him and attracted to still more heretical and legalist theories of ecclesiastical order, ones that recalled the arguments of William of Ockham and Marsilius of Padua alongside those of Philip the Fair's anticlerical advisors. These theories viewed the popes as simply useful instruments of the Church at large, which, through the agency of General Councils—and the State standing behind them—could judge pontiffs and limit or even withdraw their powers should necessity demand it.

By this point, however, sincere and less radical supporters of the *Via Cessionis* were encouraged by hopeful noises coming out of Rome. Boniface had steadfastly refused all proposals for healing the split, profited from his competitor's woes, and seen his prestige rise through the relative success of the Jubilee pilgrimage to the Eternal City in 1400. But now his successor, Innocent VII (1404–1406), claimed that he would never even have been elected had Benedict XIII shown some readiness to resign. Innocent thus pledged his full support to a swift and peaceful resolution of the dilemma.

Benedict, alas, had now once again given his heart over to the *via facti*, and was making military advances into Italy and pumping reliable financial resources to fund them. Renewed indignation over his selfish inflexibility stimulated the radicals of the University of Paris and the Burgundian party allied with them to seize the advantage, open direct negotiations with Innocent, and declare a second withdrawal of obedience from Avignon in January of 1407. Irritation with Benedict became more strident still due to his strange tango with Innocent's successor, Gregory XII. This began in December of 1407, when both men agreed to meet together to discuss the *via cessionis* at Savona. Benedict's subsequent delays and hedging led to Gregory's annoyed abandonment of the project. That renunciation was followed by the Avignon pope's dubious change of heart, his swift appearance at the designated meeting place, and the shedding of many crocodile tears over the absence of his Roman sparring partner. Dietrich von Nieheim, in a satirical *Letter of Satan to Giovanni Dominici of Ragusa* (Gregory's nephew and advisor), expressed the nagging belief of many horrified observers that this comedy of contradictory moves may have been a fraud contrived from the very outset by two incomparably hypocritical pontiffs to stymie real efforts to obtain their resignations.

By 1408, all Christendom was in a *via conventionis* uproar, moderates and radicals alike. The Avignon and Roman popes were left dependent on local support, Benedict retiring to Perpignan, in the safer territory of his native Aragon, and Gregory to the cities of a variety of Italian patrons. Given these unfortunate circumstances, seven of Gregory's cardinals and four of those from the Avignon line gathered at Livorno, in Italy, to begin negotiations for a way to end the farce on their own steam. Their number eventually reached nineteen, and, with the help of both political as well as theological and canonical backing, these princes of the Church called the Christian world to Council in Pisa on March 25, 1409.

Almost five hundred fathers sat at their assembly, twenty-two cardinals and eighty bishops among them, though scholars predominated, jurists most noticeably. Moderates like Gerson and d'Ailly were present alongside more radical heretical and legalist elements, including the president of the gathering, the seemingly ubiquitous Simon de Cramaud. All, whether reluctantly or jubilantly, knew that they were there to judge, rebuke, and potentially remove both claimants to the Papacy. Witnesses were heard testifying to papal cruelties, secret agreements, perjuries, and even dabbling in sorcery. Benedict and Gregory, both of whom refused to answer the Council's order to appear, were jointly condemned and excommunicated on June 5, 1409. The cardinals who summoned the council were thereupon delegated to select what the canonist Francesco Zabarella now called merely the principal minister and servant of the Church. Their choice, on June 26, 1409, fell on Peter Philarghi, the Greek-born Cardinal Archbishop of Milan, who took the name of Alexander V. Alexander's short reign was followed, in 1410, by the election of the man who many suspected of having poisoned him: Baldassare Cossa, the governor of Bologna, thereafter styled Pope John XXIII.

Despite the fact that the Pisan popes were able to gain considerable European-wide backing, and John XXIII even to establish himself in Rome, their two competitors remained a permanent nuisance. Gregory and Benedict retained support in important countries. Both held or tried to hold councils of their own to back up their legitimacy. Moreover, the Pisan faction was itself very quickly plagued by internal disputes. Everyone came to loathe cardinals of all description as an extraordinarily venal, ambitious, and incompetent body of men. Many Italians militating in Pisan ranks bristled at French influence and the spread of heretical and legalist ideals therein. While reform was on the lips of all, each national group had different ideas of what constituted a scandal requiring instant action: for some, it was the pro-papal teaching of the omnipresent Franciscan friars; for others, it was the failure of the Church to secure positions for the graduates of the vocal University of Paris. A new reform council, which his Pisan electors obliged John XXIII to hold, met just long enough in Rome to turn disgustedly against this pontiff as the chief obstacle to purification of the Church.

Finally, the perennial struggle for the Neapolitan throne having taken a perilous turn, the Pisan pope was forced to quit the Eternal City and petition the rulers of Europe for new political protection. Help, under the circumstances of that particular moment in time, was only available from Sigismund, Holy Roman Emperor since 1410. Sigismund was personally eager to rebuild the shattered prestige of his realm and contribute to doing so by finding a definitive way out of the continuing papal horror show. He and his Empire had never accepted the results of Pisa, so their defense of John XXIII was a tricky one to say the least. It came to entail the summoning of yet another Council, which opened at Constance on November 1, 1414, with the usual suspects from throughout Europe—practically all of them—in attendance.

John initially presided at Constance as the legitimate pontiff. Nevertheless, Sigismund and the Council Fathers, Gerson and d'Ailly prominent among them, soon saw the abdication of all three popes as an essential prerequisite to enjoyment of a single universally recognized head of the Church. Hopes for the success of this renewed appeal to the *via concessionis* were temporarily complicated by the fact that the erratic John, who swore to abdicate in March of 1415, changed his mind and fled the city for the Black Forest to try his luck anew. His efforts floundered, and, becoming aware of the desperation of his position, he ultimately threw himself on the Council's mercy. Its fathers found him guilty of being an unworthy and unlawful pope, removed him on May 29, and popped him straight into prison.

Events now took a dramatic turn. The aged Gregory XII spontaneously and unexpectedly offered his own abdication. Interestingly enough, though already considered deposed by Pisa, he managed to bow out in a manner that most subsequent writers argue to have bolstered Rome's claim to possess the legitimate line of pontiffs. Ludwig von Pastor describes the abdication scene as follows:

> The way in which this was done is of the highest significance, and must by no means be viewed as a concession in non-essentials to the assembled Bishops. Gregory XII., the one legitimate Pope, sent his plenipotentiary, Malatesta, to Constance, where the prelates of his obedience had already arrived, and now summoned the Bishops to a Council. His Cardinal-Legate, who had made his entry into the city as such, read Gregory's Bull of Convention to the assembled Bishops, who solemnly acknowledged it. Malatesta then informed this Synod, [i.e., the beefed-up Council of Constance] which Gregory XII. had constituted, of his abdication (July 4, 1415). His summons had given the Synod a legal basis. [12]

Only the Avignon pope, now in Aragon, was left. Personal efforts by Sigismund to obtain Benedict's voluntary withdrawal delayed proceedings against him for some time. Negotiations having finally failed, the Council tried him *in absentia*, declaring his deposition by July of 1417. Support for de Luna faded away, and he himself fled, along with three remaining Cardinals, to the fortress of Peñiscola. The way was thus sufficiently well cleared for Odo Colonna to be elected the sole truly serious pope on November 11 1417, though by an innovative method involving the addition of national representatives to the cardinals united in conclave. He took the name of Martin V (1417–1431). The new pope confirmed the Council's grant to the ex-Gregory XII of the Cardinal Bishopric of Porto and made him permanent papal legate in the March of Ancona. John XXIII went from prison life to the position of Cardinal Bishop of Tusculum. Benedict lived unreconciled until his death in 1422 or 1423, leaving two warring successors behind him. One of these, a mysterious Benedict XIV, lived and died somewhere in France. The

---

12 Pastor, vol. 1, 200.

other, Gil Muñoz, Pope Clement VIII, finally abdicated in 1429 and was rewarded with the Bishopric of Majorca. Clement VIII's College of Cardinals then brought a final and rather unsurprising end to the Great Western Schism by entering into conclave in Peñsicola and formally electing Martin V as his successor.

But the Schism, so many decades in duration, had not, exactly, ended "by the book," according to crystal-clear existing canonical rules. Just look at the complications involved in the solution to the problem again. How "legal" was the pressure exerted by Sigismund and the other secular powers and university scholars in gaining the desired results? Had it not precisely been the contention of the Church, since the time of the reforms of the eleventh century, that such intervention in the affairs of the Papacy was nefarious? What rendered this particular involvement permissible? What was the legality of the strange addition of national electors to the College of Cardinals in the Constance conclave? And what about the man elected? If Gregory XII really was the legitimate Pope, what did this have to say about the actions of Odo Colonna, one of his renegade cardinals? The future Martin V had, after all, fled Rome, taken part in the Council of Pisa, and helped to elect Alexander V and John XXIII. Why did he not have to do penance for his "schismatic" activity before becoming Supreme Pontiff? But, then again, how could he have humbled himself without rendering the abdication of his former master, Gregory XII, itself ludicrous? And what should one think of Alexander V? The next universally recognized Clement and Benedict took up the numbering that had been used by the Avignon pontiffs of those names (VII and XIII), therefore, historically identifying them as anti-popes. On the other hand, the next Alexander, Rodrigo Borgia, who ought, by right, to have styled himself the fifth of that line, assumed that he was the sixth. Does this mean that he believed Alexander V to have been legitimate? Apparently. If so, then how could the simultaneously reigning Gregory XII have also been the true pope? And why was Alexander's successor, John XXIII, not valid, as Angelo Roncalli appears to have made clear in 1958 by adopting the numbering previously used by Baldassare Cossa?

What all this says to me is that the Church recognized that she was dealing, in the Great Western Schism, with a specific historical problem for whose resolution she did not have all the answers at her fingertips. Under these trying circumstances she therefore had to rely solely on the one thing that she knew to be absolutely certain: that Christ would never abandon His Bride. Just because there was confusion and division over who, exactly, the pope might be, such perplexity did not signify that there was no pontiff at all. There had to be a legitimate pope, but the immediate problem was obtaining a legitimate pope to whom everyone would give his obedience. Just because existing, fallible Canon Law and its interpreters could not adequately and effectively identify him did not mean that the Mystical Body had to throw in the towel and close up shop. The Word was more powerful than the words of the law books and the dicta of the canonists. And if keeping the Bride of Christ alive and well temporarily involved a bewildered respect of the otherwise problematic interventions of Parisian pedants, renegade cardinals, puppet electors promoting parochial national causes, and emperors evoking powers rejected several centuries earlier, all could be forgiven in the end. What counted in the uncertainties of the perplexing moment was the sanctity of the absolutely proper goal of reestablishing a unified Papacy. Judged in this context, the actions of Pisa, Constance, Sigismund, and Odo Colonna to end the Great Western Schism come off fairly well. They bore little resemblance to other, more wickedly irregular maneuvers in the Church's past, such as those which the famous Robber Council of Ephesus permitted itself in the Fifth Century. Does this mean that there were no bad motivations and heretical, legalist, or simply wrongheaded theories whatsoever at play in the conclusion of the Great Western Nightmare? Not at all. There were plenty. But a Church which did not know precisely how to confront these ills while seeking to emerge from her practical labyrinth seems to have thought their judgment best left to history and Almighty God.

NO AWAKENING "ON THE CHEAP"

But this decision did not mean that firm correction of the spiritual, intellectual, political, and social problems giving birth to the nightmare of the Great Western Schism in the first place could be avoided. The Church's main task, as always, was that of offering salvation and reconnecting with the profound work of giving flesh to the consequences of the Incarnation which the medieval reform movement understood to be central to the task of saving souls. If she her to shoulder this burden properly, then it was essential for her to digest the lessons of her recent divisions, to understand all the forces working against transformation in Christ, including those in her own bosom, and to seek advice from every single bit of wisdom offered by her Sacred Tradition.

Unfortunately, however, her ability to grapple with this crucial but daunting mission had been crippled through the recent chaos. The entire reputation of the Papacy and all those forces historically allied with it had been dragged deeply into the mud by the forty-year schismatic circus. Martin V was left to return to a still troubled and half-devastated Rome practically penniless and unprotected. He and most of his immediate successors saw no other choice than to bury themselves in petty financial concerns and peninsular politics merely to be able to survive.

Meanwhile, opponents regularly called up heretical and legalist conciliar theories to keep the ever-suspect "chief minister of the Church" in line. The Council of Basel, which stayed in session from 1431 until 1449, soon went so far down the road of anti-Romanism as to depose the "tyrannical" Eugene IV (1431–1447) and create a new schism under the antipope Felix V (1441–1449). Curia and cardinals remained universally detested and viewed by nations and cities merely as tools to be manipulated to attain papal approval of their own parochial desires. And while a conciliar reform of Church and society to restore a happier, mythological Apostolic Age was very vocally discussed, the world weariness, cynicism, and anti-incarnational outlooks of powerful ecclesiastical and secular forces made swift, substantive improvement an absolute impossibility. The Council of Basel, as Geiler von Kaysberg, a contemporary critic noted, was not even powerful enough to reform a single convent of nuns in the city in which it was still in session, once the municipal council stood in its way. There simply appeared to be no element of late medieval society, ecclesiastical or secular, healthy enough to think through and give sufficient support for Christendom's climb above petty concerns to more lofty heights. The view would be wasted on those who arrived there under current circumstances anyway. Hence Ludwig von Pastor's citation of John Nider, a Dominican thinker dedicated to Church reform, with respect to the hope of improvement:

Is there any hope for a general reformation of the Church in its Head and its members? "I have," answers Nider, "absolutely none in the present time, or in the immediate future; for good-will is wanting among the subjects, the evil disposition of the prelates constitutes an obstacle, and, finally, it is profitable to God's elect to be tried by persecution from the wicked. You may see an analogy in the art of building. An architect, how-ever skillful he may be, can never erect an edifice unless he has suitable material of wood or stone. And if there is wood or stone in sufficient quantity, but no master-builder, there will be no proper house and dwelling. And, if you knew that a house would not be fitting for your friend, or, when built, would be a trouble to him, you certainly would be prudent enough not to build it." [13]

Pastor, mercifully, has another more encouraging reason for quoting this passage from Nider. He wishes to show that, despite the enormous obstacles in their way, some contemporaries who grasped the importance of the earlier medieval reform movement were quietly and slowly once again working to effect serious change according to its precepts. Such men understood that the Church took a self-destructive "low road" when she gave her primary attention to fallible political, legal, and administrative means of carrying out her mission. A primary attention to such measures overturned the hierarchy of values and opened her up to the cyn-icism of those who really in their heart of hearts did not believe in raising nature to the greater glory of God. They wished her to move boldly and confidently down the "high road," to become a "fool for Christ," to subordinate her natural tools to the greater task of making all of nature a conduit for grace.

"High road" reformers constructed out of the rubble of the Great Western Schism the magnificent achievements of Christian Humanism, the Tridentine Reformation, Baroque culture, and the post-French revolutionary Catholic revival. Over the centuries, they have given to the Church a deeper knowledge of everything in her jewel box: Scripture, Patrology, Scholasticism, and Classical culture, proving nature's ability to cooperate with grace. They have shown her how all of these jewels compel her to more vigorous missionary work and the creation of a social order open to Christ. Perhaps

---

13   Pastor, vol. 1, 356.

most importantly for practical purposes, they have delineated for her, more clearly than ever before, exactly who her chief enemy is, and where his greatest strength lies.

That enemy, at the beginning of the Twenty-First Century, is the same one identified at the opening of this article. It is the union of all those world-weary, cynical, hypocritical and heretical forces which either practically or theoretically deny that transformation of all things in Christ which is so central to the work of saving souls. It is that alliance which had already become immensely powerful and troublesome in the age preceding the years of the Great Western Schism. It is that coalition whose power was increased by certain aspects of the Renaissance, and even more strengthened by the Reformation, the Enlightenment, and the playing out of all of their manifold anti-incarnational and naturalist presuppositions from the 1500s down through to the present.

We, the living, are the unfortunate inhabitants of an age when this alliance has had its most striking, shocking, and complete successes. Anti-incarnationalist forces have, by our time, dismantled Christendom and turned the society in which we seek our salvation into a battleground of various forms of unbridled, naturalist willfulness. They have managed to do their work, in pluralist-dominated lands, while claiming to have shaped the most suitable environment for living the Catholic life. Horrifying to say, they have seduced both prelates and most members of the laity into praising and aiding their labors. They have reduced the Church to the sociological significance of a cheerleading squad for a technologically advanced but barbarian civilization, whose warehouses are filled with intellectual and material goods which lead men away from the light and back into the darkest recesses of Plato's cave.

The turmoil and confusion experienced by Catholics in the last forty to fifty years of conciliar disaster have exposed us to a situation analogous to that faced by our ancestors of six centuries ago—even if the specific difficulty of the legitimacy of the current Pope is, thankfully, not one of our problems. How can this disaster be turned round? Should it be any wonder that a proper response to and awakening from the contemporary ecclesiastical nightmare may be just as complex a matter as that experienced by our forebears? Will it really be any surprise that substantive improvement may require much criticism from scandalized believers? Can anyone honestly be stunned that some horrified men and women will not follow the advice of "moderates" who wish to make a hopelessly illogical distinction between an "acceptable" criticism of one or two abuses and their perpetrators and an "unacceptable" critique of the entirety of the scandal as far up on the totem pole as it extends? May it not also be the case that laity similar to the interfering Emperor Sigismund and prelates like the schismatic Cardinal Odo Colonna end up, in the long run, in the Church's list of historic "good guys"? Alongside other noble figures working for high road reform more quietly "by the book"?

Our reform-minded brethren emerging from the Great Western Schism knew that there was no "cheap" way for them to exit from their ecclesiastical nightmare. Our only hope today lies in taking the same "high road" that they preached. This entails tearing ourselves away from a fixation on merely one or two of our immediate problems whose solution will not address our more fundamental woes. It requires recognition of the fact that our battle is part of a centuries-old fight for the right of the Incarnation to do what it must against enemies who will not allow it to work its miracle of grace, and that we need to use all the tools that Sacred Tradition and a natural world allied with her have to offer to win it. But are we really willing to take up such a challenge?

The history of the Church since the late Middle Ages has indicated that we are not yet ready to do so. For despite the glorious work that has been done in the past six hundred years to make Catholics more aware than ever before of the jewel box Tradition places before them, they have stubbornly persisted in making the stingiest use of it possible. Some have appealed to the desires of the reigning pope but not to those of past pontiffs; some to Scripture but not to the living authority of the Bride of Christ; some to St. Thomas but to none of the Church Fathers; some to St. Augustine while reviling the Scholastics; some to dogmatic purity but not to the social doctrine that teaches us how to practice our Faith; some to theology but not to history; some to the Holy Spirit in history but not in fixed and unchangeable truth. Everything truncated tempts us to put on blinders and eventually return to the "low road." Only exposure to the fullness of Tradition can allow us to move from merely keeping the ecclesiastical boat afloat to winning the war for the soul of modernity.

The modernist vision is ultimately a willful one. Modern man does what he does because he chooses to do so, calling his choice "natural" and even dictated by the Holy Spirit. Perhaps God wishes us to redeem the willfulness so essential to modernity by an honest act of Catholic will: the will to pick up and read the whole book of Tradition; to appreciate all of the spiritual and natural wisdom to be found working together in its various chapters; to open up its jewel box and use the gems that shine so brilliantly therein. If now is not the time to make such an act of will, when will it arrive?

RECOMMENDED FOR FURTHER READING

Georges Duby, *France in the Middle Ages 987–1460*, trans. Juliet Vale (Oxford: Blackwell, 1991).

Hubert Jedin and John Dolan, eds., *A History of the Church, vol. 4, From the High Middle Ages to the Eve of the Reformation*, trans. Anselm Biggs (New York: The Crossroad Publishing Company, 1982).

Jean-Marie Mayeur et al., *Histoire du Christianisme, vol. 6, Un Temps D'épreuves (1274–1449)* (Desclée/Fayard, 1990).

Francis Oakley, *The Western Church in the Later Middle Ages* (Ithaca: Cornell University Press, 1979).

Ludwig von Pastor, *History of the Popes, from the Close of the Middle Ages, vol. 1* (London: Keegan Paul, Trench, Trubner & Co., Ltd., 1938).

Walter Ullmann, *A Short History of the Papacy in the Middle Ages* (London: Methuen & Co. Ltd., 1972).

Walter Ullmann, *The Origins of the Great Schism: A Study in Fourteenth-Century Ecclesiastical History* (Archon Books, 1967).

10

When the Catholic Church Makes Merry

A PILGRIMAGE REFLECTION
FROM AN INTERNET CAFE[†]

"THIS IS THE DAY WHEN THE CATHOLIC Church makes merry." Such was a common phrase used in the early centuries of Frankish Christianity to describe each Sunday and major feast of the liturgical year. Was such a statement just a cavalier call to meat and ale by flippant and still semi-barbaric secularists merely playing at being servants of the one true God? Given the unremitting exposure of all of the inhabitants of Gaul, high and low, to the insecurities of life; given the reverence with which the Franks approached the relics of the saints and the ceremonies of Holy Mass; and given the enthusiastic response of a significant part of their nobility to the rigorous demands of St. Columbanus when he wandered into their kingdom with his brand of Irish monasticism at the turn of the sixth and seventh centuries, I somehow think that this was not the case.

Rather, I believe that it reflected a real appreciation of the basic Gospel teaching that Christ's yoke is easy and His burden is light. Yes, the Frankish Christians were saying, the drama of life is generally a laborious and often gruesome spectacle. Still, for those who are ready to play their role in it properly, even its sufferings and tragedies can be seen ultimately to be part of a Divine Comedy. How could merriment *not* be an integral aspect of one's response to an Easter Sunday or a Christmas Day, when the entirety of the supernatural plan, both its passing sorrows and its glorious eternal end, were presented to men, women and the community in which they lived with full liturgical splendor?

Fortunately, the members of the Catholic Church can experience something similar whenever God's plan and the proper hierarchy of values are pinpointed accurately for them. Such clarity of vision is very much offered on the pilgrimage that has serpented its way from Paris to Chartres on Pentecost weekend

---

† First published in *The Remnant*, June 30, 2006.

for the past twenty-four years, with a delegation from *The Remnant* tagging along.

Now, everyone who has taken part in that pilgrimage will readily admit that it promises nothing other than three days of almost unremitting misery. The food is always monotonous and meager, the sleeping accommodations atrocious and the pain often mind-boggling and bloody. By the latter half of the second day, many pilgrims look like Chinese women with bound feet, hopping, in kangaroo-fashion, from one point on the route to Chartres to the next.

The campsite that second wretched night resembles the moon. This year, with my baggage temporarily lost, I had a chance to bop my bound feet back and forth along its mile-long campus of craters seven times before I was finally able to find my pallet and take it off to *The Remnant* tent to sleep. Sleep? Sleep? The tent was pitched on the slopes of one of the campsite's craters, so that pilgrims slid slowly outside its confines, becoming sitting ducks for the operator of a waste disposal truck seemingly determined to drive his vehicle over their helpless bodies and prevent their ever seeing the great Gothic cathedral almost visible over the horizon. And all this after repeated prayer had led them to think deeply about their personal sins and their pitiful failure to live up to the mission that God had given them.

The upshot? Why, as the Franks of old could have told them, sheer merriment of course! It is always "the Catholic Church making merry" which wends its way through the fields and woods of northern France, her sons and daughters laughing like children skipping through Oz as they do so. I do not think that I have ever felt as uninterruptedly happy and carefree about life as I have on those days of pain en route to one of Christendom's most beautiful temples.

I finally had, even if for just a few wondrous days, "eyes to see and ears to hear" things—not as I, with all my limitations, conceived of them, but as they *ought* to be. I knew, for a brief moment in time, what God wanted of me and where I was going. The route was long, laborious, and, for many, filled with blisters. But it would come to an end. And then one could, perhaps, learn how to make merry for the duration of life and be rewarded by nothing less than a seat at the eternal High Table of the Lord.

Pre-revolutionary Catholic Christendom was a civilization on permanent pilgrimage to God. It was outfitted with institutions that made God's plan so crystal clear and so integral a part of the framework of people's existences that they could keep their eyes and ears open and live a life of merriment through all their terrible pains and tragedies.

Every year, *The Remnant Tour* provides its participants a chance to glimpse what such a civilization actually meant in practice. Our visit this June to Ireland was no exception. Anyone temporarily awakened by pilgrimage to Chartres to that which really makes men and women happy and fulfilled in this valley of tears could not have failed to see in the historical structure of Ireland, in the demeanor of its more tradition-minded inhabitants and even in the terrain of Counties Clare and Mayo themselves that basic happiness which the Franks understood to emerge from a true submission to the will of the Incarnate God. So very much was still in its proper place, neither too packed nor too spread out, too rich or too poor, too sober of too intoxicated. And this in a land which had known so many hardships, ranging from invasion and expropriation to the unfathomable horrors of years of body-killing famine. There was no endless crescendo of cavalier giddiness, typical of the songs and jingles of Our Global Fatherland, to be found in the good cheer of the true sons and daughters of Hibernia. Everywhere, it was the hard-earned and long-lasting joy of the children of the merry but realistic Catholic Church which was on prominent display.

I am writing these brief comments in an Internet Café on a traffic-packed road in modern Rome, next to a cinema showing the *Da Vinci Code*. No one is merry around me, though some are laughing loudly. A truly joyful Frank from Merovingian Gaul would probably be thought to be stark-raving mad by the staff and ejected from the premises as a public nuisance. In fact, I notice that I am snarling at the man across from me as much as he has begun to glare at me. Everyone seems well-off and free from bodily pain. A vision of the shopping malls, mega-houses, pornographic entertainments and calls to false happiness which I saw advancing everywhere on the Emerald Isle is rapidly killing the memory of the doomed, chain-free towns and merry Catholic people which had filled my eyes and ears during my brief stay in and amidst them.

My three-day eye and ear opening to God's reality, to the way that God sees the earth and His children on their pilgrimage through nature, to the true vision of life which we, in our false wisdom, dismiss as impractical and nostalgic, is fading. How I long for the hungry days of the march to Chartres. How I yearn for next Pentecost, my dilapidated tent, my hard bread rolls, and my crater-filled campsite where the Catholic Church makes merry!

11

Is the Pope Greek?
AND CAN A GERMAN PRESIDE OVER
A SIMILAR SUCCESS STORY?†

POPE BENEDICT XVI IS DEEPLY INTERESTED
in closer relations with the Eastern Churches, and in this
enterprise I wish him very well indeed. Both parts of Christendom were meant to be together, and not simply because of the
doctrine of papal supremacy. At certain times in history, either
the East or the West has been in highly specific need of "its other
half's" influence.

What immediately (and amusingly) comes to my mind in this
regard is the action of an eastern prelate at a patristics conference
in Oxford several decades ago when the western clerical passion for self-destruction was perhaps at its height. The hall was
filled with modernist European and American theologians dealing
with the subject of Hell. "If you believe what you just said," this
unrepentant descendant of Athanasius shouted to one of his *per-
iti* who was attempting to mimic his western heretical colleagues,
"I excommunicate you." How glorious to hear the words *anathema
sit* in the mouth of a bishop who really still knew how to "bish"!
And where else in the delirious Christendom of the 1970s would
such clarity have come from other than some intransigent eastern
diocese evoking ancient or exotic splendors?

Many Roman Catholics are skeptical of regular, serious, friendly
contact between East and West, fearful, especially, of its long-term
anti-papal consequences. They could take heart from the study of
a lengthy period of time, from the 640s down to the 750s, when
Greeks, Greek-speakers and Greek culture in general not only
co-operated with Rome but actually came to dominate it. This
domination turned out to be a glorious thing. Far from destroying
the Latin Church, it enriched her, filling contemporary gaps in her
knowledge and practices and thereby contributing mightily to her
further perfection and efficiency. Far from crushing the Papacy

---

† First published in *The Remnant*, November 15, 2006.

in the name of that often shapeless collegiality more frequently associated with Eastern Church principles, it exalted the image and powers of the Holy See beyond previous levels.

A number of works deal in great detail with "Greek Rome," including the monumental thirteen volume *Histoire du Christianisme* recently completed in France under the direction of Jean-Marie Mayeur. The most accessible is a book by Jeffrey Richards, Professor of History at the University of Lancaster in the United Kingdom. Richards' *The Popes and the Papacy in the Early Middle Ages*, pages 476–752, comprehensively treats this subject. In the process, he also dispels the still all too common notion of some Iron Curtain having suddenly descended with the appearance of the German barbarians in the 400s to hermetically seal off West from East and the medieval from the ancient world.

Yes, Rome and Italy as a whole did experience some barbarian-induced disruptions, but both were highly prosperous and peaceful from the latter part of the Fifth Century through the middle of the 530s. It was at the latter date that the emperor Justinian fatefully decided to dispense with the fiction that German Ostrogoth "agents" were actually governing the peninsula in the name of the Empire. He was determined to restore substantive, direct Roman rule, guided from Constantinople and working through a governor (Exarch) in Ravenna. Twenty years of warfare were unexpectedly required to break Ostrogoth resistance. A "re-conquered" though devastated Italy then fell prey to a new German invasion, that of the Lombards, in 568. This finally resulted in an uneasy and regularly troubled division of the peninsula into two spheres of influence, with the eastern Roman forces remaining in control of the coastlines, as well as much of the south and Sicily as a whole.

As a result of the re-conquest, Rome and other imperial-ruled sections of Italy played host to administrative and military personnel from the East, many of them Greek-speaking. Nevertheless, the really significant culturally active Hellenes with whom we are concerned in this article arrived in one impressive wave in the early 600s. These were Greeks or Greek-speaking Syrian, Palestinian and North African migrants coming to Italy for two related reasons. One was to escape disastrous invasions of the eastern parts of the Empire, first by the Persians and, immediately after their crushing defeat at the hands of imperial forces, by the more successful Arab

Moslems. Another was to flee imperial religious persecution, about which more anon. Many Greeks and Greek-speakers headed for Sicily and the South. Those who went to Rome tended to settle at a spot which had already become a small Hellenic neighborhood beforehand: the foot of the Aventine Hill, where numerous traces of their presence remain today.

The Roman immigrants included numbers of very energetic monks, shaped by a Palestinian spirituality which taught them to embrace the idea of life as a pilgrimage; as a wandering, challenging "exile" for Christ's sake. Having reached the Eternal City, they took over and transformed some already existing monasteries, such as that of St. Anastasius ad Aquas Salvias, St. Erasmus on the Caelian Hill, and Saints Andreas and Lucia, which they renamed Saints Maria and Andreas. The older Boetiana Monastery was not only taken over by Greek-speaking Syrians, but, as it turned out, by heretics chased out of the East by the stronger defenders of equally unacceptable errors. New Roman monasteries, perhaps as many as ten, like those of the Domus Arsicia and St. Saba, were Greek foundations from the outset.

Greek-speaking monks and clerics swiftly rose to importance in the seventh century Roman Church. Abbot John Symponus became a kind of "secretary of state" to Honorius I (625–638) and John IV (640–642), while the deacon Sericus was sent to by the former pontiff to Constantinople as papal ambassador (*apocrisiarios*) to the imperial court. By the reign of Pope St. Martin I (649–653), Sericus held the key position of Archdeacon of the Roman Church. Greek officials were henceforth omnipresent, in Rome, as papal envoys abroad and as representatives to General Councils, freely and fluently translating from Latin into Greek and back again. St. Maximus the Confessor (580–662), who arrived in Rome at that same time, found that there were so many Greek-speakers active in the clergy there that he could play a central role in Church affairs without knowing any Latin.

Greek influence in Italy extended beyond Rome to the Italian episcopate. Important Hellenic bishops included John of Portus, Nicetas of Silva Candida, and the southerners Leontius of Naples, Abundantius of Tempsa and John of Rhegium. So many were these local and peninsular "Greeklings" that "Eddius Stephanus, the biographer of St Wilfrid of Hexham, noted rather disapprovingly that when his hero presented himself to a synod in Rome in 704 to argue his case against deprivation of his see, the bishops present chatted and joked amongst themselves in Greek."[1]

More than this, however, Greeks and Greek-speakers soon became popes themselves. Although the first of these, the Palestinian refugee Theodore (642–649), was elected in the first half of the century, and Pope Agatho (678–681) from Sicily may also have been of eastern Greek origin, it was not until 685 that the "Hellenic Papacy" really began. At that time, the Archdeacon John V (685–686), born in Antioch in Syria, ascended the papal throne after a normal career in the Roman clergy. He was followed by Conon (686–687, a Greek speaker from Sicily), Sergius I (687–701, Syrian/Sicilian), John VI (701–705, a "Greek" of unknown origins), John VII (705–707, "Greek"), Sissinius (708, Syrian), Constantine (708–715, Syrian), Gregory III (731–741, Syrian) and the extremely impressive Pope Zacharias (741–752, "Greek").

Eastern influence in Italy, whether under Greek- or Latin-speaking pontiffs, was felt in four specific ways, the first of which was in devotional life. Eastern festivals, such as those of the Exaltation of the True Cross and the Annunciation, Dormition and Nativity of the Virgin Mary were introduced. The cults of saints popular in the East, such as the martyr, St. Symeon, the doctors Cosmas and Damian, and a battery of warrior heroes venerated by the army, like Saint George, also took root. Saint George became so popular that Pope Zacharias himself carried his head in a grand procession from the Lateran to install it in a place of honor in the Church named after him.

A second influence was exercised over the liturgy. This took shape in two ways. One was through music, and not simply because of the appearance of Greek-inspired hymns, in Latin translation, for use in the Mass. Music was affected by the eastern presence more due to the greater honor that it now received from high Church officials. Pope St. Gregory the Great (590–604), for all of his association with chant and his creation of a Schola Cantorum, was worried about the clergy's over-involvement with singing, and wished to control and limit it. From the time of Pope Vitalian (657–672) onwards, however, a new eastern-inspired spirit

---

1   Jeffrey Richards, *The Popes and the Papacy in the Early Middle Ages, 476–752* (London: Routledge & Kegan Paul, 1979), 277.

dominated. This so exalted the role of music that achievements in its realm were seen as superb preparation for higher office. Men like John, Archcantor of the Roman Church, were sent on important diplomatic missions under their cultural cover as musicians. Gifted singers such as Sergius I became popes themselves.

Liturgy was affected by the Greek-speaking presence through the influence of elaborate eastern ecclesiastical and court ceremonials on the various rites of the generally more sober Latin Church. Imperial splendor was especially noticeable in those ceremonies emphasizing the exalted position of the Papacy, rites then enshrined in the mass books of the Latin-speaking Pope Gregory II (715–731). These headier, formalized liturgical practices were then carried out in churches beautified in the magnificent and icon-friendly eastern manner:

> It has been described as "a rigid etiquette admitting neither change nor improvisation on the part of the assistants, an awe-inspiring solemnity of ceremonies and a unique grandiose *organum* chant [which] become symbols of Papal sovereignty in the West turning the congregation into spectators and listeners."[2]

Associated with this development was a major artistic movement, spurred on by the arrival of refugee Alexandrian artists. It centered on church decoration and in particular the painting of frescoes and images and the designing of ikons in the Byzantine fashion. At its height during the reign of John VII, it was to become in part an element in the assertion of orthodoxy against iconoclasm, but it was also a supreme reflection of the Hellenization of the church and city of Rome. The basilicas of the city, handsomely endowed and lavishly decorated by the Greek popes, became in their oriental opulence veritable Byzantine temples, shimmering with silk gauze draperies, glittering with jeweled chalices, embroidered altar cloths, hanging crucifixes, inlaid silver roof-beams, gold and silver ikons, and ornamental arches, iridescent with multi-colored frescoes and mosaic floors.[3]

Yet a third eastern influence came in the form of the popularity of certain Greek Church institutions and missionary practices. Easterners were very much active in creating *xenodocheia*, hospices

---

2 Richards, *The Popes and the Papacy*, 279.
3 Richards, 279.

for foreigners and pilgrims, of whom there were, of course, many in Rome. These were often related to *diaconia*, charitable organizations, often monastic in character, providing aid to the poor and the sick, attached to Greek churches and chapels in the Eternal City such as St. Maria in Cosmedin, St. George in Velabro, Saints Cosmas and Damian, Saints Sergius and Bacchus, St. Theodore and St. Hadrian. Moreover, the vision of life as a voluntary exile, popular with the easterners, led to the (admittedly not very well known) work of men from the Greek-speaking world in northern Italy. Under the name of *decumani* and *pellegrini,* such people played a role in the evangelization of the Lombards.

Finally, and most importantly, the Greek-speaking migration had a significant impact on learning of all types. This influence overturned the anti-elitist tendencies favored by Pope St. Gregory I, who had denounced the classical training of the older intelligentsia—still overwhelmingly strong in the 500s—as an obstacle to the catechizing of common people and an invitation to heretical hair-splitting in dogmatic theology to boot. Learning was affected, as we know by now, first and foremost through making the Greek language and Greek theological arguments well known in Rome once more. Whereas men like Popes Vigilius (537–555), Honorius, Martin, and probably Gregory himself, could not understand Greek, this was no longer the case by the late 600s, when an "elitist" classical training had once again become a ticket to higher office and deep esteem. Hence, the election of a man like Zacharias, who, ironically, translated Gregory's *Dialogues* into Greek, and the praise given by the *Liber Pontificalis* to Pope Leo II (682–683), who rendered the Greek proceedings of the sixth General Council into Latin:

> A most eloquent man, adequately instructed in the holy scriptures, erudite in the Greek and Latin tongue, outstanding in chant and psalmody and polished in those senses by the most subtle exercise of them; also learned in language and polished in speaking by greater reading, the encourager of all good works and he brought knowledge to the people splendidly.[4]

Eastern learning gained its new renown, more than anything else, due to its absolute indispensability in dealing with the Monothelite

---

4 Cited in Richards, 281.

flip on the Monophysite Heresy troubling the Christian world throughout the 600s. Monophysitism attacked the decision of the Council of Chalcedon defining Our Lord's possession of two natures, human and divine, united in the single Person of the Word. Monophysites emphasized the "one incarnate nature of the Word." Monothelites confirmed the same basic Monophysite position, but by speaking specifically of Christ's possessing only one divine will. Seventh Century Roman Emperors, starting with Heraclius, gave support to Monothelitism in order to overcome divisions in the Middle East, the bulk of whose Christians were Monophysites of one sort or another.

Rome felt specially bound to the decisions of the Council of Chalcedon due to Pope Leo the Great's central role within it through his famous *Tome*. It would never willingly oppose Chalcedon's orthodox decrees. Nevertheless, Gregorian anti-intellectualism had given all dogmatic theological speculation a bad name in Roman eyes, as something manipulated by pointlessly subtle snobs. It did not take the issues that were at stake in Christological disputes all that seriously, and missed the central points being made by participants in the Monothelite struggle. Hence the confusion of one of Gregory's most loyal followers, the hapless Pope Honorius, whose dismissal of the whole battle as the work of "croaking frogs,"[5] made him an unsuspecting agent for Monothelite attacks on Chalcedon and penetration of Christendom.

It was the learned, persecuted, pro-Chalcedonian migrant monks of the East, especially the great St. Maximus the Confessor, who saved the day for Rome and for Orthodoxy. They were the force inspiring Pope St. Martin I to call the Lateran Synod of 649 to attack both Monothelites and their imperial supporters. They were the ones most active at that Synod, through the *primicerius notariorum*, Theophylact, the senior notaries (Paschal, Exuperius, Theodore, Anastasius and Paschasius), the four Greek abbots, "longtime resident in the city of Rome"[6]—John of St. Saba, Theodore of St. Saba in Africa, Thalassius of Saints Maria and Andreas, and George of Aquae Salviae—and, most significantly, the memorial signed by thirty-seven monks demanding pro-Chalcedonian action. Greek-speakers like Theodore, Bishop John of Philadelphia,

5   Cited in Richards, 260.
6   Cited in Richards, 277.

Theophanes of St. Caesarius ad Baias, George, priest and monk of Saints Maria and Andreas, and the monks Conon and Stephen of the Domus Arsicia, were appointed as Roman envoys dealing with fall-out from Monotheletism by Popes from St. Martin to Agatho from the 640s down through the end of the century.

All of the influences of Greek-speaking monks, clerics and popes in the life of the Latin Church were of enormous importance in building the prestige and glory of the Papacy, ceremonial and substantive, in the eyes of Christendom at large. Such work to enhance the role of the Roman Pontiffs was a conscious one. Everything, from the writings of St. Maximus the Confessor regarding papal authority and the need to flex it, to Pope Sergius I's translation of the body of Pope St. Leo the Great to a new, splendid and more prominent tomb, illustrates this truth. Despite occasional setbacks, owed more to the age and personality of certain Greek and Latin-speaking popes than anything else, the reputation of the Papacy was infinitely higher by the end of Pope Zacharias' reign than at the beginning of Pope John V's. That enhanced status continued further to inspire great eastern friends of the Papacy, such as St. Theodore the Stoudite (c. 758–c. 826), in their struggle for Church autonomy against Caesaro-Papism.

But what are we to learn from all this today? A great deal, I think; if nothing else, the fact that help for Rome frequently comes from what one might at first glance think to be unexpected sources. We are, after all, supposed to beware of Greeks bearing gifts. Nevertheless, we have seen that the question-—"is the Pope Greek?"—had to be answered "yes" in the late 600s and 700s, and the person responding to it would have been forced to add—"and thank God for it!"

If we were to speak of that Greek domination of the Roman Church using modern terminology, we might say that it presented a multicultural success story. It showed that "multiculturalism" can be a positive force for good, so long as it allows one culture to give needed backbone to and thereby raise the level of another one which is in trouble. This is what Greek learning in particular did for Rome in the age in question. Perhaps Greek Rome is not so well known precisely because it does not fit the *pluralist* multicultural call for cultures to melt into some degenerate, least common denominator "mush."

"Foreign" domination of seventh and eighth century Rome was a blessing for the Eternal City, leading to her splendid beautification. It was a blessing for the Church, both Universal and Latin, as well. Not only did it add a great deal, theoretically and practically, to the doctrine of Papal Supremacy. Interestingly enough, it also contributed much to the defense of local Latin Church customs against Eastern Church "imperialism." It was the Greek-speaking Pope Sergius who fought against the outrageous condemnation of western customs by an arrogant East eager to foist its peculiar traditions on everyone in the so-called Council in Trullo of 692.

One final and perhaps obvious comment. "Foreign domination" of a Rome gone sloppy was again beneficial for the Eternal City and the Universal and Latin Church in the Eleventh Century. It was at that time that superior cultural influences arriving from the north, using the good offices of the Kings of Germany, injected their cultural medicine into the devastatingly parochial and corrupt climate of contemporary Rome. Can we hope something similar may happen in our own day, with a new, outside, German influence shaking up a Rome of "business as usual" for the better? May we someday be able to answer the question—"is the Pope German?"—with an equally enthusiastic "yes, and thank God for it!" Let us pray so, since prayer is basically all that we have at our disposal at this dramatic juncture in Church History. Such junctures have been reached before, and have seen taken an equally dramatic turn for the better. Led by Greeks. Led by Germans.

12

The Last Crusade†

*"The place for me, as a minister of peace, might
not be so much in the midst of arms and artillery
pieces. But I am the minister of God, and one
must remember that this God who calls himself
the God of Peace is also the God of Armies.
And one must always fight against evil."* [1]
—PIUS IX blessing the Roman artillery

B EFORE THE LATE WALTER MATT DIRECTED
my anti-modernist polemics against enemies closer to home,
I was much more occupied with an assault on modernity in the form
of the nineteenth century Italian unification movement. That so-
called *Risorgimento* or "resurgence," was important to me as part of
the political environment in which Pope Pius IX, the subject of my
doctoral dissertation, reigned and suffered. It was also of great
consequence to my own intellectual development, this because its
ability to confuse the real nature of our modern culture wars and the
true character of its opposing forces under a mountain of grotesque
lies helped open my eyes to the similar Americanist/Pluralist con-
game. So blatantly mendacious and harmful to the Faith was this
inglorious movement that it brought into being an international papal
army sworn to battle its overall hypocrisy and many specific anti-
Catholic depredations. This army fought what some authors have
identified as the Last Crusade.

Thankfully, anyone interested in further accurate information on
the *Risorgimento* can find it today in almost any serious mainstream
scholarly work. Denis Mack Smith's book, *Cavour and Garibaldi
in 1860: A Study in Political Conflict* (Cambridge: Cambridge
University Press, 1985), and, for those who can read Italian, Angela
Pellicciari's *L'altro Risorgimento: Una guerra di religione dimenti-
cata* (Casale Monferrato: Piemme, 2000) are good places to start.

---

† First published in *The Remnant*, May 31, 2007.

---

1 Cited in Jean Guenel, *La derniere guerre du pape* (Rennes: Presses
universitaires de Rennes, 1998), 120–121.

All such works show that this "resurgence," which supposedly reflected a widespread outburst of popular enthusiasm for the creation of an independent Italian nation, was actually the project of a small group of liberal and nationalist conspirators backed by an ambitious dynasty of otherwise solid legitimist credentials—the House of Savoy in the Kingdom of Sardinia. The *Risorgimento*'s revolutionary ability to flip reality upside down under a seemingly conservative banner, as well as its skill in manufacturing unnecessary wars, makes its leaders worthy predecessors of the Cheney, Rumsfeld, Perle, Feith and Wolfowitz Gang,

Most students of the *Risorgimento* argue that it took its first practical steps to maturity through the work of Napoleon. Bonaparte's concern for a more efficient military exploitation of a "liberated" Europe led him to create a Kingdom of Italy, with himself as monarch, in the northern part of the peninsula. Needing assistance in administering his new realm, he sought and gained the aid of members of the Italian bourgeoisie and nobility who, for varied reasons, were sympathetic to certain revolutionary changes, and thus were willing to tie their future to the founding of a "Greater Italy." Napoleon's fall in 1814/1815 and the restoration of most pre-1789 legitimist governments foiled the dreams and ambitions of these collaborators.

Their disgruntlement was shared, but also given a much more profound and consistent ideological character, by men like Giuseppe Mazzini (1805–1872). Mazzini was convinced that his Enlightenment God's plan for universal harmony was dependent upon the establishment of independent, ethnically pure, democratic nation states. Only when these building blocks were in place could the music of the cosmic spheres be heard and appreciated. For Mazzini and similarly evangelical Freedom Fighters around the western world, anything that aided their cause was morally good; anything standing in its way fetid and vile. All those in opposition to this holy unification movement were destined for elimination; all who were indifferent to its goals in desperate need of consciousness raising at the hands of democratic nationalist prophets.

But the vast bulk of ordinary Italians, both high and low, were hostile to or uninterested in Mazzini's dream. Moreover, to make matters still worse, many of the "practical-minded," liberal bourgeoisie and nobility who were friendly to the idea of a Greater Italy feared Mazzini's democratic and conspiratorial approach to the project. Mazzinianism, to them, was disruptive to the pursuit of that individual liberty and material prosperity which they understood to be the chief long-term blessing of Enlightenment naturalism and the French Revolution. They deemed it hopelessly utopian to boot.

The dangers and futility of Mazzinianism was driven home for such moderates by the debacle of democratic nationalist uprisings in the Revolution of 1848. Hence the efforts in the 1850s of the Sardinian Prime Minister, the Count Camillo de Cavour (1810–1861), to work for change through the existing monarchy; to develop King Vittorio Emmanuele II's (1849–1878) openness to the idea that a liberal and moderately nationalist *Machtpolitik* might increase the prosperity and strength of his previously quite counterrevolutionary dynasty. Hence, also, Cavour's successful conversion of a number of disappointed democratic conspirators to cooperation with the Sardinian Monarchy through the establishment of what was referred to as the Italian National Committee. Perhaps the most important revolutionary won over to the moderates' strategy was Mazzini's dashing military associate, Giuseppe Garibaldi (1807–1882).

Cavour was convinced that nothing could be accomplished for the cause of liberalism and the moderate nation-building of the House of Savoy without the support of one or two of the Great Powers of Europe. This he tried to secure by embroiling his country in the Crimean War against Russia on the side of Great Britain and France. The Kingdom of Sardinia had no quarrel with the Czar, but who cared about such petty details? What Cavour needed, as he openly stated in letters to his wife, was enough dead soldiers to give him a place at the subsequent peace conference, during which he could bring up the so-called "Italian National Question" and work to expand Sardinia's borders and power. He was deeply distraught that the war ended before the cadavers could pile up in sufficient numbers to achieve this laudable goal.

Luckily for Cavour, Napoleon III decided to take up the Freedom Fighter's Burden on his own steam. He did so partly in the hope that a cute little war on behalf of a seemingly disinterested cause might calm some current political storms at home. He did so also, however, because broad assistance to nationalist movements had, after 1815, become a Bonapartist trademark, and an Italian nationalist, irritated by the emperor's failure to live up to family responsibilities, reminded him of his duty by means of an attempted assassination. Napoleon got the hint, put on his body armor and packed his bags for a visit with Prime Minister Cavour.

The Congress of Vienna had given to Austria the mission of propping up the existing Italian order of things. Altering the peninsula's political geography therefore required weakening or eliminating Hapsburg influence therein. Austria, alas, was a stubbornly peaceful power in the 1850s. Some fictional excuse for a war against her had to be invented. Emperor and Prime Minister met in a mountain lodge in 1859 to crawl over a large map of Europe to discover some spot, any spot, where a *casus belli* could be manufactured *ex nihilo*.

Where there's a will there's a way, and an obscure dynastic dispute was pounced upon with WMD enthusiasm. An otherwise unwilling Emperor Franz Josef was forced to the battlefield to save Austrian honor. Nothing went according to plan. Nevertheless, events ended up working towards the creation of a Kingdom of Italy both faster and much bigger than anyone in his wildest nightmare could ever have imagined. But this new nation would pay the price for its comic opera birth for decades—perhaps centuries—to come.

Napoleon had gone to war to hand over the Austrian-ruled Veneto and Lombardy to a Greater Sardinia masquerading as a new, little Italian nation. Disturbances to central Italy troubling the security of the Papal States were expressly prohibited by the emperor, eager as he was to quiet the fears of French Catholics. But even the "moderate patriots" of the Italian National Committee still operated with Mazzini's notion that promises were meant to be kept or broken in so far as they were useful to promotion of the Grand Cause of complete unification. War with Austria was much too useful for nationalist boat rocking to limit their ambitions to the Lombard plain. Hence, their agents in central Italy exploited the war environment to stir up troubles in this region as well. An agitation was fomented, which the extraordinarily peaceful governments of the region had little police and military force at their disposal to calm. Nationalists then wrung their hands in outrage over the inability of these "incompetent" and "backward" states to suppress the disorders which they themselves had organized. They said that only the intervention of a real army of a true, modern

State—that of the Kingdom of Sardinia—could assure that return of peace and prosperity desired by all men of good will.

Altruistic Sardinia now took up the Peacekeeper's as well as the Freedom Fighter's Burden, leaving an outraged Napoleon to fight Austria practically on his own. The angry French Emperor determined to back out of the conflict at the first moment that a victory permitted him honorably to do so. He punished his unruly ally by leaving the Veneto in Austrian possession, and further humiliated Sardinia by handing over a Lombardy which Franz Josef ceded directly to him as a "gift" from France. Napoleon also demanded that the House of Savory fully comply with its part of the highly secret pre-war bargain. This meant surrendering Sardinia's territories on the "French" side of the Alps, with the very, very Italian city of Nice prominent among them.

Here lay another rub. For Nice was the birthplace of Garibaldi, who saw that his hometown would never be part of the Italian nation to whose creation he had dedicated his life. For a man already peeved by Sardinia's failure to use his military skills during the war with Austria, this cession of sacred Italian soil was the final straw. Garibaldi returned to his radical roots, taking his vengeance by tossing moderate strategy still further to the winds than the Italian National Committee had done. He did so by recruiting a private army and setting sail in 1860 to invade the southern part of Italy—the Kingdom of the Two Sicilies—something which was totally alien to absolutely everyone's plans before and during the war with Austria.

Off Garibaldi went. In typical, hypocritical, *Risorgimento* fashion, a Sardinian naval force was sent after him with the order vigorously to stop his venture if it appeared as though England or France were going to make moves to do so—but to aid it if they did not! They did not. Garibaldi was thus able to land in Sicily and then on the mainland, taking advantage of a monarchy whose administration and army were seriously infiltrated by liberal, democratic and nationalist fifth columnists. Despite heroic resistance at the fortress of Civitella del Tronto on the border with the Papal States, the Kingdom of the Two Sicilies swiftly fell.

Sardinian troops, already involved in Peacekeeping Missions in central Italy, now rushed south. The nature of their task depended upon what Garibaldi intended to do with his conquered territories.

The army might be going to stop a "madman's" march towards Rome; a march that would obviously require Sardinian peace-keeping troops on papal soil as well. On the other hand, the army might also be going to aid a patriot's brilliant, liberating advance from the south. The man the troops encountered turned out to be the "patriot," who handed the Kingdom of the Two Sicilies over to Vittorio Emmanuele and his ministers, almost as though their previous quarrel had been a staged one all along.

Plebiscites were held in the lands fortunate enough to have had peace finally restored by the troublemakers who had first disturbed it. By 1861, a small number of voters, picked for their reliability and highly cognizant of their nationalist duty, yielded 99% majorities in favor of membership in a new Kingdom of Italy. This Kingdom's real character as a conquest by Sardinia was symbolically illustrated by Vittorio Emmanuele's continued use of his designation as "The Second" of that name. It did not take long before the average man understood what the new liberal government from the north meant in practice: a carpetbagger administration, high taxes, universal conscription, attacks on priests and the general freedom of the Church, economic policies harmful to agriculture and favorable to capitalist industrialists, and anticlerical destruction of the complex network of social services provided over the centuries by the Catholic charitable vision. Bloody rebellions, identified by the new government as mere terrorist and criminal rampages, erupted throughout the 1860s and were brutally suppressed. Mass migration to the Americas followed thereafter. Another victory for modern Progress!

It was in the troubled atmosphere of 1859–1861 that Msgr. Xavier de Merode, a member of a great Belgian family serving in the entourage of Pope Pius IX, had the idea of inviting Louis Christophe Leon Juchault de La Moriciere (1805–1865) to take charge of and reorganize the decrepit Papal Army. General de La Moriciere was a hero of the French colonial war in Algeria. De Merode had met and appreciated the undefeated record of de La Moriciere while himself serving under the French flag during his own rather dashing and eclectic pre-clerical career.

Pius IX rejected Secretary of State Cardinal Giacomo Antonelli's scathing criticism of the absurdity of any armed defense of the Papal States, detached responsibility for the army from his control and appointed de Merode as his Minister of War. The Belgian then made a formal offer to the French General, who accepted it in March of 1860. De La Moriciere, who had himself served as French Minister of War during the Second Republic, and disapproved of Napoleon III's *coup d'etat*, refused to ask permission from his "illegitimate" sovereign before taking up the new assignment.

Arriving in the Eternal City the next month, he found the existing Roman Army of six hundred men in an absolutely appalling state. It was badly armed, badly dressed, highly undisciplined and ready to drill only "if the weather remains good."[2] De Merode and de La Moriciere realized that many new and more enthusiastic recruits were desperately needed if the Roman Army were to become a serious fighting force. With Italians, both high and low, despising the career-at-arms, an appeal was thus sent out for support from Catholics the world over.

By May of 1860, eighteen thousand men, French, Belgians and Irish prominent among them, were at the Minister and General's disposal. But problems with the quality and organization of the recruits, along with difficulties of armament and supply, made it clear that many months would be required to shape them into a competent military machine. "I will count upon Providence," the realistic Vicomte Louis de Becdelievre, veteran soldier and commander of the Battalion of French-Belgian Sharpshooters, said when contemplating the obstacles to success; "and march nonetheless."[3]

Such acts of faith were indeed needed, because time to effect serious improvements proved to be totally lacking. The Italian National Committee, as we have seen, had been hard at work stirring up in the Papal States the kind of disturbances which required Sardinian armed intervention to suppress. Conspiratorial rabble rousers were already expressing anguish at the general sufferings of these huddled papal masses yearning to be free. Imagine their added sorrow at the thought of the new torments to be faced by the average man at the hands of the violent, foreign mercenaries called in to aid the cause of the cruel clerical tyrant! It was just

---

2   Guenel, *La derniere guerre*, 28.
3   Cited in Guenel, 29.

too much for an *agent provacateur* to endure! Hence, on September 10, 1860, the Kingdom of Sardinia informed the Papacy that its forces would occupy the two provinces of the Marches and Umbria, thereby ending all the agonies, present and future, of their honest and long-suffering citizens.

Sixty thousand well-trained "natives" entered Pius IX's territory to stop the mercenary threat from the antipodes. "I lead you," their leader, General Cialdini, said, "against a band of foreign drunkards whom thirst for gold and the passion for pillage have drawn into our country."[4] They met and overwhelmed a large chunk of the new and all too green papal forces on September 18 at the Battle of Castelfidardo near the great port city of Ancona. The results for these young units were catastrophic, with two thirds of the Battalion of Franco-Belgian Sharpshooters, to take but one major example, killed or seriously wounded. Ancona, under the circumstances, saw no further chance of holding out. De La Moriciere, mortified by what was, one has to admit, not a particularly unexpected failure, returned in sorrow to France. He remained keenly interested in the sequel to his work up until his death in 1865.

For sequel there was. The de La Moriciere episode proved to be just the beginning of the story. The old core of the Roman Army remained intact, with two divisions, one under the command of the Swiss General de Courten, the other under the Roman General Zappi. Moreover, the disaster at Castelfidardo gave an excuse for weeding out any remaining undesirable elements in the ranks of the recently formed and now decimated papal units. Louis de Becdelievre, in January of 1861, was able to reconstitute a new force from the survivors of the St. Patrick and Franco-Belgian Sharpshooter Battalions. These he outfitted with a popular Algerian uniform initially used by Zouaoua Berbers serving in the French Army, winning for those wearing it in Rome the name of Papal Zouaves. Six hundred strong to begin with, the Papal Zouaves were an extraordinary international brigade:

> The recruits belonged to twenty-five different nationalities. Curiously, although their country had a Protestant majority, the most numerous were the Dutch. Then came the French and the

---

4   Cited in Guenel, 69.

Belgians. The Italians, almost all Romans or Neapolitans, are well represented, above all in music (a question of competence). But one finds also Swiss (among them the officers of high rank), Irish, Austrians, Germans, among whom the Prussians and the Bavarians are the most numerous; Poles, Spaniards, a number of British, whether English or Scot, eight Americans, these above all from the southern states. From South America, Peru, Chile and Equator are each represented by one volunteer; Brazil by two. One finds also seventeen Maltese, one Abyssinian, a Turk, a Moroccan, and an Indian from Madras. Finally, one must speak of the one hundred thirty Canadians from Quebec, who will arrive in 1868. They will not have the chance to fight, but some will participate nonetheless in the siege of Rome. Another wave of one hundred twelve volunteers left Canada in August of 1870 to engage.[5]

Msgr. Pie, Bishop of Poitiers, well describes the atmosphere of religious enthusiasm in which these new recruits left for the Eternal City. "[Rome] for us," he said, "is another, better Jerusalem, more necessary than that of Palestine. Palestine is a great relic. Rome is the living and permanent seat of the light, the grace and the authority of Christ."[6] All social classes took part in what most volunteers firmly believed to be a Crusade, although the nobility, almost all of them supporters of the Legitimist Pretender, Henry V, predominated among the French recruits. Perhaps the most famous—and certainly the most popular—of the legitimist volunteers was the Baron Athanase Charles Marie Charette de la Contrie (1832–1911), great-nephew of the general and martyr of the Vendee rising. Some families, including Charette's, sent multiple members to the Zouave ranks. Most recruits were very young, and reengaged willingly when their initial time of service was finished. Their transport, and eventually much of their regular support, was provided through the work of the *Denier de Saint-Pierre*, which was first organized by Montalembert in 1848; through Mgr. Pie and his *Comite de l'artillerie pontificale*; and, ultimately, through the Baron Onffroy and his *Oeuvre des volontaires pontificaux*. All Zouaves were bound by a solemn oath, first taken on January 9, 1861, at St. John the Lateran:

---

5   Guenel, 40.
6   Cited in Guenel, 44.

I swear to Almighty God to be obedient and faithful to my sovereign, the Roman Pontiff, our very Holy Father, Pope Pius IX and his legitimate successors.

I swear to serve him with honor and fidelity and to sacrifice my life for the defense of his august and sacred person, for the support of his sovereignty and for the maintenance of his rights.

I swear not to belong to any civil or religious sect, to any secret society or corporation, whatever they might be, having for its direct or indirect goal to offend the Catholic religion and to corrupt society.

I swear not to join any sect or society condemned by the decrees of the Roman Pontiffs.

I swear also to the very good and great God to not have any direct or indirect communication with the enemies, whoever they might be, of religion and the Roman Pontiffs.[7]

The Zouaves and their Moslem-like uniform were not to the taste of everyone in the papal government, some cardinals seeing them as merely the eccentric product of overly romantic French minds. De Merode, however, was charmed by them, and eager to put them to the test. Against the better judgment of Becdelievre, who called for much more time for their basic training, de Merode sent them instantly on the offensive. They crossed into "Italian" territory at Passo Corezze on January 26, 1861, immediately creating an international uproar. This did, at least, have the side effect of once again arousing Catholic opinion in France and forcing Napoleon III to send contingents of the regular Army to guard the borders of the Papal States, now limited basically to Lazio, the so-called Patrimony of St. Peter. Unfortunately, it also brought Becdelievre and de Merode's disagreements into public view, leading to the sack of the Zouave founder. Although the legitimist Charette was the obvious replacement, political considerations brought about Colonel Allet's appointment as commander. Allet's Swiss origin could not bring down upon him the French Government's accusation of anti-Bonapartist Bourbon sympathies.

Despite the Becdelievre sack, his insistent request for more training for his troops was answered. This lasted for longer than anyone could have wanted. A three and one half year period of frustration opened for the Zouaves, during which they were kept

---

7   Cited in Guenel, 53–54.

inactive or used merely to frighten away the brigands plaguing the papal countryside. Constantly caricatured as low-life intruders by the Italian nationalist Press, the Zouaves were also subject to revolutionary bomb threats and nighttime personal assaults. Health problems were among their biggest "peacetime" difficulties. One can well understand what these might have been like when musing on the fact that one of their physicians left for medical training at Louvain in 1869—after nine years already as their surgeon. Still, as the diary of the Abbe Jules Daniel testifies, religious enthusiasm and practice remained consistent and fervent. So did contempt for the *Risorgimento*, its naturalism, and its anticlericalism. And their personal bravery, displayed in self-sacrifice in aiding the sick and burying the dead during the cholera epidemics of the late 1860s, won the Zouaves much love from the people in their garrison towns.

Everything changed for the Zouaves and the Papal Army as a whole in September of 1864. It was at that point that a Convention providing for the departure of the French Army from the Papal States in exchange for an Italian promise not to violate its borders was signed by Napoleon III and Vittorio Emmanuele. Pius IX, convinced that the Emperor had betrayed him, felt that there was nothing left for him to do but to rely on his own forces. On the one hand, this meant the encouragement of mass ceremonies strengthening awareness of Rome's role as the Capital City of an international Catholicism. On the other, it entailed directing still more attention to the Roman Army.

With de La Moriciere out of the picture and de Merode too cranky and eccentric for further martial labors, Pius IX, on October 28, 1865, put the Ministry of War and the Army under the control of General Hermann Kanzler from the Grand Duchy of Baden. Kanzler loved the Zouaves, and did not hide the fact that he considered it to be the Roman Army's elite unit. Zouaves were therefore brought into more serious service, both in Rome as well as on the southern and northern borders of the Patrimony of St. Peter. Enrollment once again soared, aided, at this point, by the encouragement of the Zouaves themselves in their private correspondence to friends and family, the crusading fervor of prelates like Mgr. Mathieu, Archbishop of Besancon, and the efforts of Committees of St. Peter to "buy" recruits out of their required military service in the regular French Army. Down to five hundred in 1865, Zouave numbers reached 2,289 by 1867 and 3,000 by 1870. Yes, some bad eggs inevitably entered the ranks along with zealous crusaders, but so did sincere "converts" from among the Italian nationalist ranks as well. One honorable and extremely interesting volunteer, who called himself Watson, turned out to be a J. B. Surrat, wanted by the American police for complicity in Abraham Lincoln's assassination—a charge that he was eventually able to prove to be a false one.

Kanzler's Army was called to the test in 1867. Giuseppe Garibaldi spent much of that year traveling round Italy, lamenting the fact that "several thousand mercenaries, the refuse of all the sewers of Europe"[8] were crushing the inhabitants of the Patrimony under their tyrannical heel, and proclaiming the need for liberation under the slogan "Roma o Morte!" ("Rome or Death!"). His campaign for an immediate attack on the Patrimony of St. Peter culminated, curiously enough, with an incendiary address to the Congress of Peace at Geneva on September 9. At this point, the Italian Government, eager to avoid international repercussions from his incurably bad manners, took the firebrand into custody. It nevertheless allowed his son, Menotti, and the international band of volunteer anticlerical "crusaders" he had recruited, to cross into papal territory on October 1 to see what mischief they might successfully be able to stir up. The Papal Army was sent to face them at the town of Bagnorea, which they had occupied. Zouaves, prominent in its ranks, sang the following song en route:

> Hear these cries of alarm,
> which bring horror into our hearts.
> Bretons, it is an appeal to arms.
> It is an appeal to our faith.
> Shall we allow our Father
> To fall under the blows of Piedmont?
> Better death, better war
> Than to suffer such an affront.
> Proud children of Brittany
> Valliant defenders of the Faith.
> God wills it! Let us enter into the campaign.
> Let us depart for the Pope-King.[9]

---

8   Guenel, 69.
9   Cited in Guenel, 94–95.

Bagnorea was regained, but the experience was a nasty one. The Papal Army saw, with horror, that the Garibaldians were ready to use civilians as human shields to protect them from danger, and that they had desecrated the churches of the occupied town. Zouaves suffered their first casualty, a Dutchman named Nicholas Heycamp. Further give and take in the next few weeks left seventeen Zouaves dead. Seventy Garibaldians paid for their revolutionary crusading with their lives.

Napoleon III, always the diplomatic card player, had balanced his 1864 betrayal with further help for the Papal States. First of all, he gave permission for a new force of one thousand French volunteers—known both as the Roman Legion and the Legion of Antibes—to go to the aid of the Holy See. Now, in face of the Garibaldian incursion, Napoleon went further still. He publicly encouraged Pius IX to resist the radicals' aggression with all the means at his disposal. Moreover, he prepared units of the regular French Army for a return to Italy.

On October 17, while that French force was being readied. Giuseppe Garibaldi "escaped" his protective custody and made his way to take charge of his son's somewhat demoralized crusaders. Garibaldian hopes were also encouraged by preparation for an uprising at Rome itself on October 22. Weapons for that uprising were to be provided with the help of a special group of volunteers, under the leadership of veteran conspirators, who had made their way to Monte Parioli, just outside the center of the Eternal City.

Fortunately, everything went badly for the Garibaldian enterprise, and on every front. The column at Monte Parioli was defeated. Arms for the uprising were limited. With the strong points of the city firmly under papal army protection, and an almost total hostility on the part of the Roman population, it never actually took place at all. The sole serious incident of the day was the blowing up of the Serristori Barracks, near St. Peter's and Castel Saint Angelo, with the tragic death of the twenty-five Zouaves who had the misfortune to be present there at the time of the explosion. Their deaths were avenged on the 25 and the 30, when two Garibaldian hideaways inside Rome were discovered and eliminated. The massacre of the Zouaves, of course, meant nothing to the government-controlled Italian Press. The vengeance wreaked on the Garibaldians, however, was immediately turned into another proof of these foreigners' incurably criminal wickedness.

Calamity for the rest of the Garibaldian Crusade came at Mentana, near Monte Rotondo, north of Rome, where Garibaldi had arrived on October 23. The ten thousand men gathered there were soon confronted with the varied military forces now at the disposal of the Pope. This included the French forces, under General de Failly, which arrived at Civitavecchia on October 28 and marched on November 2 towards the front, together with the Papal Zouaves. They were followed on the third by General Kanzler and the regular Roman Army. Both Zouaves and regulars distinguished themselves in the ensuing battle, but the walls of Mentana being strong, the assistance of the French with their new, rapid-firing Chassepot rifles, was also crucial to the coming victory. When the fighting ceased, one thousand Garibaldians lay dead and wounded. Losses on the papal side were less than forty dead and thirty wounded. Garibaldi was nowhere to be seen. Under what conditions, honorably or dishonorably, he got away, have been greatly debated ever since.

After the grand victory parade, the 1,398 Garibaldian prisoners were all too magnanimously sent home—those who did not promise to take up arms against the Papal States again along with the many who did. Catholics the world over took courage from the defeat of the revolutionaries at Mentana. New recruits for the Zouaves again came pouring in. Even if Canada now headed the list of nations sending its sons to help St. Peter, the whole of Catholic Christendom remained enthusiastic in its participation. The only exception to this rule seems to have been the bishops of the United States, whose coldness to the venture, when approached regarding it in 1868, seems to have stemmed from their fear of appearing to the American Government to be divided in their political loyalties.

Revolutionary forces, like those of Garibaldi, could indeed be stopped by the Papal Army, probably even without French help, especially given the lack of native popular support. Units of the regular Italian Army were, however, a different kind of foe. It was to be with their entry onto the scene that the history of this Last Crusade came to an end.

The final, tragic episode in the story began with the outbreak of the Franco-Prussian War, Napoleon III's recall of all French troops and their complete departure from Rome by August 6, 1870. Disaster might still not have ensued if France had come out of the conflict with Prussia victorious. Alas, it did not. News of the French debacle at Sedan in early September demoralized the French members of the Papal Zouaves who did not know where their first duty now lay. On the other hand, it once again wildly encouraged the ambitions of both the radical Garibaldians and an Italian Government eager that the House of Savoy and not the radicals reap the benefits of French defeat. Vittorio Emmanuele II sent the Count Ponza di San Martino to Rome on September 9 to present to Pius IX the by now familiar argument that threats from wild radicals required Italian intervention and the occupation of the Patrimony of St. Peter by more moderate Italian Peacekeeping Forces. "What good is this attempt at useless hypocrisy?," the Holy Father responded to the emissary. "Would it not be worth more simply to tell me that he would like to strip me of my kingdom? I can indeed surrender to violence, but to accept injustice? Never!"[10]

By September 10, the Italian war machine was in movement. General Cadorna was to move against Rome, while General Bixio, a ferocious anticlerical, headed first towards Civita Castellana and Civitavecchia. Sixty to seventy thousand soldiers would be fighting somewhere between seven and thirteen thousand Roman troops. General Kanzler, ordering a merely honorable show of resistance against violence in other places, decided for a battle to defend Rome alone. His great hope was that no one would actually dare to cause damage to the Eternal City.

Troops were recalled from all around the Patrimony, Charette making a particularly daring escape with his men through enemy-occupied regions. By the night of the nineteenth, with the loyal Trastevere population begging for arms to defend itself, and the army alive with crusading fervor and desire for martyrdom, Pius IX gave an absolutely horrified Kanzler his final orders. After a token show of resistance to indicate opposition to unjustifiable aggression, the Papal Army in Rome, just as its units outside the city, was to surrender to the invaders.

At 5:00 A. M. on September 20 the Italians opened fire at the walls, bombarding and thus causing much damage in Trastevere as well. The weak fortifications at Porta Pia, not that far from Termini Station, were breached by 9:00 A. M. By 9:30, the white flag was raised over St. Peter's. Troops from one end of the city to

---

10   Cited in Guenel, 133–134.

the other, none of whom knew of the pope's order to Kanzler, were now commanded to stop firing. Many refused at first to do so, just as Bixio, for a time, refused to end the fun of bombarding Trastevere. Sixteen men died on the papal side, eleven of whom were Zouaves; fifty soldiers were wounded. The Italians lost thirty-two dead and one hundred forty-three wounded.

Treatment of the vanquished Zouaves who did not manage to escape beyond the Tiber to the Leonine City and Trastevere was often unpleasant. Many were insulted, beaten and had their decorations ripped from their chests, even by segments of the previously loyal Roman population now ready to ingratiate themselves with the victors. Men went rummaging through the city over the course of the next week or more to find and punish any of these "brigands" who might have gone into hiding. "Pacification" was swiftly followed by the usual farce of a plebiscite:

> The Italian Government fixed for October 2nd, the date of the plebiscite destined to legitimize the annexation of Rome. The Holy Father formally forbade Roman Catholics to take part in the vote and the electoral lists were drawn up according to the good pleasure of the patriots. The citizens reputed favorable to the pope did not figure in them. In contrast, all Romans absent from the city and called to Rome to vote had to spend the night in cafes and in public squares. Porters on the eve of the vote had distributed a profusion of ballots marked with an annexationist 'yes', and individuals circulated through the streets wearing a slip of paper with 'yes' attached to their hats in the manner of a cocarde. The day of the plebiscite a large urn was placed on Capitol Hill to receive the ballots, but there were others in the offices of the quarters of the city, and since, to vote, one had to present a ballot of elector which was rendered to you without having been cancelled, it was very easy to place votes in many successive offices. The results were published on the 7th by the new junta established on Capitol Hill. They were in conformity with what had been sought: the partisans of annexation carried away an overwhelming majority at Rome (77,520 yes against 857 no) just as in the rest of the pontifical territory where the same means had been employed. But Victor Emmanuel had not even awaited those results, since a decree of the 2nd of October had already proclaimed the annexation of Rome to Italy.[11]

11   Guenel, 158.

Kanzler, in the capitulation agreement, consented to the departure of the Zouaves gathered on the Vatican side of the Tiber by noon on the 21st. After a final blessing by the pope whom they idolized, but who had prevented them from fighting, they were taken to the Porta San Pancrazio. Officers sailed from Civitavecchia and took leave from one another in Toulon. The mass of Zouaves sailed via Genova, where they were badly insulted by the population on the docks before repatriation. Zouaves who had the misfortune of being captured by the enemy outside Rome were thrown, for a time, into cellars at Lake Como, refused help in leaving Italy, and eventually walked barefoot back to their homelands.

Thankfully, those returning to Belgium and Holland received a rapturous, crusading heroes' welcome. Those returning to France were treated equally well, because their fighting skills were appreciated and the country was still at war with Prussia. Hence, Charette, the *de facto* leader of the Zouaves back in France, was allowed to form the men into a unit called the Legion of the Volunteers of the West, which was consecrated to the Sacred Heart of Jesus. Within a few months he had become this Legion's general and a Chevalier of the Legion of Honor as well. The French Government would have liked his Legion to continue after the war's end, but Charette, seeing its duty still to be primarily papal and Catholic in character, could not bring himself to agree. Despite a temporary cooling of his personal relationship with the pope, due to his marriage to an American Protestant, he remained forever true to the Zouave crusading vision and his legitimist political convictions, promoting them in a journal called the *Avant-garde* (1892–1932). After Colonel Allet's death in 1878, he became the honorary Commander of the Papal Zouaves as a whole, both inside and outside France.

General Kanzler, commander of the Papal Army, shared Pope Pius IX's fate as prisoner of the Vatican, remaining inside its walls until his death in 1888. Ninety-nine of the Zouaves he loved so dearly eventually became priests, monks, missionaries or missionary assistants. Five were consecrated bishops. Many of those who remained dedicated to a military career went to Spain to fight for Don Carlos, inspired to do so not just by his Catholic commitment, but also because his brother, Alfonso de Borbon, had fought in their ranks. All Zouaves cherished the memory of what they had done. Charette held regular reunions on his property at Basse-Motte. So did the very large number of his Dutch and Belgian comrades. The Netherlands, Belgium and Canada created museums to honor their cause, and the city of Nantes commemorated the work of de La Moriciere with a cenotaph in its cathedral.

Very little of the story of the Papal Army and its elite Zouave unit is remembered by anyone in 2007. Most Catholics, both in Italy and the United States, have too little energy left over from all the time they spend honoring "great historical figures" who considered our Faith to be an absurdity to waste the precious moments that remain to them on the likes of de La Moriciere, Becdelievre, Kanzler, Charette and even Pius IX. Garibaldi is now their Kanzler. Lincoln is their Pius IX. And for this failure to give honor where honor is properly due, they pay daily and dearly.

13

313 AD

THE END OF THE BEGINNING†

CALLING ATTENTION TO SPECIFIC DATES, such as 1789 and 1914, is a necessary means of underlining major developments in the history of the world. Nevertheless, further study regularly indicates that men require much more time before they can properly digest the changes that such dates do indeed foretell. Rather than summing up the full import of the intellectual, spiritual, political, and social revolutions to follow, what they really point to is the end of the beginning of a new era long in preparation and still pregnant with many more questions for the future.

Such is the case with the so-called "Edict of Milan" of the Christian Constantine and the pagan Licinius in 313, issued hot on the heels of their joint victory over their rival, the persecutor Maxentius. The exact form this measure took is presented to us in somewhat different forms by the early Christian historians Lactantius (c. 240–c. 320) and Eusebius of Caesarea (c. 263–339). Whatever its shape actually was, it confirmed that liberation for Christians that had begun two years earlier with Galerius' resigned admission of the failure of the policy of harassment in the eastern part of the Empire. Freedom to worship and to possess property for Christian purposes was awarded the faithful, while goods that had been confiscated were ordered returned. But what this all really meant was going to take a long time to grasp. In fact, if the truth be told, it still is not fully appreciated in the Year of Grace, 2013, and by believers and non-believers alike. Still, as indicated above, the Edict of Milan did clearly mark the end of the beginning—the beginning of that radically new phenomenon called a "relationship" between Church and State. This was so startling an innovation—and how could it not have been so, brought about as it was by the Incarnation of the Second Person of the Blessed Trinity as Jesus Christ, the God-Man—that the

---

† First published in *The Angelus*, February 2013.

Roman State had fumbled for almost three hundred years trying to figure out some coherent way to respond to it.

In many respects, the Empire did not tackle its task that badly. The imperial authorities recognized the dependency of the commonwealth upon the good will of religious-minded men and women, and wanted no troubles with the gods as such. Once they understood that Christians were distinct from Jewish zealots in full revolt against Roman rule, they recognized that believers were actually law-abiding individuals upon whom no ordinary criminal accusations could be pinned. Many of the state authorities' best instincts told them to leave these wretches to their "superstition" without interference.

But the new reality the Christians represented was just too much for the pagan community as a whole peacefully to bear. How could pagan magistrates easily comprehend the idea of a religious force organized in a supranational body of an army-like quality truly separate from the State and eager to evangelize not just a single city or ethnic group but the whole of the imperial population? How could they grasp the mentality of a Faith that would not accept and enjoy nature "as it really was," but wished to judge its "flaws" and supposedly correct them? And how could they consistently resist the pressure to crush these "haters of mankind" that came from defenders of "the ways of the ancestors," Roman and non-Roman, high born and low, the Empire over? Hence, the periodic outbursts of persecution that struck at believers whom magistrates knew to be the easiest of men to rule in every normal respect.

With the Edict of Milan, all this centuries-long fumbling came to an end. That end was a dramatic one, not because it called a halt to the persecution of Christians, welcome though this cessation of hostilities obviously was to those who had suffered from its ravages. It was really dramatic because it gave official state recognition to the existence of the Church, the Mystical Body of Christ, as a legitimate and different kind of social entity. Something "other," claiming to have its roots in a world beyond and above nature, was given *droit de cité*. A greater theoretical blow to the entire earth-bound pagan mentality cannot be imagined.

Very swiftly, many of the longer-term consequences of this death knell began to be felt, apparently demonstrating the growing influence of the Christian "body" and mentality upon the State.

Not only was the Church allowed to own property; Emperor Constantine himself began to augment her holdings considerably, as, for example, through the grant of the properties around the Lateran. Not only did bishops now become respected imperial personages, with highborn men from the senatorial aristocracy gradually aspiring to enter the ranks of the episcopacy; diocesan courts and the validity of their judgments were soon given imperial approval as well. Even ordinary priests were awarded the privileges of local notables. Not only was the weekly Christian holy day made into an Empire-wide festival, but belying the Edict of Milan's claim to offer a general "religious liberty," pagan religious practices began, bit by bit, to be circumscribed as "superstitions," and all this in Constantine's own lifetime.

Unfortunately, other things were happening during the reign of that same Emperor indicating that the full significance of the existence of a truly "separate," supernaturally grounded Christian body and mentality had by no means yet been digested by the State. Constantine's support for a revision of the Council of Nicaea's anti-Arian definition of the Son as being of the same substance as the Father is, of course, the chief case in point. It was one thing to grant the clergy special benefits when they could be handed secular administrative responsibilities that laymen in the late Empire were fleeing as intolerable burdens along with them. It was quite another to treat prelates with respect when they might use their supposedly favored and independent positions to oppose the imperial will. For as real as the recognition of the separate role of the Mystical Body of Christ in the Edict of Milan may have been on the theoretical level, that separate function was still looked upon as one that must be guided by the State and for the narrowly perceived political well-being of the State.

To give to Constantine and his successors down to 2013 their proper due, this attitude is understandable and, in effect, "comes along with the job." Weighing, measuring, and submitting to supernatural guidance always requires serious effort for all of us in each and every one of our natural daily activities. This can be especially problematic when we realize that that guidance that we as believers must acknowledge comes at the hands of men who themselves have their own temptations to misuse their vocations and can therefore badly muddle their work as transmitters of Christ's message.

Quite frankly, as far as I am concerned, the biggest obstacle to digestion of the full meaning of the Edict of Milan and the consequences this should have for the transformation of all things in Christ—right down to the present—has always been the failure of the episcopacy to do its job properly. From the very outset, all too many prelates whose chief "job hazard" and flaw ought to have been that of exaggerating the power of the Church have dedicated themselves to weakening ecclesiastical authority.

Some of these "court bishops," such as that Eusebius of Nicomedia (d. 341) who stirred up the Arian revision movement in the first place, may have been fundamentally concerned with heretical principles. Nevertheless, they clearly understood how the State machinery could be mobilized against the free action of the Church as a whole. They provided a model for that horde of prelates who joined in the ecclesiastical destruction game for the sake of personal riches and glory and made the whole of the Fourth Century one long and unnecessary battle to return (admittedly in enriched form) to the original Nicaean formula.

Particularly disturbing is the damage done by more well-meaning court bishops. Eusebius, the Bishop of Caesarea (c. 263–339) and the first great Church historian, stands at the head of the list of offenders in this regard. He, whatever his personal Arian convictions, seems to have been motivated much more by awe before the fact that a Roman Emperor with the age-old majesty of the Imperial State behind him, now called himself a Christian. This awe led him to create an aura surrounding the "Christian Emperor" that was crucial to the transformation of his responsibility from one of simple protection of the Pax Christi—a difficult enough task—to that of playing an unacceptable "apostolic" role in shaping it. Eusebius expressly rejected discussing anything in his Vita of Constantine that could be unedifying from a Christian standpoint, even though the full story might have sent the orthodox believer hunting for a much more certain shield and buckler. Having assured us of Constantine's beneficence by suppressing any evidence that might contradict its validity, he then moved on, in the Laudes, delivered on the thirtieth anniversary of the emperor's reign in 335, to set a tone in praise of the faith-friendly ruler destined for a long history of imitation down to the present day. One passage from Johannes Quasten's *Patrology* reveals the attendant problems neatly:

Eusebius begins with the assurance that he intends to avoid any display of rhetoric. He believes that the Emperor is a human being set apart from other human beings in that he is "perfect in wisdom, in goodness, in justice, in courage, in piety, in devotion to God: the Emperor truly and he alone is a philosopher, for he knows himself, and he is fully aware that an abundance of every blessing is showered on him from a source quite external to himself, even from heaven itself." Eusebius compares him to the sun: "Thus our Emperor, like the radiant sun, illuminates the most distant subjects of his empire through the presence of his Caesars, as with the far piercing rays of his own brightness." His Empire is "the imitation of the monarchical power in heaven," because he has consciously modeled his government after that in heaven. [1]

To paraphrase a line from the old film, *Cool Hand Luke*, "what we have here is a failure to communicate"—in this case, a failure to communicate the true path to that corrective and transformative impact of the Church on the State that the Edict of Milan ought to have made possible in practice as well as in theory. Eusebius of Caesarea was a "court bishop" of the most dangerous sort—most dangerous because he actually *believed* in the error that he was communicating. He told the imperial State that called itself Christian that its mere "words" ensured the victory of the Word Incarnate. Unfortunately, he was but the first of many such prelates. Future court bishops would serve the interests of national monarchies on the one hand and democratic "Catholic" political parties on the other, granting the same twisted "apostolic powers" to their "Most Christian Systems" that Eusebius awarded to his. In our own time and place, similar prelates promote the cause of supposedly God-fearing Founding Fathers who were really servants of the anti-Catholic Whig Enlightenment.

The Edict of Milan was indeed only "the end of the beginning" in terms of the history of the complex relationship of Church and State. Still, let us not allow a recognition of the problems that continued to trouble the interaction of these two institutions after 313 AD to tempt us to the conclusion that the collaboration of the earthly political authority with that of the Mystical Body of

---

1 Johannes Quasten, *Patrology, vol.* 3 (Westminster: Christian Classics, 1992), 326–327.

Christ necessarily weakened and corrupted the Church's liberating spiritual mission. One might just as well use recognition of the inevitable difficulties of harmonizing the exercise of parental and ecclesiastical authority as an excuse for calling for the separation of Church and Family.

No, the Edict of Milan was "the end of the beginning" of something more than a simple revelation of the pains involved with struggling towards eternal life in a sin-stained valley of tears. It was also "the end of the beginning" of the construction of that magnificent society that we call Christendom. Construction of that new social order had begun the moment that the Apostles, Apostolic Fathers, and their successors understood that our earthly environment was meant to be corrected and transformed through the message and grace of the Incarnation, thereby providing us a training ground for Heaven as opposed to Hell. Plans were laid intellectually and even carried through practically, to a certain narrow degree, within the precarious Catholic enclaves of the pre-Constantinian world. But the Edict proved to be the crucial step by means of which "Christendom" left its parochial club-house to conquer the public spaces of the world at large. And the rest is history.

14

Innocent III, Marriage, and Militant Christendom[†]

FOR THE POPULAR MIND, NO POPE SYMBOL-
izes the majesty and glory of the Roman Catholic Church at
its height more than Lothario dei Conti di Segni. Born around 1160,
the future Innocent III was educated in Rome, Bologna, and Paris.
Cardinal Deacon at the age of twenty-nine, he became Supreme
Pontiff a mere decade later, while still under forty (1198–1216). Caricatured by enemies of the Faith as a purely secular-minded "lord
of the world,"[1] presiding over a power-hungry Catholic political
machine with an admittedly great energy and efficiency, Innocent
III was actually an icon of the entire spiritually-focused reform
movement of the High Middle Ages. It was transformation of all
things in Christ that was his primary concern, and he underlined
this theme in writing with reference to the topic of central importance to this issue of *The Angelus*: marriage.

One cannot look to the pope's most famous work, *On the Misery
of the Human Condition*, for proof of my point. Innocent intended to
complement this "negative" text with another "positive" volume that
he never had a chance to finish: *On the Dignity of Human Nature*.
In any case, a much more complete guide to the spirit of Innocent's
thought can be found in his *Fourfold Character of Marriage*.

For Innocent, all of life is symbolized by marriage. In this
book, he shows that (1) the marriage of man and wife is one of
the glorious, sacramental tools raising the individual to eternal
life with a God (2) who is married to the just soul because of (3)
the marriage of the Logos with human nature and (4) of Christ
with His Church. Through these marriages, the fruitful, sublime,
corrective, transforming union of nature and the supernatural can
take place and have its intended effect upon the world.

---

† First published in *The Angelus*, August 2014.

---

1 See James M. Powell, ed., *Innocent III: Vicar of Christ or Lord of the
World?* (Washington: The Catholic University of America Press, 1994).

Unfortunately, however, and precisely because of the "misery of the human condition" after the sin of Adam, the task of making all such marriages truly "fruitful" in their consequences requires a great deal of difficult and humbling effort on our part. Innocent, as pastor, always reflected a practical—and often quite humorous—awareness of the number and strength of the stumbling blocks rendering fallen man's labors towards fulfillment of the exalted goals of the fourfold union somewhat less than satisfactory. What angered him was any sign of outright rejection of the truth that everyone, and in every sphere of life, was capable of successful accomplishment of this arduous climb up Mount Tabor to ensure his transformation in Christ. Such rejection was an insult to the unlimited consequences of the marriage of the Logos with human nature in a world that was meant to serve as our pilgrim route to eternal life with the Trinity.

Two particular practical influences on Innocent's firm commitment to stimulate the multiplication of marriage and its fruitfulness in all its forms must especially to be addressed.

One of these came from Peter Cantor (d. 1197), one of his teachers in Paris. Cantor underscored the importance of developing pastoral strategies appropriately proportioned to the different character of each specific human activity. He recognized the need to expand upon the approach taken by the tenth and eleventh century monks of Cluny—in many respects, the "founders" of the medieval reform movement. Just as the Cluniacs aimed to tame the lawless soldiers of the age (whom they referred to as the *malitia* rather than the *militia*) by showing what the "marriage" of their specific military activity to Christ should really mean, good shepherds must learn how to "marry" every other human activity shaping the daily lives of men and women in their own unique ways to the Incarnate Word and make them spiritually fruitful.

It was the second influence on Innocent that confirmed his conviction that the task of making the manifold consequences of such variegated types of marriage fruitful had to be an intensely militant one; that which came from the Crusading Movement. Medieval Christian culture might have taken on a different flavor if bakers had been the initial problem for Cluniac monks rather than the *malitia*. As it was, however, once the redirection of the soldier's marital vocation to proper Christian goals became the first object of the reformers' attention, it was inevitable that a certain military "feel" would serve as a model for similar endeavors in other spheres of life, working smoothly together with the basic human sense of being engaged in a battle for daily survival.

Now the Crusading Movement was in a bad state when Innocent took over as Supreme Pontiff. Despite the labors of the Holy Roman Emperor and the Kings of France and England in the Third Crusade, Jerusalem was still in infidel hands. Worse still, the Fourth Crusade had led to a downright criminal assault on fellow believers in Zara and Constantinople. If external Crusading against the infidel was not succeeding, Innocent thought that it must be because Christians were not correcting those sins in their daily lives that prevented fruitful marriage of their souls with God; a correction that the marriage of the Word and nature made efficacious through that of Christ with His Church. This left them spiritually "asleep," in a wretched, uncorrected natural condition rendering them unworthy of success in any of their endeavors. Victory in the external crusade for the defense of the Holy Land was therefore intimately connected with victory in an internal European crusade against the individual sins preventing the transforming marriage from becoming fruitful. If sham Christians—both among the fighting men abroad and that vast majority of believers who remained at home—could honestly be turned into true Catholics, then the success of the external Crusade would perhaps be guaranteed. Victory in such an internal conflict could only be achieved by intensifying an awareness of the primacy of the spirit in every vocation in life, not just that of soldiering. Peter Cantor's variegated pastoral approach had to have a sword in its hand.

Innocent's entire pontificate must be seen from the perspective of a militant, disciplined, and highly nuanced pastoral effort to ensure the fruitful marriage of souls with God, a project always intimately connected with the other three forms of marital union. It was this that dictated his exalted sense of the role of the pope, as a figure peculiarly "married" to the Incarnate Word. It was this that stimulated his paternal concern for the rest of the Catholic clergy, "married" to their dioceses and their parishes. It was this that caused him to call the Fourth Lateran Council in 1215, the most important of the medieval councils, for the *practical* work of "marrying" individuals and societies in which they lived to God.

It was also this that opened Innocent's mind to every innovative pastoral endeavor that proved itself to be effective in ensuring an increase in the number of marriages of souls with God—with the intellectual work of the Universities of Paris and Bologna marrying men's minds with heaven, and the hands-on "marital guidance" of the mendicant Franciscans and Dominicans on every level of human endeavor at the top of the list. And given his crusading mentality, it was hardly a wonder that scholarly battles inside the university got so intense; or that St. Francis of Assisi (1181–1226) could adopt the language of a crusading knight committed to deeds of derring-do on behalf of his Lady, Apostolic Poverty, or that of a chivalric soldier on mission to Egypt to convert the Sultan; or that St. Dominic (1170–1221) and his followers would go on militant attack against Catharist Albigensians who denied that transformation in Christ was possible at all.

Despite what his detractors say, our so-called "Lord of the World" was never interested in political sovereignty over any place other than the Papal States. The "sovereignty" he sought was as Vicar of Christ standing guard against anything blocking marriage of the soul with God. Once again, his work in this regard was what our hopelessly parochial contemporaries would probably call "modern" because of its tenderness and nuance—hence, his concern for the poor, tormented more and more by usury in an ever more complex medieval economic society.

Sometimes dedication to an exalted theme—such as the marriage of souls with God—can cause a person to be rather casual with respect to its literal meaning. This was not true for Innocent. Concerned with marriage in three other senses though he was, his serious treatment of the ordinary marriage of a man with a woman was always just as vigorous. As one might expect, such concerns could take Innocent down highly nuanced pastoral pathways, as this bull of April 29, 1198 indicating his dedication, as "marital matchmaker," to the plight of ladies of ill repute well illustrates:

> Among the works of charity that the authority of Holy Scripture proposes to us, there is one of real importance, which consists in correcting him who wanders on the road of error. Thus it is necessary to ask women who live voluptuously and permit anyone indifferently and without concern to have relations with them to contract a legitimate marriage in order to live chastely. With this

thought, we decide by the authority of these presents that all who will rescue public women from brothels and marry them will be doing an act which will be useful for the remission of their sins.[2]

Let us end by noting that Innocent III's deep regard for marriage on its most literal level extended to the rich and powerful as much as to the poor and emarginated. And therefore, as Augustin Fliche notes in his entry in Powell's book, even "at the risk of wounding a prince whose friend he was and who was liable to render still greater services to the church," he considered himself a "prisoner of doctrine before whose demands the temporal interests of the church ought to bend, so imperious were they."[3] Hence, his letter to Queen Marie, the wife of King Peter of Aragon on January 19, 1213, denying an annulment because of the terrible assault this would make on the sacred marriage bond:

> He who is our faithful witness in heaven, to whom every heart is open and no secret remains hidden, that in the marriage undertaken a long time since between you and our very dear son in Christ, Peter, king of Aragon, your husband, we have never departed from the right path and we have not deviated either to the right or to the left. We have acted, as our conscience is a witness, as in all the cases brought for our examination, for, by His will, we take the place on earth of Him who, just and loving justice, judges without taking account of persons. Thus, although among other princes of this world we feel for this king, by reason of his deeds, a particular affection and we desire honors and personal advantages for him; nevertheless, from the fact that it is a question of justice, as we are not allowed to protect the poor and honor the visage of the powerful, we cannot and we ought not, neither to him nor to any other, grant the lesser favor since it pertains to the sacrament of marriage, which, instituted by the Lord in Paradise before sin, looks not only to the perpetuation of the human race but represents the union of Christ with the holy church, that of God with the faithful soul, that of the Word with human nature, according to the testimony of the apostle, who in treating of marriage expresses himself in these terms: I say that it is a great Sacrament in Christ and in the Church. (Eph. 5:32).[4]

2 Cited in Powell, *Innocent III*, 70.
3 Cited in Powell, 69–70.
4 Cited in Powell, 69–70.

Hence, a pope caricatured as being obsessed with political issues would not curry the favor of the *true* sovereign powers of the world if such fawning threatened the sacrament of marriage, even in its most obvious form. He duty to protect marriage weighed heavily upon him, because he, as pope, was married with the Incarnate Word in a special way, and responsible for multiplying the number of souls married to God more than anyone else on earth. Nothing would cause him to mar his militant commitment to his own special marital vows. Let us pray that the example of Innocent will influence his contemporary successor to defend all four forms of marriage with equal crusading zeal. The task of dealing with the powers of this world in a way that avoids currying their favor and protecting the marriage of the Papacy with the Incarnate Word is never an easy one—but *Deus lo vult!*

15

Charlemagne and the Long Frankish Pilgrimage to the Just War[†]

I F ROME WAS NOT BUILT IN A DAY, NEITHER were the Christian Middle Ages. One prime example of this truth is the time that was required for the Eldest Daughter of the Church—the Franks—to produce one of medieval man's major achievements: the concept of the just war and warrior. The fact that the path from the original Germanic glorification of pure butchery to a sense of noble Christian military mission was both purposeful as well as immensely problematic can be seen through the background history and actual career of the "second founder" of the Roman Empire—that Frankish King from the Carolingian Family that we know as Charlemagne (742–814).

"Charles" had a head start towards becoming "the Great" in matters combining Christianity with military action due to a number of already well-rooted stimuli directing the Franks towards using their massive physical power in a focused and proper manner. The primal stimulus in this regard was the tribe's passionate, open commitment to the True Faith, along with the realization that that commitment had manifold practical consequences. This was stated clearly in the Prologue to the revised version of the "Salic Law" (763)—the basic "constitution" of the so-called "Salty" Franks—prepared by Charlemagne's father, Pippin.

> The illustrious people of the Franks was established by God himself; courageous in war, steadfast in peace, serious of intention, noble of stature, brilliant white of complexion and of exceptional beauty; daring, swift, and brash. It was converted to the catholic Faith; while it was still barbarian, it was free of all heresy. It sought the key of knowledge under divine guidance, desiring justice in its behavior and cultivating piety.

---

† First published in *The Angelus*, October 2014.

It was then that those who were the chiefs of this people long ago dictated the Salic law.[1]

Thankfully, public Frankish dedication of both law and sword to Christianity benefited from a second stimulus of equal importance: the assistance of courageous teachers possessing a sound understanding of all that was needed for the education of their pupils, and no illusions regarding their ignorance and recalcitrance. St. Boniface's (c. 672/680–754) extensive correspondence—all of it available online—gives us a clear guide to the tack such teachers felt they had to take. This "Apostle to the Germans" was absolutely certain that the Christian missions established by him required Frankish military protection for survival. Further still, he saw that the ability to mobilize such help in and of itself made an immense impression upon the power-worshipping barbarians, highly useful to their evangelization.[2] I would venture to add that Boniface recognized that the teachings of the intellect and the spirit are *always* "weak" in this, our valley of tears, and will, therefore, *always* need to demonstrate that they can call upon the aid of physical strength to give them practical backbone.

Nevertheless, Boniface was simultaneously aware that he was summoning up the physical strength of a warrior tribe that was to a large degree only nominally—though enthusiastically—Christian. The Franks were tempted to make an exact equation between the message and victory of the Gospel with the extension of Frankish borders and the consequent satisfaction of the political and financial needs of their ruling elite. Hence the willingness of the latter to combine physical support for the Church with the confiscation or misdirection of ecclesiastical property for military purposes and the appointment of unworthy but influential men to key bishoprics. The exaggerated physicality of the Franks made campaigns of forced baptism seem logical to them, along with the imposition of tithes upon those forcibly converted before such new "believers" were even taught what their new "faith" was. The Apostle to the Germans was disgusted by the inversion of the hierarchy of values that his dependence upon military clout might seem to

1 Cited in Pierre Riché, *The Carolingians: A Family Who Forged Europe*, trans. Michael Idomir Allen (Philadelphia: University of Pennsylvania Press, 1993), 83.
2 Richard A. Fletcher, *The Barbarian Conversions: From Paganism to Christianity* (Berkeley: University of California Press, 1999), 236, 242–243

condone. As a sound Christian teacher, he therefore exploited every opportunity he could find to change the "structures of sin" of the Frankish Kingdom and the still-pagan mentality of his frightening and often perverse guardians. He had to show "might" that it only had meaning in the service of "right." And, once again, precisely because the intellect and the spirit are *always* weak in this, our valley of tears, this meant that evangelists must unceasingly teach, chastise, and correct, in season and out of season, whatever the recalcitrance of their pupils.

A third and crucially important stimulus to purposeful direction of military action, long at work among the Franks before the accession of Charlemagne, was a commitment to the concept of life as a pilgrimage. The tribe inherited this vision from Christian Roman Gaul, which had produced some of the earliest pilgrims to the Holy Land to write extensively about their experiences. This Gallic "pilgrim spirit" taught the Franks that they were indeed on a journey through life, that that journey was by no means easy, that it had to be organized properly, that they had their own special role to play in its organization, and that their own salvation as a people hinged upon whether they fulfilled this role properly. All these themes were spelled out for them by members of the Christian teaching "college," with reference to a body of works with enormous influence throughout the Middle Ages ascribed to the man we call Pseudo Dionysius the Areopagite.

Charles the Great *inherited* such stimuli. He lived and breathed them from birth. Still, he impressed them upon the new alliance of Christian, Roman, and Germanic elements forged in the lands of the old Empire with a particular intensity and strength of will that—as the great Carolingian scholar Pierre Riché insists—identify him as the true father of that socio-political entity we call Western Christendom. It was he who confirmed the goal of reunification of the whole of the old imperial *ecumene* through purposeful use of the power of the Frankish Army; an army referred to by the tribe with the biblical name of "the Host." It was he whose regal and imperial legislation showed that the power of the Host must be placed at the service of a comprehensive extension of Christian principles into every sphere of life—economic life included. It was he who most effectively made an attempt to provide serious education for the clergy, and to raise the moral and cultural level of the active population in its entirety, encouraging the merging of a *mélange* of superior intellectual influences from Byzantium, Egypt, Lombard Italy, Visigothic Spain, Ireland, and Britain into a new Christian whole while doing so. It was he who invited teachers like Alcuin (735–804), the great English Benedictine, to head his so-called Palace School at Aix-la-Chapelle, and give new and eloquent expression to the pilgrim spirit so important to understanding the Frankish sense of mission:

> If your intentions are carried out, it may be that a new Athens will arise in France, and an Athens fairer than of old, for our Athens, ennobled by the teaching of Christ, will surpass the wisdom of the Academy. The old Athens had only the teachings of Plato to instruct it, yet even so it flourished by the seven liberal arts. But our Athens will be enriched by the sevenfold gift of the Holy Spirit and will, therefore, surpass all the dignity of earthly wisdom.[3]

Yes, Charlemagne put all of the essential elements of international medieval Christendom firmly in place—and he did so, first and foremost, as a military man; as commander of the Frankish Host. "Might" was publicly identified as being at the service of Christian "Right." Still, it was "might" that nevertheless continued to pronounce the final word in determining what "right" actually meant in practice. The Frankish "old Adam" was, to a large degree, the same recalcitrant student that St. Boniface had had to confront. Hence, Charlemagne, as bitterly lamented by Alcuin himself, continued to pursue policies of forcible baptism and imposition of tithes, fostering the impression that submission to Christianity and the payment of taxes redirected to the military goals of the conqueror were one and the same thing. Alcuin, like Boniface, knew that "might" was there to be instructed, not to instruct. But Charlemagne, good-willed Christian though he was, could never quite seem to grasp that fact. After all, how could someone publicly recognized as a Christian Emperor violate his charge?

Such a mentality showed that the task of putting "might" at the service of "right" was not complete, and, quite frankly, given fallen human nature, can never be "completed." Our pilgrimage

---

3   Alcuin of York, "Epistle 170," cited in Dawson, *Religion and the Rise of Western Culture*, 65.

never ends, even when we call ourselves Christians. Not surprisingly, the failures of the Carolingian system and the first Father of Christendom would become all too clear as the chaos of the ninth and tenth centuries progressed.

Nevertheless, the Eldest Daughter of Christendom survived the age of iron that followed this first attempt to build a Catholic society. It was to be in the Second Age of Christendom, the High Middle Ages, that the heirs of Charlemagne—saints like the Emperor Henry II and King Louis IX, along with the monks and popes who served as the Bonifaces and Alcuins of the new era—were to build a more solid concept of the just war and the just warrior. This concept, constructed around the idea of the Crusade and the crusader, was destined to become so Christian in character that a St. Francis of Assisi could happily adopt its themes and its literary expression, mobilizing them for his own spiritual combat.

Such a purified vision of the just war and warrior was obliged to temper the spirit of "exceptionalism" that Pippin's Prologue to the revision of the Salic Law and Charlemagne's carrier reflect; a spirit that claims that once a people like the Franks proclaims itself to be Christian, it has by that fact alone escaped all need for further correction and transformation in Christ; an erroneous spirit that is, unfortunately, a temptation to *all* Christian men and women in *every* age, American Catholics today included.

But our *purified* vision was also obliged to recognize that it was cleansing a spirit that was *in and of itself* a pearl of great price. That "pearl" emerged due to the incredibly courageous first step of Carolingian men of might and right to abandon their fallen human tendency to reject one another and admit their necessary interdependence. Interdependence alone gave raw power a lasting strength. It alone saved the intellect and the spirit from impotent paralysis. That interdependence, to quote Rick in *Casablanca*, "was the beginning of a beautiful friendship" that can only continue so long as the soldierly spirit thrives, Catholic teachers openly form it in obedience to the Truth, and the two work together: and this modernity abhors.

16

Is the Papacy in Turmoil?
Call in the "Outsiders"†

IN 1980, I GAVE A LECTURE ENTITLED "THE
Papacy: Beyond Weakness and Willfulness." Its aim was two-
fold, and its conclusions perhaps even more of use under current
conditions today than then.

My talk was first of all designed to demonstrate just how very
many times in history precisely those Catholics who were the most
fervent supporters of the mission and authority of the Holy See
found themselves openly critical of the statements and behavior of
reigning pontiffs. Such firm adherents of the Papacy deemed the
specific popes they were confronting guilty either of a subservience
to powerful factions, rendering illusory their role as legitimate
rulers of the Church, or of a pursuit of terribly short-sighted and
arbitrary policies destructive to the Vicar of Christ's true responsibilities, dignity, and strength.

Secondly, this lecture underlined the fact that the real friends
of a Papacy that was in self-destructive turmoil and required
serious help in bringing it back to its apostolic senses were almost
never to be found initially among "insiders" close to the throne.
Rather, they tended to come primarily from "outsiders," many of
whom learned to their dismay that their passionate love for Peter
remained unrequited all too long. The good news is that such
outsiders repeatedly emerged victorious. The bad news is that
they did so only after painfully lengthy struggles that frequently
involved desperate setbacks throwing into serious doubt the success
of their whole rescue mission. And, sad to say, their final victory
at one moment in Church History obviously did not ensure that
the problem they had seemingly solved would not arise again in
another form sometime later.

Allow me to plunder this old lecture in order briefly to outline
four examples of papal eras of weakness or willfulness and the

---

† First published in *Rorate Caeli*, February 16, 2015.

central role of "outsiders" in putting St. Peter back on his feet in each of them. Those wishing to flesh out their knowledge of the periods in question can consult my *Black Legends* book.[1] It is worth taking the time to do so when spirits sag in this current winter of our own "outsider" discontent.

I

The early seventh century Papacy was committed to a pastoral program that the eighteenth century would label as one of "noble simplicity." An important feature of this approach was a disparagement of theological disputes as nothing other than what Pope Honorius (625–638) called the exaggerated "croaking of frogs." Since such battles were precisely much more than useless babbling, Rome paid a price for her flippant negligence of doctrinal purity. She found herself a helpless puppet; the plaything of emperors who were aware of the importance of theology and sought to manipulate it for the purpose of obtaining a political solution to the highly explosive Monophysite Controversy long ravaging Eastern Christendom.

It was "outside," eastern, Greek-speaking migrants—monks and thinkers fleeing from Caesaro-Papist "croaking frogs" with swords in their hands, the most famous of whom was St. Maximus the Confessor (c. 580–662)—who saved the day. Their direct influence in Rome stretched into the middle of the eighth century. These Greeks stimulated crucial but moribund theological studies, led the fight against heresy, and enriched the Roman liturgy. A good number of them becoming popes themselves and—ironically, given the attitude of future Orthodox prelates and intellectuals—defended the Papal Supremacy and the validity of Latin traditions more effectively than many of their torpid predecessors of local origin. It was the Greek-speaking Pope Sergius I (687–701) who fought against that outrageous condemnation of western practices by an arrogant East eager to foist its peculiar traditions (including its relaxed position on clerical celibacy) on the Universal Church in the so-called Council in Trullo of 692.[2]

---

1 John C. Rao, *Black Legends and the Light of the World: The War of Words with the Incarnate Word* (Forest Lake, MN: The Remnant Press, 2011).
2 See chapter 11.

2

It is perhaps logical that a Greek "outsider," Pope Zachary (741–752), presided over the first steps towards seeking military assistance in defense of a weak Papacy against heretical emperors and hostile Lombards by means of an appeal to a second foreign source: the non-Roman, "barbarian" Franks. These Franks were themselves first converted by "outsiders"—non-Germanic bishops from Gallo-Roman cities—and then much more efficiently catechized by still other strangers—Anglo-Saxon and Irish monks. The Catholic Faith is not a xenophobic one. Strangers are always welcome.

Fervent Frankish militants of the eighth century wanted nothing better than a closer tie with the Papacy, from which they expected liturgical and canonical aid in shaping and governing their nascent Church. The military assistance provided Rome by the Carolingian Family did indeed strengthen the desired connection, although the enrichment that actually emerged from it often worked more from the outside inwards—with the Frankish Church joining the Greeks in adding her own embellishments to the still rather spare Roman liturgy. But the labors of Pepin and Charlemagne were problematic ones. Their revived Western Roman Empire was swiftly in free fall. By the end of the ninth century, the Papacy had become the puppet of feuding local political families obsessed with petty secular concerns, its universal mission reduced to practical meaninglessness. With a few exceptions—due to the temporary involvement of the forces that would ultimately turn the tide—the situation remained dire into the mid-1000s.

Once again, it was "outsiders" who came to the rescue: monks from reformed Benedictine houses in the Frankish world devoted to a role for St. Peter that went beyond catering to wretched familial material needs; Norman converts filled with love for a Papacy that they did not know had become a mere cipher; and, above all, the hands-on political interference of German King-Emperors who swooped naughtily down into the Italian peninsula, ruthlessly tossed out reigning simoniac pontiff-puppets and their "insider" advisors, and replaced them with respectable Catholics on their own authority alone. It was the most important of these reputable strangers, Pope St. Leo IX (1049–1054), who created that international curia of outsiders that developed into the College of Cardinals and demanded for what was still only a partially liberated Papacy its full independence; the independence that then placed it at the head of that glorious effort to transform all things in Christ that characterized the civilization of the High Middle Ages.[3]

3

Even the magnificent Papacy of the High Middle Ages, exercising its authority with a full consciousness of its role as guide of the Universal Church, manifested terrible practical flaws, bringing disastrous consequences in their train. St. Bernard of Clairvaux (1090–1153) already indicated his fears regarding the central cause of woe in the *de Consideratione* that he addressed to a former pupil upon his becoming Pope Eugenius III (1145–1153). Bernard saw that the danger lay in what might be labeled a kind of "practical secularization": namely, the day-to-day presumption that papal judgments, backed by canon law, a well-oiled administrative machine, and an appeal to political and military clout could be counted upon to make a neat and rather earthly-focused package of the complex work of transformation of all things in Christ. For a Papacy with its energies directed to such a mundane approach would not be looking for its chief support from whence it truly must come: Faith and Grace. It would lack the proper hierarchy of values in its activities, and in consequence, inevitably become the puppet of the legal, administrative, and political forces that it falsely thought it was merely using.

It was this confused exaggeration of the role of the Holy See and its "insider" legal and bureaucratic machine that the Consilium de Emendanda Ecclesia, produced in 1536 by the commission appointed by Pope Paul III (1534–1549) to study the causes of the Protestant Reformation, identified as the Achilles Heel of the Medieval Papacy. The disastrous funding of a hyperactive Roman Curia through appointment of its members as Ordinaries of dioceses that they robbed of their endowments and never visited or effectively governed flowed from its central axioms. So did the attempt to obtain a "perfect" political configuration in Italy, with the calling of dubious crusades in Sicily and the concocting of Renaissance conspiracies productive of nothing more than nepotism, new military dilemmas, criminal neglect of crucial spiritual responsibilities, and growing hatred for the Holy See as such.

---

3   See chapters 1, 3, and 4.

Once again, it was the work of "outsiders"—reformers of all countries with little or no initial "insider" influence—who saved the day. In this case, a tremendous amount of suffering preceded a serious attempt to drive the moneychangers from the temple. It took reformers literally centuries, during which many felt increasing helplessness and even filled with despair, before a pontiff like Paul III began to treat them seriously, allowing them to "come in from out of the cold" to make a start at showing the Papacy how to focus its attention on its primary apostolic role. For the vast bulk of the fourteenth, fifteenth, and early sixteenth centuries, these "outsiders" were treated by the "loyal" legalists and bureaucrats as naïve fools at best and traitors to the Holy See at worst. Such false friends on the inside displayed the character of their own reliability as Defenders of the Faith by so twisting papal authority out of its proper context as to award popes the right to abolish Scripture if they deemed it necessary to do so.[4]

4

Even the Catholic Reformation, guided though it ultimately was by a strengthened Papacy backed by innumerable saintly and intelligent men and women, was not without its many insufficiencies and flaws. Trent in no way resolved all the doctrinal issues that the late medieval world had engendered, the ecclesiological question of the exact authority of the Holy See prominent among them. Local political considerations and petty family concerns were never erased entirely from papal minds. Much too dependent upon the power of seemingly friendly "Catholic" States that proved to be willing to do whatever "worked" to survive, the Holy See step-by-step succumbed to monarchs' temptations to heed the teachings of naturalist Enlightenment thinkers, particularly those of the supposedly "moderate" Newton-John Locke-Glorious Revolution variety.

Very few contemporary Catholics realize that the half-century before the outbreak of the French Revolution saw popes as well as literally armies of bishops weakly and willfully backing away from support for everything that hinted of reliance on "supernatural" learning and guidance, allowing for the dominance of a Poor

---

4   See chapter 2.

Richard's Almanac, "cleanliness is next to godliness" version of "natural Christianity" to take their place. St. Thomas Aquinas was exiled from seminaries, processions and devotions that we take for granted prohibited, liturgical splendor ridiculed in the name of "noble simplicity," and effective religious orders suppressed or reduced to purely utilitarian tasks. Quite frankly, all that the French Revolution did was more violently to pursue what was already being done as an "insider job." Rome herself teemed with Jansenists and naturalists busily at work pulling the supernatural rug out from underneath seemingly hapless, supine popes behaving themselves by listening to their masters from the world outside.

Should we in any way be surprised by now that the cavalry that came charging to the rescue entered Rome from outside the Flaminian Gate? This time round, it was a team of German, French, Spanish, Savoyard, Piedmontese, and Neapolitan thinkers and activists, clerical and lay, who rediscovered the obvious: the need for the Church to root all of her activities not in the messages she receives from the naturalist powers-that-be regarding what they think "works" to gain material advantages, but in her supernatural mission to transform all things in Christ; the need for the Papacy to rise from its current dogmatic slumber to play its proper role leading the Catholic troops into battle rather than commanding them to lay down their only effective arms and embrace the enemy. It was these outsiders who created that movement of spiritual renewal leading to proper Catholic political, social, economic action, heedless of the hostility this might engender from those long habituated to keeping the supernatural monster at bay. It was they who finally came from the outside to the inside—slowly in the reign of Gregory XVI (1831–1846), and in a tidal wave during that of Blessed Pius IX (1846–1878)—thereby winning the Holy See to the job of guidance of the reestablishment of the proper hierarchy of values through such teachings as those found in the Syllabus of Errors and subsequent Social Encyclicals.[5]

---

5   See chapters 5, 7; John C. Rao, "Half the Business of Destruction Done" and "School Days," in *For the Whole Christ: Catholic Christendom versus Revolutionary Disorder* (Waterloo: Arouca Press, 2023), 179–198, 214–234; and John C. Rao, "All Borrowed Armor Chokes Us? Americanism and Christian Democracy," *For the Whole Christ* (website), April, 2015, http://jcrao.freeshell.org/AmericanismChristianDemocracy.html.

Allow me to end this brief essay by stressing two points of special relevance today.

First of all, it is not always just one specific action of a given pope at a limited moment in time that has proven to be damaging to the life of the Church in the past. It has occasionally been the whole spirit created during the course of a number of pontificates lasting decades and even centuries that has had a deadly impact—and this even without their uttering a single official statement that might be criticized as doctrinally dubious and thereby threatening to the dogma of Papal Infallibility. In other words, you cannot judge a book by its cover—even one that might be called "The Pope Speaks." What you see is what you get and have to confront.

Secondly, the "insiders" are often not to be trusted. Rather than being the loyal shields of the Holy See due to their vocal and uncritical defense of each and every one of its statements and actions they are either conscious or unconscious annihilators of papal authority. In mindlessly repeating their mantra "obedience," what they actually are calling for is a surrender to a puppet and his puppet masters.

For papal statements and actions that are weak or willful are not expressions of Christ's command to feed His sheep, and they are not infallible. In fact, they are ultimately the work of "strong man" ventriloquists holding papal marionettes in their hands. This is more clearly obvious when dealing with weak pontiffs, but it is more painfully pathetic when dealing with the willful. The weak pope may at least know that he is a coward and be ashamed by his cringing before tyrants; the willful one really thinks he is in charge, while he is merely one of Plato's classic examples of a tyrant-slave; a "tough guy" doing what the power-mad outside world tells such a figure that he must do in under to be successful. The puppet pope may be a servant of an emperor, a local Roman potentate, legalist and administrative madmen, enlightened monarchs, or a "modern spirit that has does not judge." But whoever pulls the strings, he is a puppet nonetheless, and no believing Catholic owes his puppet commands a Catholic obedience.

Traditionalist "outsiders," let us indeed recognize the gravity of the situation that we are in, while not turning ourselves into something unique in responding to it. After all, we are in one sense nothing more than the latest in a long string of outsiders that have had to deal with turmoil in the Papacy. We are in a noble company that includes Greek migrants, the conglomerate of forces behind the Frankish and Germanic renewal of Medieval Christendom, the monks of Cluny and Viking converts, the long-suffering precursors of the Catholic Reformation, and the counterrevolutionaries of the nineteenth century. Looking back to their experience, we should not be surprised that we are rejected by "insider" time servers as enemies of "traditions" of the Roman Church and a "papal authority" that are merely false and corrupt customs accepted as being baptized due to nothing other than the length of their reign of terror.

Our "outsider" battle had to come. Magnificent as the nineteenth century renewal was, it, too, did not resolve all of the doctrinal problems troubling the Church, with the ecclesiological issue, once again, being chief among them. What seemed to be a sufficient definition of Papal Infallibility—and indeed in an extremely limited fashion—did not prevent many people from exaggerating papal prerogatives into stratospheric late medieval levels anew. Hence the aid given to present-day promoters of what amounts to a Papal Stalinism in place of the actual dogmatic teaching of the Roman Church.

We will inevitably win, because we are fighting for the substance and not the mere word "Papacy" and "Papal Authority"; the Papacy and Papal Authority that stand beyond weakness and willfulness, backed by the promise and the strength that comes from Our Savior and not from Our Zeitgeist and its conscious and unconscious time servers. We will win that battle by keeping before our eyes a goal that can never change: the need to become "insiders" ourselves in order to awaken the Papacy from its current weakness and willfulness; "insiders" who, hopefully, will stand on guard against becoming the cause of future problems for our heirs in the Faith.

But the battlefield before us promises still to be a treacherous and very broad one, studded with innumerable land mines. How could it be otherwise? After all, we, like many of our ancestors, are not fighting just one statement or a given action of a single pope but an erroneous spirit and program that have all but taken Peter and most of the rest of the Church captive for over half a century.

Our task as "outsiders" is one of a painstaking reopening of the eyes of "insiders" that have been glued shut to the teaching of what St. Augustine called "the Whole Christ": the teaching of Christ in His physical body on earth and in His Mystical Body through the ages, including those rather neglected years before 1962.

Eyes that can be focused on "the Whole Christ" will readily see what the Papacy's authority and mission truly are and are not. They will readily come to recognize the protestations of loyalty to each and every contradictory word and deed of a reigning pontiff for what they really are: mindlessly recited slogans justifying weakness after weakness and willful act after willful act. Opening those eyes will not be a task for sissies. It will take a manful Catholic Faith and Reason with a proper sense of the true hierarchy of values. And it is by no means out of place in these days just before Lent to note that such a proper sense of the hierarchy of the supernatural over the natural in the final analysis means recognizing that the grave situation we are now confronting is more than human; and that "this kind can only be cast out by fasting and prayer."

17

A Very Different Francis
on a Christmas Long Ago

A BRIEF MEDITATION ON THE MESSAGES
OF THE CRECHE AND MODERNITY†

CATHARISTS WERE ONE IMPORTANT
branch of the rather large philosophical and theological "family" known as Gnostics. Their most famous twelfth and thirteenth century representatives were the people from southern France whom we call Albigensians, a name taken from the city of Albi, northeast of Toulouse. But Catharists of the High Middle Ages were very, very powerful in Italy as well, including the northern reaches of the provinces of Lazio and Umbria, lands central to the life and labors of the namesake of the current pontiff: St. Francis of Assisi (c.1182–1226).

Like Gnostics of all varieties, the Catharists loathed physical Creation, which they considered to be intrinsically evil. They considered human bodies to be the most disgusting of nature's many reprehensible elements, reviling and spitting at the pregnant women that they passed on the street for serving as the vile conduits of such corruption. No wonder, then, that the Catharists figure prominently in the history of the development of birth control methods. And it is even less of a surprise that they could not stomach Christmas.

Still, Catharists were heirs to a long Gnostic tradition of slithering slowly into their victims' psyche. This meant that they did not like to attack the writings and beliefs of a target people directly, preferring to "deconstruct" the existing order of things and gradually seduce men and women into their detestation of nature. Hence, Catharists tried to promote an understanding of Jesus Christ that encouraged thinking of His body as something that was somehow more apparent then real; something intangibly "spiritual," "mystical," and distinctly non-physical. His real birth

† First published in *The Remnant*, December 15, 2015.

as a real child with a totally real body would validate not just human flesh but the material Creation that He needed to use in order to live in general.

St. Francis of Assisi knew what they were up to. We possess a number of accounts of his sallies against these heretical haters of mankind, who realized all too well that the *Poverello* was their mortal and all too effective enemy.[1] One of Francis' initiatives, so successful that I do not know of any open attempt of the Catharists to respond to it, was the restoration in 1223 at Greccio, in northern Lazio, of a long forgotten Christmas symbol: the crèche. The following description of the event, excerpted from chapter fifteen of Frank M. Rega's *St. Francis and the Conversion of the Muslims* (Charlotte: TAN Books, 2008), and relying heavily on contemporary sources, is highly useful to the unfortunate comparison that I will then have to make with the present:

> Less than a month after the papal approval of the *Regula Bullata* [the *Rule* for the Order of Friars Minor], Francis arrived at the brothers' hermitage in the little town of Greccio—a community in the vicinity of Rieti, located about halfway between Assisi and Rome. It was now December, and Francis had long been nurturing a heartfelt desire to celebrate Christmas in a wonderful new manner. He wanted others to share his own inner joy and exaltation at what for him was the most important feast of the year, since our salvation was heralded by the birth of Christ. He conceived of a simple way to awaken everyone's love and admiration of the Christ Child, especially those who were weak in the Faith.
>
> His plan was to have Christmas Midnight Mass celebrated in the presence of a realistic representation of the humble grotto of Bethlehem, complete with live animals. "For I wish to do something that will recall to memory the little Child who was born in Bethlehem and set before our bodily eyes in some way the inconveniences of his infant needs." According to St. Bonaventure, he even obtained the approval of Pope Honorius, so that he would not be accused of willfully introducing novelty into the sacred ceremonies.
>
> Francis had arranged beforehand to have his friend, the nobleman Giovanni Velita, make the necessary preparations

---

1 See Malcolm D. Lambert, *The Cathars* (Malden: Blackwell Publishing, 1998), 171–174.

and help spread word of the event. A little manger or crib was set up in the woods near the hermitage, filled with the common, coarse hay that beasts of burden feed upon. An ox and an ass were then led to the place. Some later embellishments of the story maintain that figures of Mary and Joseph were also positioned about the manger. Francis was delighted to see everything ordered as he had wished. To the *Poverello*, "The sight of the crèche [manger scene] in its glorious simplicity was a symbol of the advent of lowliness, the exaltation of poverty, the praise of humility."

A host of brothers from near and afar descended upon Greccio, arriving from numerous friaries and villages. They joined with the crowds of local residents, field workers, and shepherds; all were drawn toward the manger where Francis knelt. The candles and torches of the onlookers brightened up the crisp night, reflecting their glow upon a light snow that had begun to fall. The sound of hymns echoed in the hollows and woodlands. Men and beasts and even nature itself radiated great joy on that special Christmas Eve—it was truly the feast of hearts. "The woods rang with the voices of the crowd and the rocks made answer to their jubilation."

The Holy Sacrifice of the Mass was celebrated at midnight with great solemnity, using an altar that had been erected over the manger. Francis, vested in his Deacon's robes, sang the Gospel in a voice characterized by Celano as sweet, clear, strong and sonorous.

He preached a touching sermon, describing the first Christmas and the humble surroundings of Mary and Joseph at the nativity of the Son of God, whom he lovingly referred to as the Child of Bethlehem. During the ceremony, Giovanni Vileta experienced a vision in which he saw a babe lying in the crib, rapt in a slumber so deep that he appeared lifeless. Then he saw St. Francis approach and take the child in his arms, rousing him from his sleep. For his biographer Celano, this vision aptly symbolized the mission of the Saint: "for the Child Jesus had been forgotten in the hearts of many; but, by the working of His grace, He was brought to life again though His servant St. Francis and stamped upon their fervent memory."

The afterglow from that evening of devotion was manifested throughout the area in the days that followed. Many miraculous healings occurred among the sick, who were prayed over and touched with some of the hay that had lain in the sacred manger.

Even infirm animals that were given the stalks of that hallowed grass for their food were restored to health.[2]

All of this was effectively anti-Catharist because of its Christ-centered focus. Francis emphasized the reality not only of the Savior's body, but His body in its most helpless, childlike state. He called attention to the Nativity in conjunction with the Holy Sacrifice of the Mass, indicating priestly ability to transform bread and wine into the Body and Blood of Christ to provide the food that men and women need to gain eternal life with God, and in their own resurrected bodies. The *Poverello* presents this teaching in a natural setting so touched by God that the hay of the manger itself became a conduit for divine assistance, and "even infirm animals that were given the stalks of that hallowed grass for their food were restored to health." No self-respecting Catharist could have anything to do with this crèche and its consequences whatsoever. That was one of the major grounds—if not, perhaps, the chief ground, given the influence of the haters of mankind in the region—why St. Francis restored its use. The population got the message, and the Gnostic game was up—at least for the moment.

Let us remember that the chief *pastoral* reason why St. Francis was anti-Catharist was because their heretical insistence upon the *complete and intrinsic evil* of Creation diverted believers away from the help they desperately needed from the Incarnate Word and the sacraments that the entry of the supernatural into daily life provided. This help was required to deal with the *grave flaws and insufficiencies of a nature* fallen from its original state due to sin. Nature's glories had to be celebrated so as to enable men to become conscious both of nature's loss, as well as the unfathomable possibility, through resort to supernatural truths and grace presented with the aid of nature, to enter into union with the Eternal God. Behind all of Francis' work is the recognition that nature could only possess—and surpass—the glory the Creator had initially intended for it by submitting itself to an indispensable correction and transformation in a Christ *divine* as well as human. With the baby who is also the Word of God as his guide, St. Francis' pilgrimage to Eternity was one wherein

---

2 Frank M. Rega, *St. Francis and the Conversion of the Muslims* (Charlotte: TAN Books, 2008), 102–104.

nature as a whole accompanied him upwards with "the music of the spheres."

"Thud" is the only musical tone that accompanies the pastoral approach offered Catholics and the world at large in Christmastide, 2015 under the reign of a pope who took his name from Francis. That "thud" is the sound that emerges from men's minds and hearts plunging downwards from St. Francis's effort to understand and celebrate nature by looking at it through the *Word* made flesh. "Thud" is the sound of the slamming of our minds and hearts into the flesh of a Creation that wants to know nothing of its sinful rejection of God's original plan for it, or what it is that it can know and do to lift itself out of the pathetic, parochial, debasing, and blinding consequences of the Fall. "Thud, and again I say unto you, thud" is the ultimate pastoral message of a pontificate that wants to go with the flow of the *Zeitgeist* rather than stand above it. "Restore all things in fallen nature" could readily serve as the official motto of the Roman Catholic Church today. And the "mercy" offered by the ecclesiastical authorities under these circumstances comes at the expense of dumping a thick, wet blanket over all of nature's healthy characteristics and tendencies—whose cultivation is treated as though it were an arrogant reproach to the poor suffering vices they would uncharitably help to repress.

The consequences of Christmas, 2015's truly anti-*Poverello,* pastoral "thud" are legion, but there is only one umbrella-like result that I wish to underline in this brief meditation here and now: its encouragement of the entire mesh of seemingly contradictory—and stark raving mad—errors that have all been in bed with one another in their production of that caricature of a civilization that we call "modernity." For the earthwards fall of those seeking to "restore all things in fallen nature" has a centuries-long history whose fundamental theme has remained unchangeable under a variety of only superficially different stimuli.

Every one of the stimuli constituting modernity involves some form or another of rejection of nature's need to learn and work together with the Revelation and Grace brought to us by the baby in the crèche. Some of these stimuli built this rejection out of a tragic *overestimation* of nature's autonomous value that itself emerged from the Christian exaltation of the value of all of the "Seeds of the Logos" to be found throughout Creation. Some rejected it out of a tragic *underestimation* of nature's ability to bear any connection with things godly after the devastating effects of Original Sin; out of a kind of semi-Catharism. The first set of stimuli moved from the Renaissance through certain forms of the Enlightenment down to the present; the second, from medieval Nominalism through Protestantism and other forms of the Enlightenment into our own times. Both denied that mixing of things supernatural and natural that demands our paying homage to the Christ child and His Kingship over Seeds of the Logos that are as dependent upon His aid as they are intrinsically valuable. And both ultimately leave man with the same guide to daily practical action: his own unchained will and the manifold bizarre pathways down which this can direct him.

Modernity's Original Sin has been that of viewing man as an isolated individual "freed" from the spell of the crèche; "free" to use his will to obtain a power over the universe that is viewed either *positively*, as something that will enable him to achieve undreamed of heights, or *negatively*, as something necessary to cultivate to protect himself from the ravages of the other depraved and willful monsters that surround him. Some men have used this autonomous modern "freedom" ironically, to invent willful machine-like explanations of the universe that enslave him to impersonal forces, and even more inescapably than they ever were enslaved beforehand. Others have used it in more immediately obvious ways, to oppress the weak to the strong, and bind everyman to his most dominant personal material passion—whatever that might be. All, together, have ripped the order of nature to shreds in the name of their "freedom" to think insane thoughts and perform insane actions, indifferent to the dictates of universal laws of Faith and Reason. Everyone demanding "freedom" for his own pet passion has helped the cause of those insisting upon other, perhaps totally conflicting "liberties." But many who have the word "freedom" constantly on their lips have kept it there precisely because they know that they possess the will, the guile, and the power to manipulate whatever its use might be to their own personal advantage.

Pope Francis' pastoral concerns in this Christmas, 2015, as during his whole pontificate to date, have been centered on "mercy" for those campaigning for various marital and sexual "freedoms," on "freedom" for the environment from the ravages of the human hand, and for "freedom" of the poor from the exploitation of the rich. This latter concern has caused many people to label him a communist pure and simple, and for those obsessed with communism to associate his sexual and environmental activism with his general Marxist tendencies.

I categorically reject the idea that the pope is a communist. Moreover, his pastoral program is not flawed because of a concern for "mercy" as such. Quite frankly, I also believe that we *are* facing a great environmental crisis, and that this is connected with the naturalist Enlightenment and an Industrial Revolution whose wretched environmental consequences Catholics were among the first who were active in lamenting. Moreover, I also am convinced that we have a global, neo-liberal, unchained free market-inspired disaster on our hands that is ensuring a massive exploitation of the poor by the rich in the developed lands as well as in the Third World.

The problem with the pope's message in Christmastide, 2015 is that he is singing the modern song of "thud." He is calling, in practice, for the need for a "correction" and "transformation" of Catholic doctrine to aid in the "restoration of all things" not in Christ but "in fallen nature." He is not telling us to pay homage to the child in the crèche and accept His corrective and transforming Social Kingship. He is not speaking in a Christ-centered fashion.

Hence, his "mercy" will ensure *carte blanche* for marital and sexual chaos; his environmentalism not only favors pagan naturalism and the validation of spiritual, film, and think-tank gurus of a simultaneously most dangerous and painfully lame taste, but also institutions like the World Bank that manipulate it for the profit of the global elite; his "humble" concern for the "poor" ends in a series of pointless gestures that every bureaucratic and capitalist card shark can find a way to profit from in the future. Sad to say, the lack of the proper crèche-centered focus also simply permits every rabid nationalist, polluter of God's earth, and libertarian to make it seem that they form the army of St. Athanasius in our own time that Catholics must support or die.

Our crèche-less modern world's willful message of "don't tread on me and my uncorrected natural will"—whether it be expressed with reference to the supposedly "Marxist" issues seemingly dear to the heart of the pope, or to those other economic and nationalist idols of the naturalist Enlightenment dear to the hearts of some "conservatives," "libertarians," or "American exceptionalists"—is always sung to the same single boring tone of "thud": the tone produced by the human mind and heart that plunged from its medieval heights on a downward trajectory to a fallen—though not intrinsically evil—earth.

Our only means of fighting the Catharist despair that must come when men realize that the endless clash of free wills that will not accept correction in Christ reveals the universe to be a meaningless entity; our only chance of pointing things into a proper hierarchy of values and hearing the "music of the spheres" is to stand above our *Zeitgeist* and judge it. And the best first step to that goal comes from turning our eyes away from the lions and tigers and bears that our current Francis shined on St. Peter's façade and focusing them on the oxen and donkeys led onto the *crèche* by a very different Francis at Greccio on a Christmas long ago.

18

Catholic Reformation and the Never-Ending Battle Versus the "Customary"†

"Christ said, 'I am the Truth.' He did not say,
'I am custom.'" [1] —TERTULLIAN

MARTIN LUTHER (1483–1546) CLAIMED THAT the reforms made by the Roman Church in his day—all of them pathetic and doomed to failure as far as he was concerned— were due only to the storm that he personally had aroused. But as much as his appearance on the historical stage was undeniably crucial to the history of the Catholic Reformation, it was totally false for him to claim that this magnificent revival was nothing other than a response to his own revolutionary activity.

Everything that was truly substantive in what is popularly referred to as the "Tridentine Reform" had a pre-Lutheran ori- gin, from the neo-Thomism that would figure significantly in its intellectual development, through the Observant Movement in the traditional religious orders and the zeal for a purified clergy displayed by the disciples of St. Catherine of Genoa, and up to and including the practical example of how to get things done on a broad scale offered in Spain by Queen Isabella and her ecclesias- tical advisor, Cardinal Ximenez de Cisneros. All that was central to this pre-Lutheran movement of thought and action would have continued to exert its influence even if the founder of Protestantism had never opened his mouth.

One prime indication of this fact: the work of St. Ignatius of Loyola, at the start of his spiritual journey from hospital-to Paris-to Rome, was done in total ignorance of Luther's teachings and importance. Moreover, a Tridentine Reform that was truly triggered and obsessed by Luther alone would have tackled many

---

† First published in *The Angelus*, March 2017.

---

1 Tertullian, "De virginibus velandis," in *Corpus Christianorum Series Latina, vol.* 2, ed. Aloisius Gerlo et al. (Turnhout: Brepols, 1954), 1209.

challenges more fully than it actually did. Abandonment of some of these challenges entirely, and failure to follow up on others among them, was to a large degree due to long term problems regarding the role of pope, bishops, priests, religious, and laity both mighty and low, in the "constitution" of the Church, as well as complexities concerning the relationship of grace and free will; dilemmas with whose intricacies a number of Catholic activists of the pre-1517 era were familiar. Problems would also have continued to present difficulties for reformers even if Luther had never raised his sights outside of his Saxon classroom. Their stubborn nature is well indicated by the fact that the same problems continued troubling the life of the Church after Luther was supposedly "answered," right up until our own unhappy time.

"CATHOLIC REFORMATION"

What both of these truths point to is the fact that "Catholic Reformation" is a never-ending battle. Its perennial necessity gives the lie to any belief that the ecclesiastical polis runs smoothly unless some villain or outside catastrophic event comes along to disturb it, and that the ills caused by such woes can be brought to a conclusion through the thunderous proclamations and apostolic assaults against them on the part of a single heroic council or saintly ecclesiastical leader. Reform was required, and projects pursuing it conceived, not only before Luther and in response to Luther, but also after the last participant left Trent in 1563, and in 1663, 1763, and 1863 as well. And among the ever-present sins making this never-ending battle for reform a constant reality is the incalculably immense power exercised at all times and in all places by familiar but erroneous "customs" masquerading as or at least accepted as the traditional teaching, administrative procedures, and moral practices proper to the Roman Catholic Church.

False "traditions," by which were meant the "customary" practices of papal and diocesan courts and curiae, along with the ideas defending them, were the bugbear of fervent Catholic reformers, including Pope Gregory VII, long before Luther, making reference to the quotation from Tertullian cited under the title of this article. All that men like Luther did, as far as reformers like Gian Piero Carafa, the future Pope Paul IV, was concerned, was to intensify their concern for a swift revamping of standard operating procedures and the corrupt canonical and erroneous theological justifications lying behind them. This and this alone could prepare the Church for the brutal war for the souls of men and the health of secular society that they saw the Protestant Reformation portended.

DOCTRINAL IMPORTANCE

In the minds of the defenders of "custom-defined-as-tradition," such Catholic critics of papal and episcopal courts and curiae were, at the very least, the sort of deluded, destructive, and even heretical zealots that centuries of papal bureaucratic prudence and pragmatism had sought to tame. At worst, they were themselves viewed as the *true* problem of the day, unnecessarily aggravating that Protestant tempest-in-a-teapot which could be quelled through the tried laws and methods of practical professionals, or through the rhetorical genius of Humanist word merchants. This latter line of argument rejected both a closer examination of Luther's theological assault and the need for proper doctrine to defend a beleaguered Church, and a defense of that doctrine as well as the demands for moral administrative procedures which respected a proper hierarchy of values through which spiritual matters were placed above mere political and economic concerns. Instead, it literally verged on the point of treating the Protestant revolt as a non-event, and its consequences were particularly deadly. For nothing, says Hubert Jedin, the great historian of the Council of Trent, furthered the Reformation more than a widespread delusion about its actual lack of doctrinal and pastoral importance among people who conceived of themselves as dealing with the "real"—*i.e.*, the customary, non-doctrinal, politically and economically relevant—problems of grown-ups.

One instance of just how thick were the "defenders of customary traditions" can be seen in their lack of reaction to the Sack of Rome of 1527. This had its origins in the French-Spanish struggle for hegemony in Italy in the fifteenth and sixteenth centuries. Its proximate cause was the clash between the political program of the harried Medici Pope, Clement VII (1523–1534), and the ambitions of Charles V (1516–1558), King of Spain, King of Germany, and Holy Roman Emperor [Charles was Charles I, King of Spain, from 1516, and Charles V, King/Emperor from 1519, both down to 1556, when he abdicated]. If its agents were actually mutinous, unpaid, imperial soldiers, these nevertheless could say that they were merely following the examples of their more illustrious clerical ally, the Cardinal Pompeo Colonna, who had plundered the Vatican side of the Tiber some eight months earlier. Whatever the specific responsibilities of pope, Catholic king-emperor, and prince of the Church might have been, the end result was indeed a nightmare. On May 6, 1527, Rome suffered the worst assault that it had ever known, far worse than anything at the time of the barbarian migrations. Nothing was spared, sacred, or profane. Clement VII's escape to and confinement within the walls of Castel Sant'Angelo until December, listening to the taunting of German mercenaries calling for his death and replacement by "Pope Luther," were the least of the indignities. Various cardinals and prelates, including one future pope, Julius III, were humiliated and tortured, altars were ransacked, the Sistine Chapel used as a stable, riches confiscated, patients in hospitals and children in orphanages gratuitously butchered. Rape and rapine, exacerbated by raids of hoodlums under the direction of the abbot of the nearby monastery of Farfa, were followed by the onset of plague. Rome and the stench of death became one.

One might have thought that the Sack would guarantee their great awakening. Nothing of the kind happened. Those whose eyes were open before the Sack may have had them opened wider still, but they were relatively few in number. With rare exceptions, men who were blind remained blind. An event of such magnitude, whose mere possibility in the abstract might have seemed apocalyptic beforehand, was digested when it finally did occur in reality as though it were simply another move on the chessboard of ordinary political life. Indeed, most Catholics, clerics and laymen alike, afterwards as before, went about their daily affairs, changing nothing, watching the collapse of the Church's position in Germany, uninspired to lift a finger to arrest it, even when possessing the authority to do so.

PASTORAL COMMITMENT

Fortunately for the survival of the Church, those treating doctrinal and spiritual matters as secondary in importance—so long as the power and political influence of the Papacy was protected—suffered at least a partial defeat at the hands of the heroes of the Catholic Reformation. As Trent, the Jesuits, St. Charles Borromeo, St. Pius V, St. Francis de Sales, and so many others progressed in influence, the "traditions" that these custom-obsessed conservatives supported were exposed for what they were: abuses fortified by many spurious, self-deceptive arguments, but used for so long as to have gained the appearance of being something sacred.

Fortunately for Rome, an effort was made to rebuild its walls with something more suitable and sturdier than whatever happened to be merely familiar: a reaffirmation of the authentic and eternal Catholic Tradition, a deeper understanding of whose *doctrines* alone revealed the *pastoral* flaws of the immediate past and indicated a surer path to a better future on both the theoretical and practical, pragmatic level. Rooted in concerns that pre-dated the Protestant revolt, Trent was deeply committed, probably more committed in a practical way than any previous council, to a thorough evangelization of a Christian world which was believed to be still all too rooted in superstitious pagan practices. Evangelization was to be accomplished by a reinvigorated clergy, episcopacy, and papacy. But already from the beginning of the Council's first sitting, it recognized that any attempt to separate pastoral activity from zeal for doctrine was impossible. The minute one touched upon the first realm, the second inexorably reared its head, the same being true when approached the other way around. The Christian evangelist had to accomplish his work with good doctrine behind him. He had to be able to teach and teach correctly.

Year by year, decade by decade, on every level, intellectual, moral and physical, we have witnessed all that we have considered to be valuable from our Christian-Greco-Roman past mercilessly attacked, torn to shreds, and mocked in its helplessness. And yet each new assault, which seems as though it ought to be the final eye-opening disaster, appears to do little to awaken us to the major cause of our impotent defense of our own heritage.

Our impotence stems from our continued support for certain supposedly practical, prudent, pragmatic "traditions"—those composed of ever more heretical interpretations of the meaning of Vatican II, marching in lock step with naturalist, pluralist, libertine, secular principles, and protected by a Stalinist understanding of the infallibility and practical wisdom of "a Pope who can do no

wrong"—which, like the "traditions" of the corrupt papal and episcopal courts and curiae of the early sixteenth century, are actually
not part of Catholic Tradition at all, but, rather, are errors and
abuses. It emerges from our conviction that critics of such false
traditions are wild-eyed and destructive zealots. It is fed by our
insistence on closing our minds to the full character of the problems that we face so as to remind one of Hubert Jedin's warning
that nothing does more to abet a disaster than an unwillingness
to recognize its real existence.

The proponents of false traditions in the first half of the sixteenth century did not see that their standard operating procedures were helpless to deal with the disaster of 1527. Thankfully,
their influence was weakened—though not by any means entirely
destroyed—by the doctrinally and pastorally solid heroes of the
Catholic Reformation. Similarly, Catholics who have accepted
the false traditions of our own time cannot understand that the
standard operating procedures of this heritage—the spirit of Vatican II—render them helpless in fending off further collapse. Any
defenders of Rome at the time of the Sack of 1527 who might
have been guided by the kinds of "traditions" defended tooth
and nail by contemporary modernist and conservative Catholic idol worshippers would have had to do their duty by joining
the mutinous soldiers in breaching the Aurelian Walls. Let us
hope that the Catholic reformers of our own day—courageous
cardinals, bishops, priests, and laity who recognize the need for
solid doctrine to back serious pastoral activity—will one day be
celebrated justly along with those who made the reform of the
sixteenth century possible.

19

World War One and the Russian Diaspora

THE WESTWARD SPREAD
OF TRUTHS AND ERRORS[†]

O NE OF THE MAJOR CONSEQUENCES OF the First World War was the tearing away of many people from the embrace of Mother Russia. Most of these men and women actually left that embrace quite happily, creating the independent nations of Finland, Estonia, Latvia, Lithuania, and Poland in doing so. Prominent among those ripped from the bosom of the old Empire very much against their will were faithful members of the Russian Church, forced out due to Bolshevik persecution. Their numbers included fervent clerical and lay supporters of an Orthodox religious revival that had seriously begun in the 1790s; believers who had been greatly encouraged in their hopes for ever more significant national spiritual growth since the relaxation of state controls over ecclesiastical life began with the first Russian Revolution in 1905.

Although this diaspora grew to be active in many places in Europe and America, France and England were its most important intellectual centers after the Great War. Especially notable in this regard were both the community of exiles in Paris, where the St. Sergius Orthodox Theological Institute was founded in 1925, as well as émigré centers in Britain, which became home to the Fellowship of St. Alban and St. Sergius, a product of the Anglo-Russian Student Conferences of 1927 and 1928. The names of those connected with these eclectic circles and institutions constitute a "who's who" of Russian Orthodox influence in the entirety of the West from the 1920s to the present, with the "founding fathers" of Sergii Bulgakov (1871–1944), Nicholas Berdyaev (1874-1948), Alexander Elchaninov (1881-1934), Georgii Florovsky (1893–1979), Lev Zander (1893-1964), Nicholas Zernov (1898-1980), and Vladimir Lossky (1903–1958) preparing the way for the next Orthodox wave, including Alexander Schmemann (1921–1983),

---

† First published in *The Angelus*, March–April 2018.

Oliver Clement (1921–2009), John Meyendorff (1926–1992), and Timothy Kallistos Ware (b. 1934).

I must confess that this Diaspora exercised a positive influence on my own development. Nicholas Zernov, probably the chief inspiration behind the Fellowship of St. Alban and St. Sergius, was one of my tutors at Oxford in the 1970s, where he had taught since 1947 and long been in charge of St. Gregory and St. Macrina House, the chief center for Orthodox life at the University. Zernov was a fine Christian man, reflecting that concern for the liturgy, the Church Fathers, and the doctrine of "divinization"—which westerners tend to prefer to speak of as "transformation in Christ"—that were central to the discussions of the local Russian Orthodox community. I look back fondly upon his forthright encouragement of a young Roman Catholic student struggling with the disaster of the Second Vatican Council, despite the disagreements that appeared through my participation in these discussions.

For disagreements there were, and of a type that I can only relate here very broadly, with reference to the "tone" coming through the diaspora message in general. That "tone" involved a marked tendency to denigrate the role of reason and communal authority in the Christian dispensation. This Russian Orthodox tendency, which was not without its influence over developments in the Roman Catholic Church from the end of the First World War onwards—and in those realms of spirituality, dogma, and ecumenism where the role of reason and communal authority were perhaps most seriously needed. Moreover, such influence seemed to me to be all too painfully manifesting its dangerous character in that first and most dreadful post-conciliar decade, which happened to coincide with my interaction with the Russians in Oxford. A brief treatment of two of the diaspora's great concerns, *hesychasm* and *sobornost*, regarding which its teachers felt something of an evangelical commitment, underline the tone and its impact neatly.

Hesychasm can be translated from the Greek as meaning "to keep still." It is an essentially quietist mystical approach, based upon both very early eastern monastic writings as well as those of Simeon the New Theologian (949–1022) and gaining its most influential expression in the work of Gregory Palamos (1296–1359). Many *hesychasts* claimed to have found a method for achieving individual union with God based upon continual employment of a simple "Jesus Prayer," along with a cultivation of the proper physical position and environment in which to recite it. They argued that commitment to their method allowed for a quiet divinization of its individual mystical practitioner, the depiction of whose sanctity, which was said to glow with the kind of light that illumed Christ on Mount Tabor, provided endless stimulation for iconographers.

Hesychasm became very strong in eastern monastic circles, gradually driving the earlier, communal-minded *Stoudite* monastic tradition into the shadows. Although they generally looked upon all things western with suspicion, *hesychasts* of the Palamos variety nevertheless shared with many late medieval Latin mystics a similar contempt for scholasticism and the role of any logical, speculative theology in paving a pathway to union with God.

But eastern critics of Palamos joined with their Latin counterparts in criticizing a spirituality one of whose main effects was abandonment of the mental tools needed to distinguish an erroneous from an acceptable form of mystical union. They were horrified by his apparent claim that the *hesychast* could achieve a union with God while on earth equivalent to that to be experienced in eternity. Worse still, they insisted that the unity he spoke of was not a complete one. Rather, it was limited to a union with God's so-called "operations"; the "uncreated light" that was said to shine down from Mount Tabor.

Palamos, in their minds, thus appeared to recoil from the idea that even the blessed in heaven could touch the actual "core" of divinity and see God fully, in His very essence. Separating the essence of God from His uncreated light was tantamount to positing the existence of two divinities: one that man could fully reach, even in this life, but through one particular anti-rational path to transformation in Christ alone; and another "god" who would remain forever unknown and unknowable. Whatever the outraged objections the passionately icon-friendly *hesychasts* might hurl at their opponents, this meant that such mystics once again had thrown the doctrinal work accomplished through the defeat of iconoclasm into jeopardy. For the total divinization of man in Christ and the proper estimation of the glory of the universe was therefore precluded, with both the individual and the fullness of nature shut off from the truly inclusive, transforming embrace of God.

Hesychasm entered dramatically into the life of the Russian Church in 1793 with Paisius Velichkovsky's (1722–1794) translation into Church Slavonic of a number of writings on the subject, most importantly, the so-called *Philokalia* or "love of the beautiful," put together by St. Nikodemos of the Holy Mountain of Athos (1749–1809) and St. Makarios of Corinth (1731–1805). Velichkovsky's writings were passed down through the Optina Monastery where he lived and worked, in nineteenth century vernacular Russian translations, by means of a popular book entitled *The Way of the Pilgrim,* and also in novels of Dostoevsky. But so was the criticism of *hesychasm's* seemingly non-dogmatic, non-sacramental approach to holiness, with its Russian mixture of individual mystical effort and obedience to the guidance of the lay monastic spiritual directors known as *startsy.* And love for the *Philokalia, The Way of the Pilgrim, hesychasm,* the Jesus Prayer and the anti-rational, quietist mysticism of its individual practitioners migrated to France and England with the Russian Diaspora, promoting twentieth century translations of their basic literature into western languages, prompted by men like T. S. Eliot among many others.

The westward movement of *hesychasm,* with its focus on individual mystical effort, was paralleled by that of the concept of *sobornost,* which aimed at explaining the nature of the "spiritual community of many jointly living people," as its name indicates. First associated with the Russian thinkers Aleksey Stepanovich Khomyakov (1804–1860) and Ivan Vasilyevich Kireyevsky (1806–1856), *sobornost* was intended to contrast an Orthodox vision of catholicity—diversity in unity—with a western presentation of the same vision that was castigated as being theologically and legally precisionist and hidebound on the one hand, yet anarchically individualist in character on the other. Supporters of the concept said that Orthodox believers forming a truly catholic community inspired by *sobornost* were united by a free and loving abandonment of themselves to the absolute values and the society that they cherished, whose bonds were cemented by a consciousness of being one, by common prayer, and by a common liturgy; not by their dull recitation of intellectual dogmatic formulae and their bending of the neck to communally-enforced legal precepts.

But critics of *sobornost* were baffled by a number of historical anomalies that the concept seemed to ignore. Why in heaven's name was the accusation of theological and legal perfectionism laid at the doorstep of a rather sleepy western world that was only awakened to the need for precision in these matters from the intellectually much pickier East of the first eight Ecumenical Councils? How was it that bending the fingers into the absolutely precise liturgical position was less legalist than accepting the Dogma of the Immaculate Conception? In what way could the "free communities of Orthodox believers" be compared to the papal "tyrants" and Catholic "robots" who so often fought heroically against the will of the Caesaro-Papists to which the Eastern Churches repeatedly subjected themselves? And how would you know if you were truly united as a loving community committed to absolute values if intellectual and legal precision regarding what these values actually might be were disdained? One was left with merely celebrating, liturgically, a union that in practical terms might not really exist.

It seemed to me, the more that I learned about the phenomenon while at Oxford, that there was no wonder that the *hesychasm* and *sobornost* promoted by the Russian Diaspora were of interest to supporters of the Ecumenical Movement, Personalists, New Theologians, and enthusiasts for esoteric spiritual insights of the years leading from the end of the First World War down to the Second Vatican Council. The anti-rational, anti-legal, anti-communal authority approach that such mysticism and such a vision of Christian society embraced allowed all of them to escape the "dry, hidebound, dogmatic and spiritual legalism" of a Roman Church bewitched by the call for clarity demanded by the modern Papacy since the days of the Syllabus of Errors. How much easier it would be for them to unite Christians in both a spirit of love as well as in a fight for the true faith if all that Roman fuss and bother regarding what such a spirit love and truth faith actually meant were to be abandoned! And what better way was there of humbling Rome's parochial pettiness by calling up the example of good-willed fellow believers who had so obviously been persecuted by secularist totalitarians!

Alas, the more I argued with precisely such good-willed, persecuted, fellow Christians at Oxford—along with their Anglican and Roman Catholic fellow travelers—the more I grew confirmed in my still embryonic traditionalist conviction that everyone succumbing to the lure of the anti-rational, anti-dogmatic, anti-legalist, anti-communal authority message that their "tone" and "tendency" dictated were doomed; doomed to see their substantive Faith and its morals dismantled around them by whatever forceful presence in the group could impose itself as an electrifying spiritual director or community guide. Any stepping back to determine whether such a *force de la nature* and his followers were rationally and morally on the right path would reintroduce the bogeyman of dogma and law back into the picture, disturbing the celebration of their community of prayer, love, and spiritual union. I know this for a fact, because having attempted to probe some of the things that I heard brought me up against the immediate reproach of "trying to pin the spirit down according the lifeless precepts of Roman Law"; of "not allowing the Holy Spirit to speak His message to me"; of "not opening my heart to the superior (and somehow never to be judged) spirituality and special mission of the East"; of "failing to grasp the special lessons an inspired Russian Church had learned about the evils of relying on the state to protect her"—as though the western concept of legitimate authority were the same as the exercise of Czarist, Caesaro-Papist power.

Once again, I am grateful for what I have learned from Eastern Christianity—and Russian Christianity in particular. I agree with the argument that the Church breathes with two lungs—one from the East and one from the West. But that means that I can take pride in a Western Church that has indeed inherited a Roman concern for law and put this to work in her understanding of authority, community, and spiritual transformation in Christ; a Western Church that has done so in union with a dogmatic rigidity whose importance she very much first grasped under pressure from her Eastern Sister of the early Ecumenical Councils. And it is these two lungs together that tell me to use all the tools of my Faith and Reason to ensure that Russia spreads her truths—and not her errors—to the rest of the globe.

20

The Renaissance of the Twelfth Century and Its Guardian Angels[†]

A NY CHRISTIAN INTERESTED IN THE springtime of western Christendom—and the absurdity of Enlightenment denigration of the "Dark Ages" along with it— should pick up the Harvard historian Charles Homer Haskins' classic work, *The Renaissance of the Twelfth Century*. This justly celebrated text, published and republished since 1927, catalogues the manifold intellectual and cultural achievements, as well as the general spirit of rebirth and hope, characterizing what was an overwhelmingly religion-driven age, Catholic to its very core.

Even if the renaissance in question brought up many problems that profound thinkers and saints would be forced to struggle to overcome from the 1100s down to our own time, these dilemmas emerged in the midst of a commitment to one unified goal: the need to fulfill the message of the Incarnation by transforming all things natural through the supernatural teaching and grace of Christ. Aside from its consequences for civilization in general, what that commitment engendered was a substantive respect for the complexity of social life and the central importance of the individual person within it underscoring our purely naturalist contemporaries' celebration of "diversity" and "human dignity" for the empty sloganeering that it really is.

Every era has its key movers and shakers—its "guardian angels"— and I would like to call attention to two of these with respect to the twelfth century renaissance, the first of whom is unfamiliar to most of us: a professor at the budding University of Paris known in his day by the name of Peter "the Cantor" (d. 1197). Peter Cantor insisted that transformation in Christ required ecclesiastical guidance not of some undifferentiated mass community, but, rather, of a multifaceted network of societies with immensely varied vocations in life, each made real through the work of its individual members, and each presenting peculiar obstacles to holiness. In short, the

---

† First published in *The Angelus*, January–February 2018.

Church had to construct as many supernatural pastoral ladders to heaven as there were distinct natural human activities, socially organized, but always with the awareness that it was the individual representatives of these activities who were destined for eternal life.

It was this project of individual redemption through recognition of different pastoral approaches to diverse social vocations that Innocent III, perhaps the most famous and grateful pupil of Peter Cantor, took up at the end of the century. Innocent applied it to individual Christians in general by means of a more refined spelling out of the basic social activity of the Church as a whole in the Fourth Lateran Council. He also utilized it in dealing with more specific concerns, as with his support for institutional guidance of persons engaged in higher education, men and women committed to St. Francis' life of Apostolic Poverty, and even the special pastoral labor involved in redemption of those who had fallen into the unacceptable "profession" of ladies of the night. If time and space permitted, it would be equally possible to demonstrate that the great scholastic systems of men like St. Thomas Aquinas are characterized by their concern for individual minds, souls, and redemption, but always in the context of a rich and diverse social order that cannot be reduced to one, monolithic Leviathan.

Our second and much more famous protagonist in this task of sanctifying the individual through a natural world of varied human vocations is St. Bernard of Clairvaux (1090–1153). Yes, it is true that that great saint's suspicion of the possibly secularizing effects of the work of contemporary philosophers illustrates the kind of battles that emerged as a result of the century's mobilization of all of the manifold natural tools at man's disposal. Nevertheless, he served as a "guardian angel" for one of the most dangerous and destructive of the many human social groups whose individual members were in desperate need of redemption; the group that historically was the very first target for transformation in Christ: the military, whose natural soldiering vocation had to be redirected from its march to hell to the service of a just cause that might actually aid it in its own peculiar ascent of Mount Carmel.

This labor—so politically incorrect in our own time, which loves to deal with its most difficult problems by refusing to acknowledge them as such—began in the tenth century through the monks of Cluny and their efforts to turn the existing, anarchic soldiery, sarcastically labeled "the *malitia*," into an honest Christian *militia*. They accomplished this work by convincing at least some members of the *malitia* to abandon their evil ways and use their arms to guard otherwise helpless pilgrims on the perilous road to the shrine of Santiago de Compostella in Spain instead. This enterprise ultimately gave birth to the crusading movement, the justification for which lay in its call to protect pilgrims en route to Jerusalem, to defend an Eastern Roman Empire under renewed threat from the Moslems, and to recover a Holy Land unjustly taken from the Christian world five hundred years earlier. And it was this work that also led to the creation of the Knights of the Temple, those "fighting men of prayer" who dedicated themselves to the safeguard of worshipers coming to King David's city and found their own individual guardian angel in St. Bernard.

Our guardian angel took up this role in a letter to Hugues de Payens (c. 1070–1136), the Templars' founder, entitled *In Praise of the New Knighthood*. Eager to aid the Knights both in their recruitment as well as in their hunt for material support, he expressed therein his admiration for their ability to root their peculiar natural vocation in its proper supernatural end:

> Thus in a wonderous and unique manner they appear gentler than lambs, yet fiercer than lions. I do not know if it would be more appropriate to refer to them as monks or as soldiers, unless perhaps it would be better to recognize them as being both. Indeed they lack neither monastic meekness nor military might. What can we say of this, except that this has been done by the Lord, and it is marvelous in our eyes. These are the picked troops of God, whom he has recruited from the ends of the earth; the valiant men of Israel chosen to guard well and faithfully that tomb which is the bed of the true Solomon, each man sword in hand, and superbly trained to war.[1]

In the long run, this "new knighthood" proved to be just as multifaceted as the Christendom Renaissance world in which it was

---

[1] Bernard of Clairvaux, "In Praise of the New Knighthood," in *Bernard of Clairvaux, Treatises III*, trans. Conrad Greenia (Kalamazoo: Cistercian Publications, 1977), chapter 4.

born, also creating a whole new genre of chivalric literature in its train, one that sang of the Christian soldiery as a force defending all that was beautiful, deserving of love, and generally weak in consequence. In doing so, it also aroused in its "guardian angel" a conscious desire to adopt—and purify—this often rather capricious troubadour tool, utilizing its theme of romantic love to lead the soldiers under his guidance to the deepest form of loving union: that sought by God Himself with each and every individual soul. Hence St. Bernard's commentary on the *Canticle of Canticles* and its symbol of human love as a ladder to conveying the loving union God set out to achieve on a higher level through the Incarnation:

> But if she loves with her whole being, nothing is lacking where everything is given. To love so ardently then is to share the marriage bond; she cannot love so much and not be totally loved, and it is in the perfect union of two hearts that complete and total marriage consists. Or are we to doubt that the soul is loved by the Word first and with a greater love?
>
> Because we are carnal and born of concupiscence and of the flesh, our love must needs come from the flesh. If this love be well guided, it will gradually become, under the influence of grace, a spiritual love, for 'that was not first which is spiritual, but that which is natural; afterwards, that which is spiritual (1 Cor. xv, 46).

Our twelfth century renaissance knew that redemption of distinct individuals through the diverse social institutions organizing their varied vocations in life gains its crucial aid from the revelation and grace coming through the Mystical Body of Christ the Incarnate Word. Hence, it cannot come as a surprise that a man like St. Bernard would probe these for an ever-deeper understanding of their treasures. Such probing led this "guardian angel" to a study of the *real* guardian angels, to whom, as Fr. Pierre Pourrat says, "Christian piety had hardly directed its attention" before his homilies on the subject.[2]

In a characteristic application of twelfth century developments, the Abbot of Clairvaux does not discuss angels as watching over us in some monolithic fashion, but with clear distinctions. As Pourrat indicates, he sees angels as the protectors not only of the Church

---

2   Pierre Pourrat, *Christian Spirituality, vol.* 2 (London: Burns Oates and Washbourne Ltd., 1924), 60.

as a whole, but of each and every single Christian edifice in its own way, so much so that "the heavenly spirits, in choir, blend with the psalmody of the monks."[3] Marvelous as this is, their protection is distinguished still further, with St. Bernard proclaiming his astonishment with God that "his angels, those sublime spirits so happy and so near his throne, his familiar and, we may say, his intimate friends" are given the task of protecting each and every individual in each and every one of their vocations in life.[4] His exhortation to us to honor these extremely personal protectors and the incalculable aid that they offer to us can be summarized in the homily that is read in the Breviary on October 2:

> Although we may be but little children, and the way that remains for us to pass over before we reach salvation be very long, and not only very long but also full of danger—for all that, what is there for us to fear, who are guided by such guardians? It is impossible for them to be overthrown or seduced, still less for them to seduce us, they who keep us in all our ways. They are faithful, they are prudent, they are powerful; wherefore fear? Let us follow them, let us cling to their footsteps, and we shall thus abide under the protection of the God of heaven....
>
> Shouldst thou foresee a grave temptation or fear a great trial, invoke thy guardian, thy guide, thy refuge in oppression and in distress. Call on him and say, "Lord, save us, for we perish." He does not sleep, he does not slumber.... O my brethren, may your guardian angels be your intimate friends; be unceasingly with those who, when you often think of them and devoutly pray to them, guard and console you every moment.[5]

I may be wrong, but I believe that the Church has generally counseled against our attempting to dwell any further on this magnificent reality, as, for example, by "naming" our individual guardian angel. Perhaps this is deemed much too arrogant on our part. Perhaps it is due to the fact that our guardians themselves carry out their labors as members of their own diverse angelic societies, and, that it is best to make clear that they, just like we ourselves, can only be what they are meant to be individually

---

3 Pourrat, *Christian Spirituality*, vol. 2, 60.
4 Bernard of Clairvaux, "In psalm. Qui habitat, Sermo XII," cited in Pourrat, vol. 2, 60.
5 Cited in Pourrat, vol. 2, 61–62.

through the communities that God has placed them in. Perhaps any human project of personalizing them further than Scripture, which has named only a few angels, would cheapen their grandeur and work for us, just as the naturalist demand for individuals to think and act purely on their earthly plane alone actually cheapens and destroys us in the Divine plan.

Whatever the case may be in this regard, it strikes me as particularly fitting that in the mysterious Providence of God, the development of devotion to our guardian angels should have been left to the twelfth century. For nothing can be more aesthetically complete than seeing how a renaissance that achieved its work by plunging into the "dirt" of all earthly vocations marred by sin—the particularly "dirty" one of soldiering included—discovered, as it went about its labors, that all of the angels of God were there beside them, individually aiding each and every man and woman to be truly reborn and transformed in Christ.

21

À Rebours, en Route, and Very Much on Target

J-K HUYSMANS AND THE APOSTOLATE OF THE OUTSIDERS†

A REBOURS IS THE NAME OF A NOVEL WRIT-
ten in 1884 by Joris-Karl Huysmans (1848–1907). Its anti-hero,
Jean des Esseintes, namely Huysmans in disguise, is disgusted with
the dominant, arrogant, mid to late nineteenth century "positivist"
vision, which insisted that only empirical, scientifically verifiable
data could reveal the character of "nature." His reaction is to
abandon the spirit of the times, to go "against nature"—the English
translation of the title—and to indulge in a decadent, self-indulgent,
and ultimately cynical aestheticism, totally alien to the practical
"blood and iron" concerns of the mainstream positivist world.

The author of *Against Nature* and the so-called Decadent
Movement in literature he was central to creating, both traced their
initial anti-Establishment inspiration to *Les Fleurs du Mal* (1857)
of Charles Baudelaire (1821–1867). But Baudelaire, a deep admirer
of the counterrevolutionary thinker Joseph de Maistre, was ultimately encouraging more than simple decadence to counter the
modern conception of progress. Hence, Huysmans, like others in
the movement, soon realized that the fanciful excesses of the voluntary "outsider" des Esseintes, while an understandable response
to the flatness of the "insiders'" *Zeitgeist,* were not sufficient to
deal with modernity's sickness unto death. In fact, it was his own
reflection upon des Esseintes' weaknesses thus actually helped
most to convert the very author who had created this anti-hero
to Catholicism.

Huysmans traces his gradual rejection of an "outsider's" child-
ish, decadent, and nihilistic decision to live "against nature" as
falsely presented by the positivists with a life guided by a proper
understanding of the natural world as taught by the Incarnate

---

† First published in *The Angelus*, January–February 2020.

Word in four further novels: *Là-bas* (*The Damned*, 1891), *En Route* (1895), *La Cathédrale* (1898), and *L'Oblat* (*The Oblate*, 1903). Here, the main character, another autobiographical figure named Durtal, flees the dangerous flirtation with demonic forces to which his decadence has led him. He goes *en route* to a Catholicism whose full effect on nature is symbolized by the cathedral of Chartres, which inspires him to become an oblate in a Benedictine monastery. Durtal/Huysmans has come to realize that he lives in a good natural world flawed by sin where the believer has to accept the need for suffering and expiation on his way to eternal glory.

A man like Huysmans was always an outsider from the standpoint of many Catholics who did not grasp the different kind of path that people who started with Baudelaire and moved through Decadence and the subsequent Symbolist Movement had taken to arrive at the fullness of the Faith. Huysmans' truly "insider's" sense of the importance of orthodox belief and the dangers to which the dominant mentality exposed someone seeking to find and maintain it, can be seen in the alarmed warning regarding theological Modernism he sounded in *The Oblate*, which was published the year of St. Pius X's election to the See of Peter.

Biographies such as Huysmans' and his fellow Decadent-to-Symbolist-to Catholic literary colleagues are of great interest to me for two reasons, the first of which is that they contribute to an understanding of something very important in the history of the Church: the Apostolate of the Outsiders. This Apostolate has repeatedly proven to be an incomparable blessing to the Mystical Body of Christ, whose "insiders," clergy, religious, and laity alike, can often lose their way, if not in terms of "officially" rejecting the Faith and destroying the sacraments, certainly in the sense of neglecting, obscuring, and giving public scandal to them. It is at such moments that those who are "outsiders," whether through their lack of any power to correct what has gone badly wrong or their sincere longing for deeper knowledge of the substance of the Way, the Truth, and Life—and not its disfigured image—have repeatedly entered onto the scene to fulfill their role. This outsider call to "jump start" a failing engine has the occupational hazard of being misunderstood and maltreated by the insiders who are not doing their own job properly. All one has to do is to look at the accusations of schismatic and heretical behavior hurled at the monks of Cluny in the tenth century and the initial reformers of the Renaissance and Catholic Reformation era to verify this fact.

By now, it will be clear to all of my readers that the specific and incomparably important Apostolate of the Outsiders that concerns me here is the one that has been exercised for fifty years by the Society of St. Pius X. Founded by a man who never dreamed that the term "insider" could possibly be denied him, this Apostolate has unashamedly dedicated itself to teaching and doing nothing other than what Archbishop Lefebvre had had the highest official approval for preaching and promoting throughout his entire previous vocational career. Moreover, it has courageously maintained this commitment while being publicly reviled for crimes the injustice of which only its predecessors in cleaning the ecclesiastical Augean Stables in previous periods of mainstream collapse could fully appreciate.

Other contributors to this issue will outline the many particular accomplishments of the Society in very detailed ways, being much more competent to do so as day-to-day laborers in its multiple fields of endeavor. It was only after reflecting on what it was that I might possibly offer in this regard that the "outsider" Huysmans came to mind, and the second reason why meditation upon his experience and that of so many others either following seemingly "untraditional" paths to the Faith or rediscovering its fullness in times of confusion and despair is important: true Christian charity demands that they be taken seriously and nurtured. It is the Society of St. Pius X's remarkable apostolate to so many other Catholics or would-be Catholics "on the outside looking in" in the gravest time of crisis in the history of the Church—an Apostolate *of* an Outsider *to* the Outsiders—that I felt capable of recording for posterity. For there are many who are "of" the Society even though not "in" it.

This truth is driven home to me over and over again on the many occasions I attend Mass at St. Nicolas du Chardonnet in Paris. There are men and women in that congregation, very easily identified by their manner of dress and their failure to socialize with anyone after Mass is over, who are not SSPX "insiders." Nevertheless, this parish is obviously their home; I recognize their faces from year to year, and they come because St. Nicolas is where they see the fullness of the faith. They are indeed "in" this community of believers even if they are officially not "of it"; no one has turned them away, and it must be the case that this has kept them sane amidst the rubble of the Catholic Church and Catholic Christendom. The Apostolate of the Outsiders exercised by the SSPX has been exercised to and for them as well; there are concentric circles of outsiders for whom this exercise has been crucial, whether the leadership and members of the Society are aware of it or not. Although no historical record is likely ever to associate this community with the force responsible for keeping it spiritually alive, I can at least offer one bit of evidence for its existence: myself.

It must be a peculiar sensation to feel like an "insider" in one's own particular narrow time and place, but that is certainly not a feeling that I have ever experienced. Although I had good parents, a happy home, a wonderful childhood, and a fruitful educational experience, I can remember very much always thinking of myself as something of an outsider peering at a scene that was just not quite right. What, exactly, was wrong with the picture was very unclear to my immature mind, but as my entrance into high school in the dreadful Year of Modernity called 1965 led to graduation in the still more ominous one of 1969, it was obvious that the disconnect between my own life and what "nature" as my time and place was offering me was becoming more and more pronounced. And the most distressing aspect of that disconnect was the fact that nothing in my personal makeup particularly disposed me to want to be or to enjoy being "on the outside looking in."

Developments portending a still more thoroughgoing exile from the world around me were soon to follow. In the spring of 1970, my first year as an undergraduate, I was introduced by one of my history professors to the entire counterrevolutionary critique of modern civilization as a whole. Three years later came entry into Oxford and membership in an international fraternity of exiles from modernity determined to make our experience at that venerable institution an outsiders' defiance of a *Zeitgeist* that looked as though it had the full backing of the clueless powers that-be, administrative and student. This was followed at the end of the decade by the beginning of my own university career, whose lack of connection with any current-day "insider" existence can be read by anyone with the stomach to do so in the novel posted on my Internet site entitled—appropriately enough—*Periphery*. Caveat emptor! It is the bitter, sardonic, product of an outsider engaged in a total war against the distorted nature of my times; someone at that point still regularly and intensely tempted to become another—but probably much more mediocre version of—des Esseintes.

Thankfully, this pull to take the path *là-bas* was not uncontested. From the very outset of my university experiences, there were forces that were putting me *en route*. And a constant companion along the highway towards the true understanding of the meaning of nature and how to use it properly to reach eternal life in Christ, a fellow-traveler that has helped mightily to pick me up when too weary to go on or turn me around when ready to go astray has always been that Apostle to the Outsiders called the Society of St. Pius X.

For an outsider I always have been. I only learned of Archbishop Lefebvre through Dietrich von Hildebrand and the Roman Forum, having been introduced to their own countercultural fight against heresy and the *Novus Ordo Missae* in 1970 by the same university professor who acquainted me with the secular counterrevolutionary critique. I merely watched the opening of the seminary at Econe on a television screen from Oxford. It was simply as a representative of the Roman Forum that I was sent to meet and interview Msgr. Ducaud Bourget soon after the takeover of St. Nicolas and have my one and only glimpse of the Archbishop himself. It was curiosity alone that brought me to Ridgefield, Connecticut, immediately following its opening in 1979, to find out what the seminary training there was like. I was never a member of a Society parish and I am not one now.

Somehow this has never stopped the Society from always welcoming and encouraging me. In fact, it literally saved me from my most serious des Esseintes relapse, which took place between 1985 and 1987, when my revolt against an ever more wretched natural world led me entirely to abandon both my secular counterrevolutionary and traditionalist Roman Forum commitments. It did so by pressing me to come to lecture for it regularly on Church History and the problem of Americanism and reawakening my desire to get back *en route*. And it has continued to do so with an openness which I credit more than anything else for maintaining my sense of self-respect and the value of my historical discipline; keeping me, more than thirty years hence, from falling once again prey to the temptations of *là-bas*.

Openness to outsiders, according to the Society's enemies, is not a quality that it possesses. But openness is a virtue, as I believe Chesterton said, only when, like a mouth, it chomps down on something solid. At least in my experience, the Society has demonstrated precisely this kind of openness, encouraging valuable influences that it might not have considered part of its mission at the outset, and has gained strength in the process. Dare I suggest, in proof of this fact, that St. Mary's, Kansas today is a quite different phenomenon, academically and culturally, than it was some decades ago? It has benefited from this proper openness, just as the Catholic world of the turn of the twentieth century benefited from Huysmans and other outsiders like him.

But once again, these outside influences have proven their value in union with a Society committed to the *unum necessarium*: handing down the Tradition full and intact that was handed down to us, something which the mainstream Church is, to say the least, very confused about doing. Reveling in being outside and *avant garde* for their own sake, is, as Huysmans was well aware, a very dangerous game to play, with some of the would-be Catholics whom he knew who continued to indulge that narrow sport feeding the Modernist Movement he vigorously condemned. Outsiders have been a blessing for the Church only as a force working to enrich and strengthen the Tradition, ultimately from the inside.

Let us hope that it will not take another fifty years *en route* for an event to take place that so many of us "of" but not "in" the Society fervently pray to be able to see: the day when the mission of Archbishop Lefebvre is vindicated, and the errors of an ecclesiastical Zeitgeist which has truly gone *a rebours* are targeted and chastised with what Dietrich von Hildebrand labeled "the glorious and liberating words—*anathema sit!*"

22

Demolishing Thor's Oak

AN EARLY MEDIEVAL MODEL FOR
MODERN CATHOLIC "ICONOCLASM"†

S T. WILLIBALD (C. 700–C.787), FOUNDER OF
the diocese of Eichstätt in Bavaria, is our first guide to the life of
St. Boniface (c. 675–754), a fellow countryman from Anglo-Saxon
Britain. Born as Winfrid, St. Boniface was given this, his second
and better-known name—which was taken from that of an early
episcopal martyr of Tarsus in Asia Minor—at the behest of Pope
Gregory II (715–731). It was that great pontiff who appointed him
as a missionary bishop; as the Apostle to the still heathen German
tribes; the Saxons in particular.

St. Willibald tells us that in 723, quite early in his mission, St.
Boniface dealt with one specific problem in his mission territory in
a quite dramatic manner. Taking an axe into his hand, he chopped
down a sacred tree—variously named as Thor's, Jupiter's, or Thun-
der Oak—located at Gaesmere, near the present day town of Fritzlar
in northern Hesse. Modern Catholics in these current dark days
can draw three crucial lessons of perennial value from this clear-cut
act of brazen public "iconoclasm."

The first, fundamental, and perhaps most obvious of such lessons
is that there is a *good* kind of "image-smashing" alongside a *bad* one.
Affirmation of this truth flows inevitably from a faithful acceptance
of the fullness of the message of the Incarnation of the Word.
Magnificent testimony to this truth can be found in the writings of
many of the Eastern Church Fathers, especially those of St. Maximus
the Confessor (c. 580–662), elaborated upon by St. John of Damascus
(c. 675–749) and St. Theodore the Studite (759–826) in the era of the
Iconoclast Controversies (726–842). Their teachings helped mightily
to ensure the dogmatic decisions of the Second Council of Nicaea
(787) and the ultimate "Triumph of Orthodoxy" over the Iconoclasts
in 843, commemorated every year in the Eastern Churches through
the recitation of various "anathemas," such as the following:

† First published in *The Angelus*, January–February 2021.

To those who persist in the heresy of denying icons, or rather the apostasy of denying Christ, and who are not counseled by the Mosaic law to be led to their salvation, nor convinced to return to piety by the apostolic teachings, nor induced by patristic exhortations and explanations to abandon their deception, nor persuaded by the agreement of the Churches of God throughout the whole world, but who have once and for all joined themselves to the portion of the Jews and Greeks: for the blasphemies cast by the Jews and Greeks at the prototype, have been shamelessly used by the former to insult through His icon Him that is depicted therein; therefore, to those who are incorrigibly possessed by this deception and have their ears covered towards every divine word and spiritual teaching, since they are already putrefied members, having cut themselves off from the common body of the Church, ANATHEMA

This wondrous "anathema" points to the realization of Saints Maximus, John, and Theodore that there is no way that one can accurately understand that God's creation as a whole is an "icon," a sacred image, unless every one of its elements is "venerated" in its fitting and proper place in the divine hierarchy of values. This hierarchy of values, before all else, demands recognition of the need for man's Redemption from sin, and the constant, corrective, and sanctifying, transformative Grace that can only come from the greatest of the iconic elements of the natural world: Jesus Christ, who is the Incarnation of the Word, the Second Person of the Trinity, responsible for the creation of the universe in the first place.

Severing the iconic character of any given aspect of Creation from the saving and sanctifying Grace of the Cross of the Incarnate Word, and then offering to that isolated natural element an unquestioning acceptance on its own terms is a hideous error at the very least. Worshipping it as a floating bit of fallen debris that has wandered away from its true place in nature is a pagan blasphemy at its very worst, crying out to the heavens for a *good* "iconoclast" to expose and crush its hopeless but nevertheless destructive attempt at a coup d'état against the hierarchy of values. Failure to take up the "Catholic Iconoclast Burden" would be a dereliction of duty contributing to the blocking of fallen man's need to focus on the corrective and transformative work of the Incarnate Word. This labor alone clarifies the supernatural framework in which each and every specific element of nature actually can and indeed must play an iconic role reflecting and leading men to the glory of God, explaining why acts of *bad* iconoclasm against them are an insult to the Divine Plan in the process.

A second lesson of great importance emerging from St. Boniface's assault also involves the hierarchy of values, but this time with respect to the conditions under which one may legitimately undertake an act of *good* "iconoclasm." Allow me to introduce this teaching by citing in detail what Willibald tells us about the demolition of Thor's Oak:

> Now at that time many of the Hessians, brought under the Catholic faith and confirmed by the grace of the sevenfold spirit, received the laying on of hands; others indeed, not yet strengthened in soul, refused to accept in their entirety the lessons of the inviolate faith. Moreover, some were wont secretly, some openly to sacrifice to trees and springs; some in secret, others openly practised inspections of victims and divinations, legerdemain and incantations; some turned their attention to auguries and auspices and various sacrificial rites; while others, with sounder minds, abandoned all the profanations of heathenism, and committed none of these things. With the advice and counsel of these last, the saint attempted, in the place called Gaesmere, while the servants of God stood by his side, to fell a certain oak of extraordinary size, which is called, by an old name of the pagans, the Oak of Jupiter [Thor]. And when in the strength of his steadfast heart he had cut the lower notch, there was present a great multitude of pagans, who in their souls were most earnestly cursing the enemy of their gods. But when the fore side of the tree was notched only a little, suddenly the oak's vast bulk, driven by a divine blast from above, crashed to the ground, shivering its crown of branches as it fell; and, as if by the gracious compensation of the Most High, it was also burst into four parts, and four trunks of huge size, equal in length, were seen, unwrought by the brethren who stood by. At this sight the pagans who before had cursed now, on the contrary, believed, and blessed the Lord, and put away their former reviling.[1]

What we read here is very much in tune with previous and future guidelines given to missionaries from Rome, such as those provided by Pope St. Gregory the Great (c. 540–604) for St. Augustine of

[1] Willibald, *The Life of Saint Boniface*, trans. George W. Robinson (Cambridge: Harvard University Press, 1916), 62–63.

Canterbury (d. 604) in his expedition to Anglo-Saxon Britain in 598, as recorded by St. Bede the Venerable (c. 672–735), along with the *Responses* of Pope Nicholas I (c. 800–867) to the Bulgarians in 866 at the time of the Latin missions in the Balkans. Both of these pontiffs identify the role of the missionary as one requiring great caution in approaching pagans, their beliefs, and their sacred images.

Underlying their nuance is a profound perception of just how existential the truly life-changing "turning around" that "conversion" entails really is. Psychologically astute, these papal instructions drive home the fact that what one wants to do through "conversion" is to allow a man to "turn around" from a belief rooted in a valid natural desire to give meaning to his life in an impossibly false and self-destructive way to one answering that legitimate longing for existential meaning in a fully true and fruitful manner. Too harsh and too immediate an assault on a rooted pagan belief or custom could destroy these ties to a praiseworthy hunt for Truth in a dangerous way, replacing them only with a hopeless nihilism that benefits no one but Satan. But balancing prudence and evangelical zeal is not an easy task; missionary work is not to be left in the hands of unprepared sissies.

St. Willibald's account of St. Boniface's dramatic action near Fritzlar is in conformity with the guidelines of Gregory and Nicholas. For the Apostle to the Germans does not set about his obviously iconoclastic deed as a direct assault upon untutored pagans' central beliefs. Quite the contrary is true. *Willibald tells us that Boniface's primary reason for the demolition of Thor's Oak was the backsliding of German Catholics who had already converted.* These new believers were returning to blasphemous image worship, and it was they who, first and foremost, were the object of his concern. If we are to infer anything about the remaining German pagans in the region, Willibald's chronicle seems to identify a disturbed state of mind regarding the battle of divine images and whose side to come down upon definitively: that of the old pagan gods and their totems or the Cross of the God of the Christians. It seems to me that St. Boniface, completely convinced of the falsity of Thor and the truth of Christ, understood that his successful destruction of a tree whose proper iconic role in the hierarchy of values was being obscured through its improper pagan adoration, would bring these wavering pagans firmly, once and for all, into the Camp of the Saints. In short, the act of good "iconoclasm" had bad or weak Catholics as its primary target, and fence-sitting outsiders as its secondary focus.

Surely there is no doubt where I am taking this argument. Many contemporary Catholics globally—but most commonly in the formerly Christian West—have lost their Faith or are in the process of abandoning it. Perhaps even worse, those who have already left the flock often openly work to demoralize and undermine the commitment of those who wish to remain loyal members of it by disguising their very real apostasy. This apostasy, both open and disguised, is taking place from the top of the Catholic world to the bottom, displayed in everything from the adoration of Pachamama to the worship of the LGBTQ agenda as something eminently moral but long hidden from wicked Christians' world view, to the adulation of Joe Biden and his Moloch-like love for abortion as though he were the model of a solid Catholic statesman.

Our remaining brothers and sisters in the Faith are scandalized, but also demoralized by this ever-expanding madness, given that it is rarely contested by much of the Judas clergy, who lead their flock to the unquestioning veneration of patently false images. Their scandalized and endangered belief cries out to the heavens for good iconoclasts to destroy such open idolatry root and branch. Once again, a failure to answer that cry would be a dereliction of duty: not only to already existing and imperiled Christians, but also to the many, many people outside of the Catholic world who are longing for the True Faith and need its fundamental "icon"—the Word Incarnate and all that is corrected, redeemed, and transformed through His Revelation and His Grace—to shine forth and smother the dark light emitted from the manifold "Thor's Oaks" worshipped by our sick and dying world.

But there is also a third lesson to be gained from what happened at the original Thor's Oak. Let us remember that St. Boniface undertook his missionary labor after having gained the promise of military protection from the chief Frankish political leader, Charles Martel (c. 688–744), who was extending his political influence eastward into more easterly German regions at the time.

Now the letters of the Apostle of the Germans admit that this military and political alliance was a double-edged sword, since his "protector," like all men, could do bad as well as good. In point of fact, he believed that Charles Martel had all too often flexed his muscles in the religious realm in the wrong way, and to such a degree that he told his son Pepin that he believed his father was actually rotting in hell. In admitting this danger, Boniface was doing nothing other than reiterating the truth that the sacred character of each and every aspect of nature, all of which were meant to reflect and lead to the greater glory of God, political and military authority included, could only exercise their iconic roles properly under the corrective and transformative guidance of Christ and Christ's Church. Many confessors and martyrs were to drive that point home in other acts of good iconoclasm; in public preaching and exhortation designed to humble an invasive State claiming to know what was pleasing to the Lord on its own steam, and demanding worship of its improper decisions as the God's honest truth.

But exercise that role properly the State must! The Great Commission specifically indicates that it is not just individuals but *nations* that are to be converted to the worship of the Christian God. Nations involve authoritative institutions, and one of these is the State—the legitimate State—whose God-given task is to crush what harms the people that it rules. The good iconoclasm represented by the demolition of Thor's Oak—aimed primarily at saving Catholics from plunging back into the hands of the devil, and secondarily at giving the final push to those wavering between the worship of proper and improper "icons"—must ultimately demand authoritative State protection for a necessary image-smashing. If it does not do so, legitimate State *authority* is replaced by illegitimate, egotistical, arbitrary, often hidden—dare we say "Deep State"?—*force*. And this—whether in St. Boniface's day or that of Joe Biden, Kamala Harris, and Nancy Pelosi—shows no nuance or prudence in its demand for tossing the icon of the Cross at the foot of the Antichrist.

Catholics of the world! Sharpen your axes! The choice between battling for the True Faith, aided by the legitimate State, and the Bad Guys, leaning upon raw power, is all too clearly not outside Fritzlar, but at our doorstep.

23

Gerusalemme Liberata?[†]

IT WAS WITH THE ABOVE WORDS, THE TITLE of Torquato Tasso's epic poem of 1581 on the liberation of Jerusalem in the First Crusade, that the Kingdom of Italy illuminated state buildings in Rome to celebrate its British ally's capture of the Holy City from the Ottoman Empire during World War One. And indeed there were many Catholics that December of 1917 who were also ready to see the hand of God in this particular victory of the Entente over the Central Powers. To them, such a triumph meant that with Palestine in *Western* Christian hands, control of the Holy Places, which had been given by the Turkish authorities to the Orthodox in 1757, could now be returned to representatives of the Roman Church. As Pasquale Baldi wrote in *La Questione dei Luoghi Santi* of 1919:

> Today, the improbable has become a fact; today, due to a prodigious combination of events that we regard as providential, Italy, France, and England, three nations that took part in the Holy Wars, hold Jerusalem under their dominion. Today, then, the Catholics of the whole world can expect that the hour of justice may finally sound. Today, they can finally hope that for the Sanctuaries of Palestine the splendors of the era of Constantine may be renewed.... Today it no longer matters how many Greeks there are in the Ottoman Empire, but how many Catholics there are in the entire world. [1]

Unfortunately, the Great War was actually to prove to be the catalyst of a twentieth century Jerusalem and Palestinian nightmare that still frightfully shakes the peace of the globe in 2021. This is due to the fact that Britain made not one but three plans for the postwar future of the Arab region of the enemy Ottoman Empire. Worse still, all of these plans rudely conflicted with one another

---

† First published in *The Angelus*, July–August 2021.

---

1 Cited in Silvio Ferrari, "Pio XI, la Palestina, e I Luoghi Santi," in *Achille Ratti, Pape Pie XI* (Rome: École Française de Rome, 1996), 909.

and could not therefore bode anything but long-term trouble for Palestine and the Middle East as a whole; trouble that almost immediately saw understandable Catholic hope for control of the Holy Places take second place to fear of a much more worrisome threat.

Pasquale Baldi built his hopes upon the Sykes-Picot Agreement of May of 1916, as modified by the events of 1917–1918. That agreement had envisaged a joint Anglo-Franco-Russian responsibility over the Arab regions of the Ottoman Empire. The Bolshevik Revolution in the fall of 1917, and then the Soviet signing of the Treaty of Brest-Litovsk with the Germans the following year, removed the chief defender of Orthodoxy from the consortium of future guardians of the Middle East, leaving Britain and France as sole custodians of the region. It was from their cooperative western hands that justice for the Roman Church's rights was expected.

The Balfour Declaration, outlining a second British plan for a major part of the Middle East, posed the new danger. This was contained in a letter of November 2, 1917, from the British Foreign Minister, Arthur Balfour (1848–1930), to Lord Walter Rothschild (1868–1937), meant for transmission to the Zionist Federation of Great Britain and Ireland, led by Chaim Weizmann (1874–1952). It committed the United Kingdom to working with the Zionist Movement for the creation "in Palestine of a national home for the Jewish people."[2]

Before that Declaration, Pope Benedict XV (1914–1922), looking forward to western control of the Middle East, discounted any danger to Christian interests from the existence of small Jewish agricultural settlements in Palestine. Unlike Theodor Herzl (1860–1904), the founder of the Zionist Movement, who did not find St. Pius X (1903–1914) in any way receptive to his plans, Benedict, in May of 1917, gave a friendly welcome to Nahem Sokolow (1859–1936), another major Zionist leader. He told him he thought that Jews and Catholics would be "good neighbors" in the Holy Land.[3] But after Balfour's letter, as Cardinal Pietro

---

2   Arthur James Balfour, "Balfour Declaration 1917," The Avalon Project, https://avalon.law.yale.edu/20th_century/balfour.asp.
3   Cited in Sergio I. Minerbi, *The Vatican and Zionism: Conflict in the Holy Land, 1895–1925*, trans. Arnold Schwarz (New York: Oxford University Press, 1990), 112.

Gasparri (1852–1934), Benedict's Secretary of State, explained to the Belgian Ambassador to the Holy See, the danger that Turkish rule would be replaced by "the transformation of Palestine into a Jewish State," was perceived as being a deadly blow to Christian rights in the region.[4]

Both the Sykes-Picot Agreement *as well as* a Jewish "homeland" or "State" were distressing to the overwhelmingly Arab population of Palestine, whose postwar future had been envisaged very differently by the Hashemite Family, the third "partner" of the British in their varied plans for the post-Ottoman Middle East. That third plan was actually the earliest in time chronologically, sealed as it was by an agreement concluded in 1915 with Hussein bin Ali al-Hashimi (1854–1931), the Hashemite leader and Sheriff of Mecca, and his two sons, Abdullah (1882-1951) and Faisal (1885–1933). It was this pact that unleashed the revolt that was supposed to ensure the creation of an Arab Kingdom in the region under Hashemite rule. But how could Palestine figure into that Kingdom if it were simultaneously going to be under joint Franco-British guidance and also provide a national home for Jews as well?

Rome's fears for the Holy Land, awakened through the Balfour Declaration, were further intensified due to the accord sealed by British Prime Minister Lloyd George (1863–1945) with French Premier Georges Clemenceau (1841–1929) of 1918 and validated by the Supreme Allied Council in San Remo in April, 1920, awarding sole control of Palestine to Great Britain. This decision would inevitably strengthen the supporters of the Anglo-Zionist agreement. And given that Greece at that time looked as though it could gain possession of Constantinople, and that one major segment of the Anglican Church was becoming more and more friendly with the Orthodox theologically, the Vatican worried that an Anglo-Orthodox union might use British power in Palestine to crush Roman claims to guidance of the Holy Places. Catholics would lose footing in the region in two distinct ways.

Mustafa Kemal (1881–1938), the "Father" of the Republic of Turkey, soon dashed Greek designs on Constantinople, eliminating one of Rome's fears. Nevertheless, the Vatican intervened as strongly as possible to try to block the League of Nations'

---

4   Cited in Minerbi, *The Vatican and Zionism*, 119.

confirmation of Britain's so-called "Mandate" to sole rule in Palestine in 1922. The Mandate articles under consideration gave to Britain the task of creating political, economic, and administrative conditions for the constitution of a national Jewish home in Palestine (Article 2), establishing a Jewish entity to collaborate with the Mandate authority in all questions relevant to the development of Jewish interests and the execution of works of public utility (Articles 4, 11), and favoring Jewish immigration, settlement, and acquisition of Palestinian citizenship (Articles 6, 7).

Cardinal Gasparri, in his observations to the Council of the League of Nations of May 15, 1922, explained that the Holy See had no objection to equal rights for Jews, but the articles in question went beyond equality, giving the migrants a special position to the detriment of what were referred to as the "non-Jewish communities existing in Palestine"—namely, 83% of the current population. The Secretary of State noted that Article 22 of the Treaty of Versailles spoke of Mandates as having a "sacred, civilizing mission." And yet such a goal would seem to be trampled if the present, indigenous, and overwhelmingly majority population were subordinated to a new, minority national group. "Civilization" would be equated with exploitation.

Vatican objections were powerful enough to cause the League to delay approval of the Mandate. Chaim Weizmann, by then the head of the World Zionist Organization, found that he could now not even arrange a meeting with Pope Benedict—who apparently was upset by the way in which his earlier encounter with Sokolow had been used to exaggerate his approval of Jewish migration to the Holy Land—to negotiate a change of policy. Yet despite this setback, Sir Herbert Samuel (1870–1963), the British High Commissioner for Palestine, did meet with Benedict's successor, Pius XI (1922–1939), on July 6, 1922, and somehow succeeded in calming Rome's fears sufficiently to allow for the League's final approval of the Mandate without further Vatican intervention.

There were two schools of thought in Rome regarding the situation in interwar Palestine, whose basic premises can be followed in the pages of the two most authoritative Roman "mouthpieces": the *Osservatore Romano* and *La Civiltà Cattolica*, A minority judged Zionism positively, considering the return of the Jews to the Holy Land to be providential; a passage towards their general conversion, and a sign of the imminence of the Second Coming. Supporters of this view called the conversion of Theodore Herzl's son a "logical" consequence of the return to Zion. Opponents contested just how logical this conversion actually was, given the vehemence with which it was vehemently denounced within the *Yishuv*, the Zionist Community in Palestine.

The majority view, favored by *La Civiltà Cattolica*, was extremely hostile to the entire Zionist Movement. It continued to see the Jewish Diaspora as a punishment of the People of Israel for Christ's Crucifixion. Moreover, the Jewish migration into Palestine was attacked for its blatant secularism, and its consequent promotion of a modernization of the region destructive of the sacred and moral character of the Holy Land. In an article of 1937 entitled "The Jewish Question and Zionism," *La Civiltà Cattolica* condemned the Movement as nothing other than a third example of secularist Jewish effort to dominate the world, the occupation of the globe's most sacred space accompanying its monopolization of the capitalist financial world and its role in promoting revolutionary Bolshevism: "There is no disguising the fact—the British representative to the Vatican admitted in 1923—that the jubilations which greeted the British occupation of Palestine has given place to a noticeable uncertainty and suspicion; a feeling, too, that there was greater liberty for the Church and religion under the regime of the Turks."[5]

British Mandate rule in Palestine in the interwar period was plagued by an indecision leading to drastic changes of policy that ended by alienating every party concerned. Pro-Zionism characterized its approach in the 1920s, so much so that in 1924, the Jerusalem correspondent of the *Osservatore Romano* complained that Europeans were underestimating the seriousness of the efforts of the Jews to gain full control of Palestine. The public authorities of the *Yishuv*, aided as they were by the World Zionist Organization, were said to be so sophisticated that the Arab opposition would not be able to arrest their advance by one step. This warning was confirmed by the Italian Consul General in 1927, who advised his government to work together openly with the Jews, since they would, without a doubt, be the future leaders of the Holy Land.

5 "The Jewish Question and Zionism," *La Civiltà Cattolica* 88, no. 2 (1937): 418–31.

Riots in 1929 brought about a British reconsideration of its policy in Palestine in a way that first looked to limiting Jewish immigration and settlement. Pressure from the World Zionist Organization caused the United Kingdom to abandon this change of policy, sparking the Great Arab Revolt of 1936–1939. Suppression of that rebellion caused the Mandate authorities to cultivate the services of the officially illegal *Yishuv* military defense organization, the *Haganah*. But with the revolt subdued, and the chief Moslem Arab leader, the Grand Mufti (Judge) of Jerusalem, Mohammed Amin al-Husseni (1897–1974), in exile in Berlin, British plans then changed drastically anew. They now envisaged an immediate end to Jewish immigration, and the creation within ten years of an independent democratic Palestine that the Arab population, still 70% strong, would unavoidably control.

Hence, just at the beginning of the Second World War, the Jewish settlers, friendly to the British in their conflict with Germany, were to turn against them inside Palestine. This meant not only potential trouble from the *Haganah*, under the control of the Old Zionists, but also from the *Irgun*, the paramilitary force of the much more militant Revisionist Zionists, founded by Ze'ev Jabotinsky (1880–1940). Both these Zionist forces were to cause problems for the Mandate authorities, the Arab population, and one another, beyond the creation of the State of Israel in 1948, and right up until the present day.

In 1943, in the midst of the war, Monsignor Domenico Tardini (1888–1961), the assistant for external affairs under Pope Pius XII's Secretary of State, Cardinal Luigi Maglione (1877–1944), reaffirmed Rome's position unambiguously: "The Holy See," he said, "has never approved the project of making Palestine a Jewish home."[6] He also made it clear that the Vatican disapproved of suggestions for partitioning the region, given that there would be Christian minorities in both a Jewish and a Moslem Palestine. Rather than either of these options, the Holy See preferred that the British remain in control as the Mandate authority. That still seemed to be the best guarantee of a "free Jerusalem" where Christians could worship God with some semblance of security.

But what if a continued British presence in the area were to

---

6 Cited in John F. Morley, *Vatican Diplomacy and the Jews during the Holocaust, 1939–1943* (New York: KTAV Publishing House, 1980), 92.

prove to be a pipe dream? That was a distinct possibility. World War One had already convinced the Papacy that Europe was dedicated to its self-destruction and that the future of the Roman Catholic Church had to be secured through its worldwide development. It was this sober assessment that lay behind Rome's more conscious commitment to ensuring an indigenous episcopacy and clergy throughout the globe, Palestine included. It was this judgment that also caused the Holy See to befriend the national movements that it deemed more and more inevitable, and to find ways to steer them from potential union with purely secularist forces, especially Marxist parties. Rome's anti-Mandate intervention in the early 1920s had stressed concern for the exploitation of the majority Arab population in Palestine—the exact same complaint that this community's own representatives in London had simultaneously expressed. In the interwar period, both the Latin Patriarch, Msgr. Luigi Barlassina (1872–1947), and Eastern Catholic prelates like Bishop Gregorios Hajjar (d. 1940), favored an alliance with the Arab Moslems in a joint, religious-focused, anti-Zionist and anti-Marxist union.

As the war came to an end, the thought that support for a religion-friendly, Arab-dominated Palestine might be a suitable guarantee of a *Gerusalemme Liberata* after all was beginning to take root. Little could anyone in the still Catholic pontificate of Pius XII imagine that in the not-too-distant future, the dominant opinion within the Roman Church would view secularist Pluralism as the best support for the freedom of the Christian world, and the Old Covenant as an equal with the New—-and this, just as Jewish and Arab Moslem religious revival were reaching their peak. Little could anyone then have foreseen that the Vatican would consider prayer at the Holy Places as "non-essential" as prayer anywhere else under the tyrannical reign of the Covid god—regardless of who might be in control of them.

24

What a Woman Must Do

THE FEMININE MYSTIQUE VERSUS
THE BRIGADES OF ST. JOAN OF ARC?[†]

F ORGIVE ME FOR BEGINNING THIS ARTICLE
for *The Angelus* issue on women with reference to a term
associated by most Americans with the title of a book published by
Betty Friedan in 1963 that played a central role in launching the
Feminist Movement in the United States. The reason why I feel
compelled to do so is because the word "mystique," employed in
this context, has a very serious and specifically twentieth century
Catholic history to it. A brief glance at this background intro-
duces us to a modern Catholic teaching concerning what it is
that a woman who wants to be a "real Christian woman" must
do if she wishes to "fulfill her potential" and perfect herself. Not
surprisingly, that teaching is totally contradictory to traditional
Catholic thought on this subject, the nature of which I would
like to illustrate through an example offered by Mexican women
at the time of the Cristeros War of 1926–1929.

Use of the word "mystique" was popularized in the 1920s and
1930s, primarily in France, Germany, and Belgium, from three
interconnected sources: the lay promoters of the many-headed
philosophy known as "Personalism," Dominicans and Jesuits spreading what eventually became known as the "New Theology," and
monks eager for a "pastoral" as opposed to a God-centered liturgical reform. Those embracing this term pressed both missionaries
as well as militants engaged in so-called "Specialized Catholic
Action" among youth and workers to the conclusion that their
essential evangelical task was that of recognizing the particular
"spirit"—again, the "mystique"—most passionately stimulating the
distinct group to which they ministered. Once that specific, invig-
orating mystique had been isolated, the labor of the activist then
became one of "witnessing" to its obvious inherent value, since it
could not possibly exercise the vital, passionate impact that it did

---

† First published in *The Angelus*, September–October 2021.

on the groups in question unless the Holy Spirit were somehow behind it, moving its members away from narrow, self-interested, purely individual goals towards full Christian perfection as communal-minded "persons."

What might be labeled the ideology of "mystique-ism" is really nothing more than yet another naturalist Enlightenment recipe for accepting *fallen* nature on its own marred terms, dressed up rhetorically by modern sophistic arguments. Its association of the voice of the Holy Spirit with "vital passions" cannot help but hand over the teaching and sacramental office to the strongest, most willful, most bullying elements of the communities that it targets, with all serious correction of truly narrow sinfulness and real transformation in Christ being abandoned as obstacles to the development of a Divine Plan whose real character it so badly distorts. Under its spell, the duty of Catholics becomes that of keeping their mouths shut, "witnessing" to the triumph of the human will masquerading as that of God, and "accompany-ing" unrepentant bullies in their work of oppression and ultimate self-destruction. "Mystique-ism" leads to the perfection of monsters, not of Christians.

"Mystique" hunters of the 1920s and 1930s were excited by the thought of witnessing to and accompanying all the contemporary vital forces around them, with Fascist and Communist groups at the top of the list. Let us briefly explore the deeply anti-Catholic consequences for all communities following such distorted guide-lines for perfection by returning to our current topic concern-ing the large community encompassing half of the human race: women. Under "mystique-ism's" dictates, willful, bullying women ready to impose their uncorrected and sinful desires upon all who share their gender become the determinants of the "feminine mystique" to which all Catholic evangelists must "witness." The Holy Spirit will brook no obstacles being placed in their totally inward-looking, elitist, self-degrading path. Both the Magisterium as well as a pastoral-minded Liturgy must be reshaped according to the purely naturalist truths the oppressors reveal to us, along with the ever more grotesque practical and moral changes these entail. Toughness, corporate aggressiveness, unrestrained ambition economically and politically, as well as joyful openness to sexual promiscuity and abortion become the marks of the fulfilled and perfected woman. Indeed, they become the signposts pointing to the female Catholic saint as well.

Honest believers can easily smell a rat and understand that "mystique-ism" exalts a revolutionary travesty of the meaning of feminine fulfillment and perfection. For, as St. James tells us in the Epistle bearing his name, every good and perfect gift comes from outside of us, from above, from the Father of Lights, and not from heeding the inward desires of souls that have been directed away from the achievement of God's good plan for man and nature by Original Sin. When we look purely to ourselves for the source of our perfection, we condemn our souls to shriveling and death.

A truly Catholic example of identifying "what a Christian woman must do" in this earthly valley of tears, and at a moment when changing circumstances seemed to call for further and possibly unconventional action on her part, comes from Mexico, in the very same years that "mystique-ism" was rising to the fore in Europe. Those wishing to explore in greater detail what I will merely summarize below should read an article by Sister Barbara Miller, "The Role of Women in the Mexican Cristero Rebellion: Las Señoras Y Las Religiosas," published in *The Americas* in January of 1984.[1]

Most Americans are unaware of the brilliant Mexican Catholic Social Movement born in the years preceding the Revolution that erupted in 1910. This came to full maturity in battles against an increasingly anticlerical government in the decades that followed; a conflict at first fought peacefully, but then ultimately by force of arms in the Cristeros War of 1926–1929. Part of that Movement was distinctively feminine: the Union de Damas Catolicas Mejicanas. Founded in 1912, the *Damas Catolicas* really blossomed from 1920 onwards as one of the four central branches of Blessed Anacleto Gonzalez Flores' (1888–1927) national Union Popular and then his Liga National Defensora de la Libertad Religiosa.

The Damas Catolicas recognized that Mexican society was facing many new problems raising social justice and moral questions, including those connected with young women independently entering more and more into the public workforce.

---

1   Sr. Barabara Miller, "The Role of Women in the Mexican Cristero Rebellion: Las Señoras Y Las Religiosas," *The Americas* 40, no. 3 (January 1984): 303–323, https://doi.org/10.2307/981116.

Their answer to these developments was not to investigate their own passionate feelings about such matters, followed by a call for alterations in Church teaching, liturgy, and morality to respond to them. Rather, it was to promote more extensive access to quality Catholic education and devout reception of the Sacraments so as to be able to confront the changing world around them with a deeper understanding of the Faith and the need for Grace: both of them coming from outside themselves, "from above, from the Father of Lights."

It was to assure the proper fulfillment of this outward-looking, basically educative mission that the Damas in 1926 became more activist than they had ever dreamed possible beforehand. During that year, the revolutionary government significantly tightened its controls over the Roman Catholic Church, closing large numbers of Catholic schools and expelling the teaching religious, many of them women, many of them foreigners, from their houses and the churches serving them. The *Damas* moved from dispatching simple letters of protest to militant street action, blocking the doors to schools and churches to the entry of the troops sent to dislodge religious from them. These latter actions resulted in dramatic encounters with soldiers and government ministers who often treated the protestors brutally, beating and imprisoning numbers of them and even threatening them with sexual violence. "Men of the whole Republic, there are your models," their journal, *La Dama Catolica*, proudly boasted on May 1, 1926, after the first of their women had taken to the streets. "Go hide your shame in the dark caverns of our forests."[2]

Calls to further, still more unconventional feminine action came by the end of that year with the outbreak of actual hostilities in the Cristeros War, to which the *Liga* gave its full support and sought to direct. Once again, women judged what was proper for them to do in the midst of this terrible crisis on the basis not of their passionate internal feelings, but with reference to what needed to be accomplished to ensure external access to the teachings of the Faith and transforming sacramental grace. Dealing with the latter necessity became particularly dramatic since the government's effort to determine which clerics it would or would not

---

2   Cited in Miller, "The Role of Women," 310.

allow to perform Church services had gone so far that the bishops suspended all regular sacramental activity to avoid it.

By June of 1927, Mexican women had formed Las Brigadas Femeninas de Santa Juana de Arco, to whose success they bound themselves with vows to resist the revolutionary government to the death. At their height, these "Feminine Brigades of St. Joan of Arc" numbered fifty six squadrons enrolling twenty five thousand militants. But their story is a complicated one, their members including or at least being aided by three types of women: the *señoras*, the *religiosas*, and the *jovenes*.

As far as I can determine, the Damas Catolicas composed mostly of middle and upper class women from the very start of their apostolate, formed the bulk of the *señoras*. These women could not bring themselves to accept an actual fighting role in the Cristeros War, but did absolutely everything that they could to support the cause. The Damas courageously remained the active, open "voice" of the movement for the defense of Catholic freedom, printing broadsheets against the government and even organizing illegal processions in honor of Christ the King. Members hid hunted priests and wounded fighters, raising money to ransom captive prisoners and provide for the families of those who were fighting.

A second militant component, that represented by the *religiosas*, the female teaching religious, played a less passive role. Unlike the *señoras*, they either had to flee to Cristero-held territory or go underground, often living under conditions of extreme harshness, moving from den to den, and sometimes suffering an imprisonment and bestial treatment therein. Their chief apostolate was to sustain the spirit of the soldiers. They prepared meals for and nursed Cristeros in towns in which they could function openly, organizing espionage networks for them in places where they had to hide. In fact, they even told the great Cristero General, Enrico Goristieta (1888–1929), that they were ready to take up arms alongside the regular male soldiery if absolutely necessary. "We were young," one of them said later, "but we suffered for Christ enthusiastically. I am happy to have suffered in that time."[3] They were ready to carry on "until victory or death."[4] "Fulfillment of their personal needs" meant nothing to them whatsoever.

---

3   Cited in Miller, 314.
4   Miller, 313.

Finally, the third segment, the *jovenes*, the young, overwhelmingly lower class in background, while also seemingly mostly engaged in gun and ammunition running, as well as nursing, openly fought as well. In June of 1929, one of the founders of the Brigadas, Luz Laraza de Uribe, better known as "General" Tesia Richaud, was captured, beaten and tortured. She died not for the victory of the feminine mystique but for the glory of her Savior, her final words of "Viva Cristo Rey" preparing her path to true perfection and eternal life in heaven. Is it any wonder that one of the Cristero leaders rhetorically asked the question: "What would the Mexican men be if the Mexican women did not exist?"[5] One answer to that query is that they would have lacked a brilliant example of what all Catholics must do *properly* to "fulfill themselves."

Señoras, religiosas, and *jovenes* all did what they believed that they had to do in to keep the outside channels of the Faith and Grace open to themselves and their loved ones. Although the end of the Cristeros War was a messy one, involving much in the way of betrayal of the cause by an all too accommodating Vatican and those Mexican bishops in alliance with it, by 1940 the situation of Catholics in that troubled country had significantly improved. Mexican women of all of the three categories that appear to have played some role in the general labor of the Brigades of St. Joan of Arc then asked nothing better than to return to more quiet educative tasks to perfect and transform themselves in Christ.

Although an examination of the collapse of civilizations provides us with the dreary sight of one sinking ship after another, such gloom and doom is usually relieved by the identification of at least some political, social, or cultural vessel still sufficiently seaworthy to allow those seeking to escape a given historical tsunami some viable ark on which to survive. What comes most readily to mind in this regard is the situation in the Western Roman Empire in the fifth century AD, where the complete ruin threatened by the dissolution of the secular imperial order under the pressure of barbarian invasions was step by step averted through the unexpected political efforts of wise and holy popes and bishops whose real mission was nevertheless dedicated to the creation of a supernatural community.

---

5   Cited in Miller, 312.

No such solace can be found in the midst of our contemporary catastrophe. Today, literally every single social pillar has been diverted from its proper function to grotesque ends. All of them—Family, Labor, Capital, Education, State, and Church—exalt naturalist Enlightenment *mystiques* demanding submission, as they always do, to the triumph of the willful, passionate powers that dictatorially define what these mean. Each has been so perverted that its chief function has become that of drowning the individuals it was meant to help clamber aboard its distinctive ark to avoid the floodwaters of earthly misery. All forces essential for the creation, preservation, and exaltation of the lives of human persons are united as never before in assuring individual degradation and destruction, with the current Pontiff serving as Supreme Spokesman for "mystique-ism," "witnessing" and "accompanying" the reigning Oligarchs in their oppression of all men and women of good will.

Good popes forced by historical circumstances in Late Antiquity to undertake certain tasks that were not intended to be part of their mission were at least themselves also servants of a living social institution and took their responsibility to maintain the full Catholic Tradition seriously. It is now atomistic individuals, stripped almost entirely of communal aid, who are in the unenviable position of having to assume a much wider gamut of responsibilities totally on their own.

What is an individual woman to do, thrown back on her own devices, under such alarming conditions? Under no circumstances is she to turn inward to consult "the feminine mystique." She can spare herself the effort, because this, as usual, will be infallibly defined and shoved down her throat by the most aggressive ideologues and criminals in union with the Global Oligarchy of our day anyway. Her effort will only serve their cause.

Instead, she is to do what Catholic women—just like Catholic men—have always been obliged to do: aim her mind and spirit outward and upward, to the correction and transformation in Christ that alone will truly fulfill and perfect her. To a large degree that means simply holding firm to the Tradition, for, as Archbishop Lefebvre said, our future lies in our past, and it is our duty to pass on what we have received from that Tradition untrammeled. But to hand down that Tradition effectively under the dictatorship of the ruling Oligarchy today will mean imitating the activist example of the Mexican *señoras, religiosas, y jovenes* at the time of the Cristeros, if only to carry on the basic familial mission of protecting one's loved ones. Mistakes will be made in the process—there is no doubt about it. But, as Napoleon was wont to say, when battle is forced upon us, *on s'y engage et puis on voit*—one engages the enemy and sees what happens. The *unum necessarium* is to look to the supernatural message of the Cross and not to the natural one of the willfully manipulated and sinful *mystique. Christus vincit; Christus regnat; Christus imperat. Viva Cristo Rey!!*

25

Truth, Custom, Trent,
Baroque Culture, and Spain?[†]

*"Christ said 'I am the Truth.' He did not say,
'I am custom.'"* [1] —TERTULLIAN

I. THE BAROQUE SPIRIT AND THE FULLNESS OF THE
CATHOLIC TRADITION

My personal awakening to the full meaning of Catholic Christendom came in the summer of 1973 on my first trip to Rome.
Trapped one particularly sultry afternoon in a welter of medieval
streets, and eager to locate some cover from the sun and a source of
liquid refreshment, I was rapidly losing all my interest in tourism.
As narrow lanes led to tinier passageways that appeared to be
nothing more than escape-tunnel size cracks between the walls of
citadel-like palaces, my frustration became ever more intolerable.
Finally, when all hope seemed lost, there I was—luxuriating in a
magnificent Baroque piazza, equipped with refreshing fountains,
watering holes, and stunning architecture, sculpture, and painting,
both religious and secular.

What soon dawned on me—and what was then confirmed
and sharpened by my reading—was that the architects who had
conceived that piazza—which lifted up the spirit while nevertheless offering all that the body could wish—were conscious of
the intricate connection of both the basic "stuff" as well as the
overall plan of human existence. Their implicit call to discover
"more than meets the eye" in the highly diverse, changing, and
often very petty components of daily existence—a call reflected
throughout the Baroque achievement—drove home the teaching
that one could only interpret the particular and often quite quirky
components of earthly life properly by looking at them through
the eyes of God. If one ignored the jumble of the human condition, in all of its complexity, good and bad, reality was lost; if

---

† First published in *Verbo*, August–September–October 2021.

---

1 Tertullian, "De virginibus velandis," 1209.

one discounted the plan behind it, the drama of existence was obscured by what could be taken for a display of nothing more than pathetic meaninglessness.

All this considered, I would argue that the "Baroque" sense of the acceptance of the complexity and difficulties of discerning the "stuff" of reality as essential parts in the divine plan is not something unique in the history of Christendom, but, rather, a brilliant, particular, historically bound *revival* and *further development* of what lies at the very heart of the Catholic Tradition in general. For the implications of this supposedly purely "Baroque" vision—one of conscious use of each and every one of the building blocks of nature, stubbornly marred by sin, to build a stairway to heaven, to achieve the "transformation of all things in Christ"—were being discussed and acted upon with ever greater refinements throughout the history of Christendom from its very outset.

A splendid *western* Christian contribution to this universal Catholic enterprise took place in the centuries beginning with the monastic reforms promoted by centers like Cluny in Burgundy from the tenth century onwards. At that time, all of the tools of mind and heart jointly needed to understand God's message, and then bring to fruition the task of transformation in Christ, found powerful intellectual and spiritual supporters, while varied pastoral approaches for embedding the Truth in the population at large also flourished. Popes like Innocent III brilliantly summarized the thrust of the entire project, vigorously emphasizing as he did the need to nuance pastoral work according to the unique problems of specific individuals and groups, those of the most unlikely candidates for sainthood included.[2]

Unfortunately, problems that became especially apparent from the thirteenth century onwards interrupted this development of the Catholic Tradition, not just stalling its further unfolding but also placing weighty roadblocks in the path of believers eager to learn of the fullness of the message. Tertullian (c. 155–c. 220), attacking flawed perceptions of the Faith in his own day, rather snidely wrote that Christ said that He was "the Truth," not what was "customary."[3] Flawed "customs" obscuring the knowledge and

---

2   On Innocent, see Powell, *Innocent III*, 1–33, 178–184; On the whole Cluniac Movement, see Rao, *Black Legends*, 117–170.
3   Tertullian, "De virginibus velandis," 1209.

pursuit of the true path to transformation in Christ took deep root in late medieval Christendom, cutting off the natural "stairways to heaven" that Baroque Catholicism was to do so much to open up and widen.

II. A DEVELOPING TRADITION OBSCURED BY FLAWED CUSTOMS

Numerous ecclesiastical and secular problems help to explain this interruption of the always difficult pilgrimage to God and its replacement with flawed approaches to learning and putting the Christian message into practice on the individual and corporate level, which, becoming "customary," were erroneously equated with Catholic Truth. Such problems include the inglorious collapse of the Crusading Movement, Church-State battles leading to the establishment of the Papacy in Avignon, the Plague, chaos in the Holy Roman Empire, the Hundred Years' War, the Great Western Schism, and ultimately the scandalous behavior of many Renaissance clerics and political figures. All of these factors contributed mightily to making the effort of working to transform nature in Christ a task that seemed to be an utterly impossible fool's task.

More important to our discussion here is the theoretical minefield laid in the lap of Catholics seeking to explore the fullness of the Christian message and put its transformative mission into action. This minefield was also complex in character, although its end effect can be easily explained. Quite simply, it blew to bits the union of the two branches of the sacred sciences whose harmonious cooperation is crucially needed to grasp the Divine Plan: the *positive branch*, which is concerned with the literary and living historical sources of the Faith, and the *speculative*, which employs human reason, logic, and philosophy as a whole to explicating the written and living message to guide its proper practical playing out in time. Hotheaded proponents of both speculative and positive theology contributed to the divorce in question.[4]

St. Bernard (1090–1153) may have been too harsh in his critique of the destructive arrogance of speculative thinkers like Peter Abelard (1079–1142). On the other hand, the complaints of John

---

4 The best text to use to follow the unfortunate development discussed below is Georges de Lagarde, *La naissance de l'esprit laïque au déclin du moyen âge, vol. 1–5* (Nauwelaerts, 1958). See also Rao, *Black Legends*, 171–246.

of Salisbury (1110s–1180), the Bishop of Chartres, ring all too true regarding an eclipse of all non-speculative studies necessary to Christian learning in the face of the Aristotelian onslaught in the twelfth century stimulated by an often exaggerated, ideological emphasis upon the value of pure logic. For a rather dry Aristotelian logic and philosophical approach to learning, isolated as it can be from Scripture, the Platonic-minded Church Fathers, the living, historical Catholic Tradition, and that feel for rhetoric which is so effective in pastoral work can never be sufficient for the complete understanding of the Christian vision and its practical application.

Nevertheless, the revenge of the enemies of speculative thought was perhaps even more deeply damaging. At the top of the list of these foes of Realist Aristotelian thinkers were extreme Nominalist philosophers who condemned the supposedly blasphemous arrogance of attempting to put the human mind at the service of the message of the Revelation, and insisted that God's inscrutable "will" must be accepted without trying to extrapolate and understand it. Alas, this apparent exaltation of "Christian humility" actually tended to lead to the equation of "God's will" with whatever it was that all too human individuals claimed that will to be.

The same was true of others who criticized the "pridefully ignorant" speculative endeavors of the Realist, Aristotelian Scholastics, and interpreted the "divine will" with their own diverse tools. These critics included a number of supporters of different schools of mystical thought and many Renaissance Humanists: the former claiming to learn of God's will by means of the messages imparted through their own interior spiritual lives; the latter through rhetorically inspiring, ancient literary works—at best, those of Scripture and the Church Fathers, and at worst texts that were purely pagan Greco-Roman masterpieces. Legal positivists who were eager to glorify the supposedly "Christian will" of whoever might hold power in the State were another all too prominent group gaining great influence from their assault on a speculative theological identification of truth and falsehood that placed obstacles in the way of the exercise of pure coercive force.

In short, the revenge of the enemies of speculative theology guaranteed the victory of the arbitrary will: the will of the ruler, whose judgments are "law" in the mind of the legal positivists; the will of the mystic, to whom God speaks directly; and the will of the Humanist, who turns beautiful words to the service of whatever seems worthy of promoting to him—and profitable to boot. And in the teaching and administrative life of the late medieval Church, what this specifically meant was the exaltation of the plenitude of Petrine Power by canonists in the pay of the Holy See on the basis of papal "will" alone; a tragic application of Nominalist theological principles to the daily practical life of the Body of Christ. Hence, the dangerous words of the canonist in the *Determinatio compendiosa* of 1342:

> Especially is he, the pope, above every council and statute; . . . he it is, too, who has no superior on earth; he, the pope, gives dispensations from every law. . . . Again, it is he who possesses the plenitude of power on earth and holds the place and office of the Most High. . . . He it is who alters the substance of a thing, making legitimate what was illegitimate . . . and of a monk making a canon regular, . . . he it is who by absolving on earth absolves [also] in heaven, and by binding on earth binds [also] in heaven. . . . Again, it is to him that nobody may say: "Why do you do that?" . . . He it is for whom the will is reason enough, since that which pleases him has the force of law (*ei quod placet, legis vigorem habet*); . . . he is not bound by the laws . . . *etc* (*solutus est legibus*). Indeed, the pope is the law itself and a living law (*lex viva*), to resist which is impermissible. This then is the Catholic and orthodox faith, approved and canonized by the holy fathers of old, from which all justice, religion, sanctity and discipline have emanated. If anyone does not believe it faithfully and firmly, he cannot be saved, and without doubt will perish eternally.[5]

"God's will," which over time was equated with "papal will," was then used to justify endless abuses, the most destructive of which was the persistent treatment of diocesan administration from the standpoint of Roman economic needs rather than local pastoral concerns. Wherever papal will could be enforced, bishoprics were often assigned either to curial officials—to provide, from their endowments, salaries the Papacy could not otherwise pay—or to friends of political allies whose cooperative behavior needed to be rewarded.

---

5 Francis Oakley, *The Western Church in the Later Middle Ages* (Ithaca: Cornell University Press, 1979), 165.

Since it was impossible for papal (or political) employees to leave their administrative positions to tend to even one diocese—much less the two or more often entrusted to their misuse—episcopal charges inevitably entailed the same absenteeism practiced by the Roman Pontiff himself while in Avignon. Perhaps the most bizarre development from such unfortunate policies was to be the creation of nominal "bishops" who were occasionally not even priests. Such "bishops" got the revenues from their "property," and then employed some consecrated hireling to do the episcopal tasks they themselves could not or would not perform. The result, in any event, was crystal clear: local bishops, whose oversight was desperately needed to bring transformation in Christ to fruition in a nuanced way in varied pastoral settings, were systematically hindered from doing what their apostolic task involved. While God might be claimed to "will this," in practice His truth was being trampled by what step-by-step had become simply papal and curial "custom."

III. SPANISH RECONNECTION WITH THE FULLNESS OF THE CATHOLIC VISION

In order to reconnect with the fullness of the Catholic vision and give it new life, thereby permitting later "Baroque" culture to do its part in developing that vision still further, two things were first necessary: a recovery of all of the tools required for a sound appreciation of Christian doctrine, and the kind of nuanced pastoral approach already encouraged by Pope Innocent III to bring that transformative doctrinal message and grace effectively into the lives of different groups and individuals. Much was done to encourage recovery of these tools at the Council of Trent. But the Council of Trent would not itself have been capable of fulfilling this task had it not been pushed to do so by outside forces active in such labor for a good long time beforehand, with Spanish influence probably the most important of all.

Let us examine the Spanish role in the recovery of this two-fold set of tools, beginning with those providing doctrinal solidity. This great achievement, like the divorce of the sacred sciences discussed above, is also rather simple to explain. Spain developed institutions and offered teachers that overcame the self-destructive intellectual battle poisoning the late medieval world, "joining together what no man should put asunder"—speculative and positive theology—to the perfection of both these partners in seeking divine knowledge.

The first of the great names associated with this fruitful endeavor is the Franciscan Church reformer and statesman, Cardinal Ximenez de Cisneros (1436–1517), who, on July 24, 1508, founded the College of San Ildefonso at the rather modest University at Alcalá de Henares that he himself had for a time attended. to enliven his foundation, he brought along with him a group of students recruited from the much larger University of Salamanca where he had also studied.[6]

Francisco de Vitoria (1486–1546), who began teaching at Salamanca in 1524, led that university into its days of greatest renown. He did so not just through his own teaching, but through those of his fellow Dominican disciples as well, especially Domingo de Soto (1494–1560), who had also done some studies at the Alcalá, and Melchior Cano (1509–1560), who was to be influential at the University of Valladolid as well as at Salamanca. The nascent Society of Jesus, so important at Trent, and central to Catholic education in the post-Tridentine "Baroque" world, was to benefit greatly from both the Alcalá and Salamanca, incorporating the "marriage" of speculative and positive theology that these institutions and their greatest representatives had effectively brokered.[7]

---

6   On the Alcalá, see "University of Alcalá," Catholic Online, accessed September 9, 2023, https://www.catholic.org/encyclopedia/view.php?id=419; Luis Fernández de Retana, Cisneros y su siglo; estudio histórico de la vida y actuación pública del Cardenal D. Fr. Francisco Ximénez de Cisneros, vol. 1–2 (Madrid: El Perpetuo Socorro, 1929–1930); and Bernhard Knorn, SJ, "Theological Renewal after the Council of Trent? The Case of Jesuit Commentaries on the *Summa Theologiae,*" *Theological Studies* 79, no. 1 (March 2018): 107–127, https://doi.org/10.1177/0040563917744653.

7   See Paul Oskar Kristeller, *Renaissance Thought: The Classic, Scholastic, and Humanist Strains* (New York: Harper & Row, 1961) and Hubert Jedin, *Geschichte des Konzils von Trient, vol. 1–4* (Freiburg: Herder, 1950–1975). Jedin's book catalogues the Spanish contribution throughout its volumes. To begin with, one could look at vol. 1, 114, 123, 129, 321, 420, 428, 445, 502, 607; Francisco de Vitoria, *Vitoria: Political Writings,* ed. Anthony Pagden and Jeremy Lawrance (Cambridge: Cambridge University Press, 1991); Norman Doe, ed., *Christianity and Natural Law* (Cambridge: Cambridge University Press, 2017); Juan José Pérez Camacho and Ignacio Sols Lucia, "Domingo de Soto en el Origen de la ciencia moderna," *Revista de Filosofía* 7 (1994): 455–475, https://core.ac.uk/reader/38842510; John R. Volz, "Melchior Cano," in *The Catholic Encyclopedia, vol. 3,* ed. Charles G. Herbermann et al., (New York: Robert

What the Spaniards did was simply to reconnect with the best thinkers of the Realist school of scholastic speculative theology, so badly neglected due to Nominalist and reductionist Renaissance ridicule, and then utilize the logical surgical instruments these Realists so well sharpened in tandem with the literary concerns and skills they learned from the Humanists. St. Thomas Aquinas was at the top of the list of the redeemed Realists, although the works of later thinkers, even Nominalist critics, sometimes expressing a specific thought that was valuable, were not shunned either. Meanwhile, San Idelfonso also promoted the studies of Greek, Hebrew, and rhetoric so dear to Christian Humanist hearts, while those attending the Alcalá, Salamanca, and Valladolid developed that interest in the Scriptures, the Church Fathers and Church History which positive theology cultivates as well. All this together enriched their knowledge of the sources of Catholic Truth, their logical ability to understand its consequences, and their talent for explaining it with a sense of proper style. Once again, what was accomplished at the Alcalá and Salamanca was digested by the Jesuits and fed the successes of their educational network later on.

Allow me to elaborate on this theme just a bit further. It was due to Vitoria's imparting to his disciples his personal marriage of speculative logic and the positive sources and style cultivated by Christian Humanists that Cano was able to produce his magnum opus, *De Locis Theologicis* (Salamanca, 1563). This work established the foundations of theological science on the basis of Scripture, Sacred History, the Church Fathers, the Councils, the decisions of other ecclesiastical authorities, and the value of Natural Reason as developed by the Scholastic theologians and science; and, as was to be expected, all presented with the best literary flair. It was Vitoria's open mind that also formed De Soto, who was influential not just with his theological works, but also through his studies of motion, which had an impact on Galileo; linguistic theory; and, by means of his book *On Justice and Law*, on future treatments of natural law.

Appleton Company, 1908), 251; Katherine Elliot van Liere, "Humanism and Scholasticism in Sixteenth-Century Academe: Five Student Orations from the University of Salamanca*," *Renaissance Quarterly* 53, no. 1 (Spring 2000): 57–107, https://doi.org/10.2307/2901533; and Nelson H. Minnich, "The Voice of Theologians in General Councils from Pisa to Trent," *Theological Studies* 59, no. 3 (September 1998): 420–441, https://doi.org/10.1177/004056399805900303.

All three of these thinkers from Salamanca were convinced that Thomism in particular—once again, a Thomism applied together with the other tools noted above—had immediate practical value for all manner of contemporary issues. Practical applications ranged from Vitoria's dealing with the proper treatment of the inhabitants of the New World in *De Indis*, to De Soto's speculations on just war theory, property rights, contractual law, and economic issues, sharpened by his distinctions of God's law, positive law, distributive justice, and commutative justice. Such men could not to be neglected by the powers that be—Domingo de Soto, for example, was Emperor Charles V's confessor—even though the secular authorities did not always like what they heard them saying.

But what about the question of bringing the transformative Christian life down from the theoretical level to the practical daily life of groups and individuals? Cardinal Ximenez is justly remembered for his praiseworthy reforming activities touching primarily on the life of the clergy, in which he benefited from the constant support of Queen Isabella (1451–1504). But for our purposes here, relating the practical revivification by Spain of a Catholic vision that would then impact upon the Council of Trent and the development of Baroque Culture as a whole, the man whose influence we must most emphasize is St. Juan of Avila (1499–1569).[8]

Born in Toledo, Juan first attended the University of Salamanca (1513–1517) and then the Alcalá (1520–1526), thus being formed by the mixture of speculative and positive theological and humanist education that both institutions favored. Ordained in 1526, he went to Seville with the idea of preparing for a life in the American missions. A Franciscan in the diocese, recognizing his superior catechetical and preaching skills, urged the Archbishop to keep him in Spain for more local missionary work, throughout the areas of Andalusia just recently brought under Spanish Christian control. He did so while living together in a loosely structured community of priests engaged in similar labors, all of whose members looked to him for spiritual guidance. His rhetorically refined sermons

---

8 For all the below, see David Coleman, *Creating Christian Granada: Society and Religious Culture in an Old-World Frontier City, 1492–1600* (Ithaca: Cornell University Press, 2003), 137–144; for Avalos, see 119–129; on his "converts," see 9–10, 93, 143–144.

were said to be "like a gun with much ammunition which when it was fired wounded many birds."[9]

Denounced by enemies to the Inquisition, Juan spent 1532–1533 in prison, a time that he claimed was the most productive in his life, and during which he wrote his major work on spiritual direction, *Audi, filia*, for a young woman living a consecrated life under his tutelage. After being absolved by the Inquisition of all charges against him, he was incardinated in the diocese of Cordoba in 1535, preaching first in that city, and then, for five years until 1541 in Granada, through all of his labors cementing his reputation as the "Apostle of Andalusia."

As a spiritual guide, Juan was eager to inspire clerics first and foremost to seek internal transformation in Christ as the absolutely indispensable prerequisite for effective pastoral activity. In this regard, like so many others in Spain in this rich sixteenth century, he was influenced by the writings of the Franciscan mystic, Francisco de Osuna (1492/1497–c. 1540). Juan was also convinced that sound intellectual training was essential to the pastoral effectiveness of a holy clergy, and this, of course, would require a mixture of speculative scholastic and positive humanist education. Avila's outstanding work during the middle years of his ministry was the establishment of schools at every level of instruction: schools of doctrine for children and adults, and colleges—the equivalent of our high schools and universities—the most notable of which was that in the Andalusian city of Baeza. Finally, he reminded the clergy under his influence that their pastoral labor had to be flexible in character; they were surgeons of souls, and the diseases that they were required to address were manifold in nature. Practical experience taught him this on a day-to-day basis as the Apostle of Andalusia, his tasks in Granada perhaps most of all.

Granada, both because of its large Moorish population as well as its influx of migrants from other parts of Spain, was a complex, challenging pastoral field of endeavor, to say the very least. Nevertheless, Juan of Avila was to have a major impact in the city, directly in the years from 1536–1541, and indirectly thereafter. His direct labor coincided with the latter part of the episcopacy of Gaspar de Ávalos (1485–1545).

---

9   Cited in Coleman, *Creating Christian Granada*, 140.

Avalos was quite different from St. John, more confrontational than nuanced in his pastoral approach. Nevertheless, with the Archbishop's assistance, Avila was able to found the Colegio de Santa Catalina in 1537, utilizing it to promote his understanding of what a holy and educated clergy should be like. During these years of personal presence in Granada, Juan also "converted" a number of men who were to follow his guidance not just with respect to the foundations of the spiritual life, but also with regard to the need for diverse, nuanced approaches to different pastoral problems.

One of these "converts" was St. Francis Borgia (1510–1572), the third General of the Society of Jesus, to whose ranks Juan of Avila warmly directed more than thirty young men. He himself would probably have become a Jesuit were it not for the illness that weakened him from 1551 onwards. John was to be instrumental in leading the Jesuits to undertake their great educational apostolate.

Another convert was St. John of God (1495–1550), a truly singular personality, who, after listening merely to one of Avila's sermons, changed the course of his whole life, dedicating it to religious self-sacrifice. His selfless work with the sick was to lead to the creation of the Brothers Hospitallers. "Will you not do something good for your brothers?" he would ask the people around him as he sought alms for his hospital in Granada; "Is there anyone who will do something good for his own brothers? . . . Who will do something good for himself?"[10] Many inhabitants at first thought him to be literally insane, and mocked him openly for his madness; but, because of his obvious surrender to Christian charitable love, the entire city was present at his funeral in 1550.

A third convert was the Dominican, Blessed Luis de Granada (1504–1588), who studied at the Colegio de San Gregorio in Valladolid. His multifaceted writings on Scripture, Church History, and dogma were crowned by his ascetical works, most importantly, *The Sinner's Guide* (1555). Luis' preaching was equally brilliant. As might be expected from a follower of St. Juan of Avila, all that he wrote and preached was done with the greatest classical style, though translated into the pastorally effective vernacular, Spanish and many others.

---

10   Cited in Coleman, 132. See also 130–137.

Avila's indirect labor with Granada intersects with the story of Pedro Guerrero Logroño Mendoza (1501–1576).[11] Guerrero, from an old family of northern Spain, had studied at Salamanca, but then moved on to the Alcalá, where he first met and worked together with St. Juan. It was Avila who recommended Guerrero for Archbishop in 1546 when the Emperor first offered it to himself. He sent his protégé a letter in 1547 as Guerrero took up his position in Granada, urging him on to constant preaching and unflagging pastoral work. "Since the wolves never cease biting and killing," he concluded, "the prelate should never sleep or shut up."[12]

Guerrero did as he was told, realizing, as a good disciple of St. Juan, to begin with that he had to focus his labor on creating a holy and educated clergy. He set up the Colegio Eclesiastico de San Cecilio for the training of clerics, insisting on the best of Humanist preparation for them. Specifying sixteen reform measures for their improvement as clerics, Guerrero sought to carry them out by means of extensive parish visitations throughout the archdiocese. The Archbishop was eager to promote all manner of nuanced pastoral activities as well, giving great support to St. John of God and his Brothers Hospitallers, and encouraging the laity in their efforts alongside those of the clergy.

Guerrero grew to be particularly close to the Jesuits. He liked their flexible confessional nuance, attended their lectures, encouraged the use of the *Spiritual Exercises*, and approved of their regular public preaching against social ills. Guerrero was deeply attached to the Casa de la Doctrina, established in 1559 by Pedro de Navarro, S. J., another of St. Juan's followers, in the heart of the Moorish section called the Albaicîn. This institution had an enormous impact on the Moorish converts because of the fact that, like St. Juan and the Archbishop of Granada himself, it placed more emphasis upon personal faith and moral reform to establish one's title to the name "Catholic" than simply that of being an Old Christian who was perhaps the servant more of "custom" than of Truth. The greatest testament to the Casa's effectiveness was the hatred that it earned from the stubborn militants of the local Moslem community, who turned against it with a fury in a short-lived revolt later in the sixteenth century.

11   Coleman, 144–176.
12   Cited in Coleman, 149.

IV. SPAIN AND THE COUNCIL OF TRENT

Trent, like many of its more ancient predecessors, was not an "easy" council. It ultimately met in three sessions—1545–1547, 1551–1552, and 1562–1563, its progress deeply disturbed by political, personality, and procedural questions, alongside bitter, substantive disputes over what the actual "meat" of its labors must be and in what kind of language its decisions should be expressed. Although it was already at the First Session (1545–1547) that the crucial determination to deal with both doctrine and reform together was taken, and the supporters of Scholasticism and Humanism established their twin, indispensable rights to participate in accomplishing this work, there were constant clashes over exactly what this labor was to entail, such disputes spilling over into and even intensifying in the Second (1551–1552) and especially the Third (1562–1563) Sessions.

Spaniards were central to every aspect of these developments, some of them active at one or two Sessions only, others for all three. Educators from Salamanca like the Dominicans Domingo de Soto and Melchior Cano were at times present and very vocal. So were Spanish members of the new Society of Jesus, most importantly Alfonso Salmerón (1515–1585) and Diego Lainez (1512–1565), the new order's second General. Learned diplomats such as Diego Hurtado de Mendoza (1503–1575) played their role also. Reforming bishops like Diego de Alaba y Esquivel (d. 1562) of Astorgas, Avila, and then Cordoba, Bishop Martin Perez de Ayala (1504–1566) of Gaudix, Segovia, and then Valencia, and, most importantly, Guerrero of Granada, president of the Spanish delegation in 1551–1552 and 1562–1563 were crucial to the proceedings. One physically absent but very clear "presence" was Juan of Avila, whose reform memorials, to be discussed below, were to be pressed by Guerrero with great vigor. All of these men, once again, combined concerns for speculative and positive theology, Scholasticism and Humanism, and the need to embed a Catholic vision founded on a sound doctrinal basis, in all aspects of life, in nuanced ways, for the sake of transformation in Christ.[13]

A more extended article would tackle how Spanish influence was central to the establishment of the basic principles of dealing

---

13   See Jedin, *Geschichte des Konzils von Trient*, vol. 2–4, *passim*. See also Coleman, 144–176.

with doctrine and reform and the use of both scholastic and humanist tools, with reference to the heated battles over the definition of "justification" which took place in the First Session, as well as to the often contentious discussions of the Sacraments over all three sittings. These can be followed most fruitfully in the appropriate volumes of Hubert Jedin's masterful work on the Council of Trent.

I think it best to focus our attention on the most explosive Session of all: the Third. By that time the Spanish delegation was not only the biggest, but also the angriest at the Council. This was because it felt that serious reform was being stalled, and that guaranteeing its taking place required tackling an extremely important doctrinal and ecclesiological issue as well, once more illustrating how doctrine and pastoral concerns were intimately connected. Let us go back a bit in time to see how this all was to play out at Trent.

For decades before the opening of the Council, reforming Spanish bishops, educators, and preachers were very much aware of the problems afflicting the Universal Church in general and the Papal Court in particular.[14] When the First Session opened, Spanish delegates immediately encountered a great deal of "pushback" from the Roman Curia and curial-minded bishops, Italians for the most part, who considered themselves to be the sole stalwart defenders of Catholic "tradition." These "spoilers," illustrating Tertullian's complaint, confused what were deeply rooted, abusive, "customary" beliefs and practices with Sacred Tradition as such. Catholics critical of existing abuses were, in their minds, at the very least, the kind of deluded, destructive zealots that centuries of bureaucratic papal prudence and pragmatism had sought to tame. At worst, the "spoilers" were themselves the true problem of the day, unnecessarily aggravating a Protestant tempest-in-a-teapot that could be quelled through the tried laws and methods of practical professionals.

When the First Session was moved to Bologna, deep inside the Papal State and therefore more subject to curial control than Trent, the Spanish deemed this to be an Italian trick to avoid reform measures, which indeed were stalled.[15] The Second Session, in 1551–1552, saw them blocked as well. It was the Third Session that was to prove definitive for reform, and this, primarily only

---

14   Jedin, vol. 1, 106–108, 123–124.
15   Jedin, vol. 2, 353–376.

in the final seven months of its proceedings after a great deal of weeping and gnashing of teeth.

Guerrero, who had been so eager to cooperate with his fellow Council Fathers at the Second Session that one of the papal legates said that nothing useful could have ben accomplished without him, had nevertheless come away disillusioned by the obstructionism he had encountered there. When he left to head the Spanish Delegation at the Third Session in 1561, he was a much more angry man, attacked by the Italians as being "harder and more obstinate than a rock."[16] He seems to have relished his reputation, writing to King Philip II: "I believe that I have made myself a troublemaker in the eyes of these men, but this fact causes me no pain whatsoever."[17] Bishop Gonzalez de Mendoza of Salamanca claimed "the Italians hate Guerrero so much that upon hearing that he wants one thing, they do the contrary."[18] The Archbishop of Granada was convinced that all this was due simply to their corruption, recipients as they were of papal bribes. In later life, Guerrero was still calling up references to his bad experiences from conciliar days:

> I have no special permission from the Holy See to dispose freely of certain goods held through the Church, although I easily could have obtained such permission during my second stay at Trent, as did all of the other prelates who graciously accepted such grants. I was likewise invited to do so, but in order to remain free to conduct the business of the council, I neither asked for it nor accepted it.[19]

Juan of Avila was deeply on Guerrero's mind at the Third Session. The Apostle of Andalusia, whom the Archbishop had wanted to take part in Trent as a *peritus*, did not attend, but did write two "Memorials," one for the Second Session in 1551 entitled "Reform of the Ecclesiastical State," and another for the Third in 1561, labeled "Causes and Remedies of Heresies" to aid the Spanish Delegation in its work. A third document in 1563 called "Treatise on the Priesthood" completed his thoughts on the subject of reform, based as they were on years of experience pursuing

---

16 Cited in Coleman, *Creating Christian Granada*, 145.
17 Cited in Coleman, 145, 147.
18 Cited in Coleman, 166.
19 Cited in Coleman, 167.

it. Guerrero took his writings, and their intimate connection of reform and doctrine, seriously to heart.[20]

As we have seen, St. Juan of Avila's ultimate goal was the conversion and transformation of all men in Christ, and this required the labor of priests who were "surgeons of souls" who could deal in a nuanced manner with a myriad of different spiritual illnesses. Hence, the deep concern for the training of the necessary surgeon-priests—the shock troops for the entire Christian project—that we have noted to be such a central part of his labor in southern Spain. That training, first of all, demanded the holiness of the priest himself. No amount of zeal for reform legislation could compensate for the lack of priests—whose chief pastoral tool was the Eucharist, and whose sacral touching of the God-Man Whom he distributed to his flock transformed his consecrated existence—who pursued the path of self-perfection as their chief personal goal.

Nevertheless, personal priestly sanctification, crucial to the work of aiding the laity, was not something that could effectively be pursued in the Mystical Body of Christ as an atomistic activity. A prayerful, communal fraternal spirit among priests must be cultivated, to serve as a most powerful stimulus to aiming at perfection. We have seen that Juan, during his early priesthood in Seville, had lived with other clerics in a loosely structured community, and for many years afterwards, disciples continued to gather around him to live a kind of non-monastic fraternal life.

Creating this life-long brotherly spirit was something that must itself be stimulated by having those training to become priests first live together before their ordination. Good positive theologian that he was, Juan cited the ancient examples of St. Jerome and St. Ambrose, who founded communities for the training of the clergy, the former telling a young man wanting to become a priest to live in a monastery in such a way that you may *deserve* to become a cleric.[21] "If we acted as they did," Juan insisted, "within a few years, there would be a different kind of priest and people than there are now."[22] As he stated in his first memorial of 1551:

---

20   Coleman, 139, 171. See also Joan Gormley, "St. John of Avila and the Reform of the Priesthood," *Homiletic & Pastoral Review* 104, no. 7 (April 2004): 18–25, https://www.catholicculture.org/culture/library/view.cfm?id=6038.

21   Gormley, "St. John of Avila," 23.

22   Cited in Gormley, 23.

If the Church wants good ministers it must create them; and, if it wants good 'surgeons of souls,' it must take the responsibility of raising them so, as well as the responsibility for the work involved; and, if not, it will not achieve what it desires. . . . A tree, in order to realize its potential, needs, from an early age, to be directed and straightened. The horse and the mule, in order that they learn to take proper steps, must first be under the hand of the trainer. [And, similarly,] In all human offices, the good official is not born already made, but, rather must be made.[23]

Bishops, as the servants of their clergy rather than their masters, had the central responsibility in this labor. Avila took it for granted that bishops entering into their dioceses understood that they, too, had to make a general examination of conscience to assure that their primary personal commitment as prelates was to the pursuit of holiness and that venal motivation was rejected in all of the decisions that they made. He then told the bishops that they must stop discussing reform, since there had already been plenty of dialogue. Now we can "excuse ourselves from deliberation and take up the task of putting into practice something that fell into disuse because of the sins and calamities of the Church."[24] There was no need either for making new regulations demanding a serious clergy in their diocese. Once again, there were already enough regulations on the law books, "yet, with all of this, everyone knows how wicked, how ignorant, and how disordered we ecclesiastics can become."[25] Assuring a holy clergy was the task before them, and this, in the long run, could only be achieved through the establishment of seminaries.

Bishops had to be aware that the cause of the ruin of the clergy had been the entrance of worldly people into its ranks; men who had no knowledge of the grandeur of the state they are undertaking and whose hearts were on fire merely with earthly ambitions. To this end, Juan recommended painstaking selection of the candidates who would receive a rigorous, communal, fraternal, spiritual and intellectual formation in the seminary precincts. No one must be allowed to enter the seminary who entered due to

---

23   Cited in Coleman, *Creating Christian Granada*, 173.
24   Cited in Gormley, "St. John of Avila," 22.
25   Cited in Gormley, 22.

property concerns or concupiscence. Hence, the widespread late medieval definition of the life of the priest with primary reference to economic questions—what kind of benefice or "living" he possessed—rather than his spiritual vocation had to be condemned, root and branch.

The Christian people pay dearly when a candidate for the priesthood enters into this path in response not to God's call, but to "the call of money and an easy life." Such priests will unworthily touch the Body of the Lord, the harm of the entirety of the Mystical Body, as "those who were supposed to be shepherds turn themselves into wolves and make carnage in the souls of those they were supposed to bring to life."[26] If bishops were going to accept men without the proper spiritual and intellectual capacity, then they should label their chief goal "the cultivation of fields in barren lands."[27]

No one with any sense, Avila says, would entrust a wounded animal to an untrained veterinarian. How then entrust one for whom Christ died to someone who has no training in the "art of arts," the care of souls?

> For a tree to grow straight, it is necessary to guide and straighten it from the time it is small. For a horse or a mule to be driven, they have to first be under the hand of a trainer. In all human occupations, the skilled person is not born ready-made but must become good at what he does. Becoming a doctor, a lawyer, a carpenter, a shoemaker, or anything else, requires its year or years of initiation and apprenticeship so that the person can learn little by little the skill that afterwards he can exercise without danger. Well, being a priest and becoming a good one is a thing of great perfection and difficulty.[28]

All seminarians, operating in a communal, fraternal, atmosphere of prayer were "vessels" which had to filled to capacity for a task in which the intellect would play its role throughout their lifetime; "so that, growing with age, goodness, and learning, the priest may speak with authority and, without danger, may exercise his high office."[29] They were, after all, learning what it was that St. Gregory

26 Cited in Gormley, 23.
27 Cited in Gormley, 23.
28 Cited in Gormley, 23.
29 Cited in Gormley, 24.

the Great called the "art of arts," the care of souls.[30] Ignorance of doctrine was a tool of the devil, and all seminarians becoming parish priests must be formed doctrinally through knowledge of Scripture and speculative studies. They also were to study "grammar" for at least four or five years, so that they would have the rhetorical skills needed to transmit what they had learned. And they needed to study practical conscience problems to address the diversity of diseases that the soul doctor had to handle. Finally, some of their number should be dedicated to higher learning in the Sacred Sciences to help the bishop and other priests as was necessary. They could be a tremendous help in avoiding the errors that can easily creep in when there is a little knowledge and in dealing with difficult cases that are sure to arise.[31]

As already noted, Archbishop Guerrero had St. Juan of Avila's reform proposals very much on his mind as leader of the Spanish delegation at the Third Session of the Council of Trent. But given the Papacy's treatment of diocesan resources as property questions, and its willingness to tolerate episcopal absence and neglect in order to support either certain bishops' work at the Roman Curia or that of curial officials who had nothing whatsoever to do with local affairs, abuses perpetrated by the Holy See had directly to be addressed as well. To do so meant that the connection of the pastoral and the doctrinal had once more to be raised, this time with respect to basic ecclesiology: namely, the very nature of the Episcopacy, its God-given responsibilities, and its relationship with the Papacy, as well as the question of whether and to what degree the Holy See could act in an erroneous and abusive manner. Interestingly enough, these concerns were in many respects very similar to the very first suggestions for reform coming from the *Consilium de emendanda Ecclesia* of 1537, commissioned by Pope Paul III, which was highly critical of papal curial practices, identifying them as the central cause of corruption in the Church at large.[32]

Before any conciliar confrontation with Rome emerged, Guerrero and the Spanish delegation actually worked in union with the papal legates over another doctrinal issue: securing the acceptance

---

30   Cited in Gormley, 24.
31   Gormley, 24.
32   Coleman, *Creating Christian Granada*, 168–176.

of the dogmatic work already done by the Council beforehand. This meant confirmation of the Third Session's continuity with the previous two rather than its convocation representing a completely fresh beginning. Battle over this matter was joined due to German and French attempts to review the Council's earlier reassertion of the Catholic Tradition because of the continuing and growing strength of Protestant forces in their own lands. Problems only began once this crucial Papal-Spanish victory was achieved.[33]

Guerrero believed that the key to moving on to serious reform required wresting control over the conciliar agenda from the pope and the papal legates and putting it into the hands of the council bishops themselves. As he wrote to King Philip II:

> We complain because we have been denied the right to propose and deal with highly necessary things that are appropriate to such councils, and very important to the well-being of the entire Church, especially regarding matters of reformation. It has been nearly twenty years now that such issues have been discussed here, but we have not yet been able to reform even a single abuse at its root among the great quantity of abuses that exist. . . . If this is the way it will be done, then it would be better if you simply ordered us to return to our churches, for nothing will be accomplished.[34]

Philip nearly convinced Rome to allow Guerrero's deeply desired right of proposal, but Cardinal Giovanni Morone (1509–1580), the chief papal legate, blocked it, horrified that such permission, rather than speeding up business, would guarantee further years of tedious and ultimately fruitless debate. Nevertheless, Pius did allow the delegates to meet unofficially among themselves to make reform proposals that the pope and the papal legates then considered, reworked, and presented for the deliberation of all.

It was because of this concession that Avila's reform memorials were made known to the Council Fathers. Some of his proposals intersected with those presented by the Portuguese Archbishop of Braga, Bartolomeo de Martyris (1514–1590). When finally brought before the Council for deliberation in July of 1563, the major doctrinal statements that Guerrero put forward regarding the

---

33   Coleman, 168 and Jedin, *Geschichte des Konzils von Trient*, vol. 4.1, 76–93.
34   Cited in Coleman, 170. See also 135 and Jedin, vol. 4.1, 76–93.

God-given character and responsibilities of the Episcopacy were strongly opposed by the "Curial Party." To complicate matters still further, although the French, led by Louis Cardinal de Guise (1527–1578), supported major aspects of this Avila-inspired reform program, his delegation's own approach emphasized a different doctrinal vision regarding the Episcopacy that almost no one among the Spanish could ever approve.[35]

French delegates at Trent did not accept the validity of the Council of Florence, with its powerful defense of papal prerogatives, and looked instead to the teachings of the Councils of Constance and Basel which affirmed the superiority of councils, weakened the ability of the Holy See to guide individual churches, and thus gave support to the rights of bishops and local concerns which in France were referred to as "Gallican liberties." A Church organized under such guidelines, they argued, followed the ancient Christian model, which was held out by the French as an object of imitation for all problems of teaching and reform.

Papalist bishops—the so-called *zelanti*, mostly Italians—wished to have Trent confirm the Florentine decrees dealing with papal authority that the French opposed. From their standpoint, support of Constance and Basel meant schismatic Conciliarism at best and heretical Conciliarism at worst. They were backed in their arguments—although more moderately and thoughtfully—by the Spanish Jesuit Lainez, who represented a reform-minded militancy that was nevertheless basically strongly pro-Roman in approach.[36]

Spanish bishops rejected what they considered to be a fanciful French divinization of an ancient Church whose actual character they felt to be still a subject more of speculation than of real knowledge.[37] Still, while accepting the decrees of Florence, they did insist upon their more precise definition of the dignity of the episcopal state as such. Thus, however much they might admit that the individual bishop owed his jurisdiction to Rome and obedience to papal doctrinal leadership, they maintained that the bishop's role as a direct successor to the Apostles placed him under divine obligation to reside in his diocese and carry out his God-given—not papal-given—responsibilities. Their arguments in this regard were

---

35 Coleman, 168–176 and Jedin, vol. 4.1, 94–263.
36 Jedin, vol. 4.1, 210–263.
37 Jedin, vol. 4.2, 37–49.

based upon that mixture of positive and speculative theology that they had learned from Vitoria, De Soto, and Juan of Avila.[38] As the Bishop of Guadix said, summarizing their position:

> Not only do bishop[s] hold all that they have by *ius divinum*, but also, though they are confirmed by the Holy See, they do not by this confirmation cease to hold divine sanction, since neither St. John Chryso[s]tom nor St. Basil nor other ancient prelates can be shown ever to have been confirmed by or even to have received anything from the Roman pontiff![39]

Even when, in the course of debate, some Spanish bishops seemed to make what could be construed as extreme statements regarding episcopal right, they did so simply because they wanted to emphasize the necessity of the urgency of the issue and the importance of accepting nuance in local applications of universal Christian precepts. Hence, a conscientious bishop would have to oppose the widespread awarding of dioceses to people who worked in Rome and never actually administered their sees, and the granting of so many exemptions to individuals and religious orders that governance by a resident bishop became frustrating and almost impossible. As an episcopal college, in council, the Spanish bishops felt called upon to demand reform of the papal court itself and eliminate the perpetuation of such abuses.

The Curial Party insisted that basing residence on divine command to bishops recognized as receiving their power as Successors to the Apostles directly from God would violate the Scriptural teaching of Matthew 16:18–19 and that it would make the papal governance of the Church impossible. Many *zelanti* loudly condemned not just the French Gallican position but also the Spanish arguments as heretical. From the standpoint of Guerrero and his fellow Spaniards, opposition to the basing of episcopal authority on divine law was itself unequivocally heretical, refusal to discuss the question outrageous, and failure to do so cause for abandoning any further stay at Trent entirely.[40] They were incredulous that the Curial Party claimed that requiring episcopal residence to guarantee good governance of dioceses would somehow

---

38 Jedin, vol. 4.1, 113 and vol. 4.2, 32.
39 Cited in Coleman, *Creating Christian Granada*, 169.
40 Coleman, 169–176.

"hurt the pope." Once again, they believed that only reason for this kind of statement was enslavement to a vision of the clerical life as primarily a property rather than a vocational matter; a vision dangerous to the eternal salvation of the priest and his flock. The debate was to prove to be a long and bitter one.[41]

Ecclesiology proved to be so productive of division that Cardinal Morone and a group of leaders of the various nations at the Council concluded that the only way to deal with the matter and achieve some measure of reform was to abandon a *direct* treatment of the doctrinal issue. Still, with the Gallican approach muffled through Guise's aid, a very good deal of the Spanish ecclesiological position entered *indirectly* into the impressive reform decrees passed in the last sittings the Council in the latter part of 1563.

Council Fathers did, indeed, lay down certain reform guidelines for the papal court itself. The authority of the bishop in the governance of his diocese and the call for his residence therein were significantly strengthened, even without any specific reference to this as a result of his God-given responsibility as a Successor to the Apostles. Exemptions that were previously enjoyed by religious orders, lay patrons, confraternities, and even the Papacy were abolished, regardless of what "immemorial custom" dictated. Permission for preaching and hearing confession was left to the discretion of the local Ordinary. Further detailed reform was left for elaboration at the local level after the Council's end, but the presence of papal legates at provincial synods seemed to guarantee continued guidance from an internationally minded Papacy.

Avila and Guerrero's influence are also clearly to be seen in the mandate for the establishment in each diocese of a seminary for the proper training of future priests. The final decree ordering this measure very much reflects Avila's particular concerns, although in less metaphorical language than noted above. It also recalls Guerrero's actual 1547 rules for the running of Ecclesiastical College of San Cecilio in Granada, stipulating that seminaries only take young men "whose character and inclination afford a hope that they will always serve in the ecclesiastical ministry."[42]

41 Jedin, *Geschichte des Konzils von Trient*, vol. 4, 1.2, *passim*.
42 Cited in Coleman, *Creating Christian Granada*, 173. See also 166–176 and Jedin, vol. 4.2, 29–189.

V. A NEVER-ENDING CONSTRUCTION OF A "BAROQUE" CHRISTENDOM: 1563–2021

Serious reform-minded bishops returned home from Trent ready to "take no enemies" in their work for correction of the many deeply rooted abuses in the life of the Church. Although certainly now in possession of an arsenal of new canonical weapons with which to battle for "transformation of all things in Christ," and well aware of being able to summon fresh, militant forces like the Jesuits to help wield them, they were very quickly to find that their endeavor would still by no means be an easy one. For nascent Baroque Catholicism, brilliant though it would prove to be, was not—and could not be—destined to provide a "final word" for a task that would have to respond to ever-new problems, alongside perennial ones, until the end of time.

Let us explore this truth briefly, in very broad strokes, focusing primarily on Spain and Spanish territories, in ways that bring us directly to the problem of our own day: the total renunciation of the central project of transformation that characterizes contemporary "mainstream" Catholicism.

First of all, no mere possession of the "right canons" could ever guarantee that those motivated by the proper reforming spirit would infallibly exercise an effective personal activity on behalf of the good cause. This is well demonstrated in the case of even such a sterling prelate like Guerrero of Granada. Weary of his constant, decades-long battle for improvements that he thought to be obviously apostolic in nature and essential to the well-being of the Church, he came to view opposition to their implementation as always explicable only by incorrigible corruption. In doing so, he abandoned the nuanced pastoral approach that he had learned from Juan of Avila and had practiced so fruitfully in the first period of his episcopacy. Guerrero now moved so authoritatively against obstacles to his will that his enemies accused him of employing as bishop the same "tyrannical" tools that he had attacked as arbitrary and excessive in the hands of the Papacy.[43]

In short, the building of effective Catholic stairways to heaven is a work "constantly in progress." It is permanently threatened not only by outright evil, but also by every flaw of every individual

---

43 Coleman, 177–180.

with free will in a world marred by sin—those of good bishops like Guerrero included. Unfortunately, this stubborn truth can—and did—lead in many cases to renewal of a frustration productive of despair; despair over the feasibility of the entire project of transformation in Christ such as already witnessed in the period of the Late Middle Ages. Why bother to work for something that seemed incapable of achievement?

Secondly, and much more importantly, doctrinal problems continued to jeopardize working with nature for the greater glory of God. The Council of Trent realized—more, I would venture to say, under the inspiration of the Holy Spirit than through the brilliance and the conscious will of its leadership, which generally fumbled its way to this conclusion—that there could be no firm foundation for efficacious pastoral work without the guidance of sound, revealed teaching, unveiled by the harmonious cooperation of speculative and positive theology. Should this foundation be lacking, pastoral initiatives could once again end by promoting merely "willful" influences which, when deeply rooted, would form "customs" falsely equated with Catholic Truth. This would revive the situation of the Late Middle Ages, but now with still more disastrous long-term consequences hostile to the transformative mission of Christ, since it would be like when "a dog is returned to his vomit."[44]

Serious dangers to the solidity of that foundation emerged from the fact that what was decided at Trent doctrinally was only accomplished through a great deal of compromise—much of it very grudging compromise to say the very least. Bitter, centuries-long quarrels over unfinished business, especially with respect to the two basic issues of ecclesiology and justification, were to demonstrate the impossibility of avoiding new disputes, and just how much the battling over doctrinal *lacunae* in the work of the Council was to be exploited on the pastoral level to subvert the work of making of nature a rock solid "stairway to heaven."

As far as ecclesiology is concerned, we have seen that attempts to tackle one central aspect of the "constitution" of the Mystical Body of Christ—the apostolic character of the Episcopacy and its exact relationship to the Papacy—proved to be so provocative as

---

44 2 Pet. 2:22 (Douay-Rheims), citing Proverbs 26:11.

almost to break up the Third Session of the Council in 1562–1563 entirely. What came from the Council remained ambiguous. The Spanish had ensured the passage of reform measures effectively enshrining the divine authority of the bishop as a Successor to the Apostles, but these were accompanied by a statement that "the authority of the Apostolic See both is, and is understood to be, untouched thereby."[45]

The touchiness of addressing the respective roles of the clergy and the laity, as primarily reflected historically in the relationship of the Church and officially Christian States whose justification of their work for the social order was deeply intertwined with religious issues, proved to be equally divisive. Both the French and the Spanish bishops were concerned about the growing power of the so-called "New Monarchies" and wished to protect episcopal authority from being usurped by them. The fact that there were problems here that needed to be clarified led Council Fathers to press for discussion of a "reform of the princes" at Trent, and Cardinal Giovanni Morone (1509–1580), who presided, as papal legate, in the Council's last nine months, to use the threat of this discussion to convince the great powers to come to terms on the episcopal-papal issue. Hence, discussion of the exact relationship of Church and State was also shelved.[46]

What did such gaps in ecclesiology mean for effective pastoral work? Everyone publicly insisted that such labor was needed, but continued to quarrel over who was to be the most important force propelling it. Was this to be predominantly the responsibility of the Pope, whose prerogatives the Council claimed to have left untouched, or the local bishops, whose authority, in practice, was indeed considerably strengthened by the decisions of Trent? But if the bishops were to be the prime movers in pastoral matters, were they really to be free to do what they deemed important, or were they to become chiefly agents of the Most Christian Kings and Catholic Majesties who generally controlled their nominations, confirmations, and the boundaries of their practical activity? Among many other problems, failure to touch on Church-State issues meant neglect of the whole question of what was going on in the worldwide missions under Spanish and Portuguese control,

---

45 Cited in Coleman, *Creating Christian Granada*, 176.
46 Jedin, *Geschichte des Konzils von Trient*, vol. 2.2, 121–139.

and whether the spiritual interests of the indigenous colonial peoples were uppermost in governments' minds or subordinated to secular ones.

Couple the confusion as to which authority should lead the crusade for the transformation of all things in Christ with the intensification of the still more basic debate over how the individual believers engaged in the construction of stairways to heaven were "justified" in the sight of God, and the result had to be a new crisis in the life of what has always been a crisis-filled Church.

Much of this latter struggle was to involve the Society of Jesus—so closely associated in the popular mind with Spain, Trent, and Baroque culture. It was also to involve St. Juan of Avila and the whole Spanish achievement of the Alcalá and the University of Salamanca, since the Jesuits, with Lainez as the chief instrument for making this a permanent project of the Society, were to "bear the burden of the schools," with a program and spirit directly red-olent of their spirit and structures for incarnating it. As the letter of August 10, 1560, cementing the Jesuit tie to education stated:

> There are two ways of helping our neighbors: one is in the colleges by the education of youth in letters, learning, and Christian life. The other is to help all universally through preaching, [hearing] confessions, and all the other means in accord with our customary way of proceeding.[47]

One of the most important Spanish Jesuits at the Council, Father Alfonso Salmerón, knew from personal experience just how much compromise had played a role in the conclusion of its dogmatic work. He cautioned his confreres against the potentially deadly divisions that could arise from too rigorous demands for sharper definitions of doctrinal matters only partially settled at Trent.[48] Nevertheless, this warning proved to be extremely difficult to follow. Jesuits, Dominicans, and Augustinians quickly engaged in conflict over a more exact identification of the relationship of grace and free will in justification in ways that impacted mightily

---

47 Letter to the superiors of the Society, Rome, August 10, 1560, in Patribus Societatis Jesu, eds., *Lainii monumenta: Epistolae et acta Patris Jacobi Lainii secundi praepositi generalis Societatis Jesu ex autographis vel originalibus exemplis potissimum deprompta a patribus ejusdem Societatis Jesu, vol. 5, 1560–1561* (Matriti: Typis Gabrieli Lopez del Horno, 1915), 165.

48 Bangert, *Storia della compagnia di Gesù*, 342.

upon sacramental and devotional practices, spiritual direction, and missionary tools—once again emphasizing the impossibility of separating doctrine and pastoral activity.[49]

Spain and Spanish territories were central to the battle that was joined, the main lines being formed in favor of or in opposition to the Jesuit Luis de Molina (1535–1600), a professor at a number of different institutions in the Iberian Peninsula and promoter of the "free will friendly" doctrine of probabilism. His battery of "grace favoring" enemies included the disciples of Domingo Bañez (1528–1604), Dominican Rector of the University of Salamanca, along with those of two teachers from the Spanish Netherlands: Michael Baius (1513–1589), the Rector of the University of Louvain in the Spanish Netherlands, and, much more importantly, Cornelius Jansen (1585–1638), Bishop of Ypres and author of the *Augustinus*, the "Bible" of the subsequent Jansenist movement.

From inconclusive disputations under the presidency of Popes Clement VIII (1592–1605) and Paul V (1605–1621), through reiterated condemnations of laxism and rigorism, semi-Pelagianism and crypto-Protestantism, the debate continued to rage though the seventeenth and eighteenth centuries. It very quickly invaded the realm of spiritual direction, liturgical, sacramental, and sacramental and devotional life, arousing the interest of kings, law courts, and all ranks of clergy and people, so that anybody who might stake any claim to teaching anything became involved. From shaky victory to temporary defeat to a renewed but fragile ascendance, the free will camp appeared to have won the magisterial doctrinal victory by the time of Clement XI's (1700–1721) powerful apostolic constitution, *Unigenitus*, in 1713. Nevertheless, unending, bitter, Janenist-led opposition to *Unigenitus* turned the tide against it, but in alliance with a variety of other anti-Jesuit forces. These, all together, whatever the particular often quite contradictory goals of each, ended by working to "liberate" pastoral activity not just from doctrinal guidance, but from every supernatural spiritual force whatsoever—grace included—interrupting once gain the project of transformation of all things natural in Christ.

They did so ultimately under anti-supernatural, anti-doctrinal, and inevitably anti-rational "willful" pressures coming, to begin

---

49   For the grace/free will discussion, see Rao, *Black Legends*, 361–367.

with, from two Protestant sources.[50] One of these was Pietism, which sought to avoid the theological disputes that were tearing the Reformation world apart by replacing them with an emphasis upon a "simple" commitment to living the precepts of a moral, charitable Christian life, regarding which everyone could still "obviously" agree. The other, itself partly shaped by Pietism, was Newtonian Physico-Theology, which claimed that God was best adored through the study of the physical, natural laws of His Creation and the practical application for the benefit of mankind as a whole that was given to them through the work of institutions like the Royal Society of London and its imitators. Both of these models placed more hope for building stairways to heaven through focusing upon what seemed to "work" on a natural level to create peace and well-being for the community at large, pointing both to their "successes" in following this path as well as the "failures" of lands still enthralled to supernatural, doctrinal concerns.

The non-Protestant world brought the Pietist and Newtonian Physico-Theological approach to practical fruition by the second half of the eighteenth century. It did so through the policies of supposedly Catholic States who joined in the anti-supernatural, anti-doctrinal, and anti-intellectual campaign out of admiration for countries such as Britain and Prussia, which were already experiencing great successes in marching down the pathway of "whatever works," without fear of being criticized for dogmatic errors with moral consequences. They did so also out of fear of losing out in the general battle for earthly power and riches if they did not follow suit.

In pursuing their goals, Catholic States found that they could rely on arguments presented to them from the alliance of forces noted above frustrated with what it deemed to be an erroneous, Jesuit-manipulated presentation of Roman doctrine. Jansenists, especially, joined in this game because a de-emphasis on doctrine allowed them a chance to pursue their pet projects under the guise of purely "pastoral" activities whose anti-free will direction, doctrinally charged though it seriously was, would be left to wreak its havoc under the rubric of avoiding "useless theological divisiveness." State and so-called "Reform Catholic" aims came to

---

50 For the whole of the following discussion, including its Spanish application, See Rao, *Black Legends*, 313–389.

mold one another, with a "truly pastoral Christianity" gradually being equated with a dismantling of the rich sacramental, devotional, and liturgical life of a "false," "Baroque Catholicism" and its replacement with a piety based on "inner feeling," "simplicity," and, inevitably, purely naturalist economic development.

Spain and Spanish territories in general succumbed to these pressures under the reign of King Charles III (1759–1788), who had already gained a reputation as a reformer while ruler of the Kingdom of the Two Sicilies (1734–1759). His effort to redirect society to the primary goal of practical, constructive labor was aided by Spaniards such as the Benedictine Benito Jeronimo Feijoo (1676–1764), author of the *Teatro critico universal*, Pedro Rodriguez de Campomanes (1723–1803), whose *Discourse on the Encouragement of Popular Industry* (1774) argued for the universal spread of the English-style cooperative scientific movement as the best means of promoting natural efficiency, organizations such as the Basque Economic Society of Friends of the Country, founded in 1763, and bishops such as José Clíment (1706–1781) and Felipe Bertrám (1704–1783). The impact of these measures in secularizing Spain, Italy, and—perhaps more than anywhere else—Latin America, cannot be overemphasized. Things spiritual were reduced to the natural in all fields of endeavor.

Thankfully, the realities of the French Revolution and the fight against it awakened the remnants of what was more than merely a "Baroque" Church to what was eternally essential in her character, long enough to recognize and deconstruct the trick being played on her, and to open the eyes of many purely "pastoral-minded" reformers as well. Rediscovery is the best word to characterize the experience of a great number of committed Catholics of the 1800s. Throughout the post-French revolutionary Catholic world, thinkers and activists of impressive caliber demonstrated a desire to learn, develop and put into practice truths which had been buried by decades and even centuries of governmental, Jansenist, naturalist, and simple parochial "custom."[51]

Depending upon energy, taste, and imagination, this drive led them back to the *doctrinal* riches of the Fathers of the Church, past the medieval scholastics, past Councils, and to a mystical,

---

51   For all of the following, see Rao, *Black Legends*, 390–631.

devotional, and liturgical life rich in practical *pastoral* lessons for both the Catholic community and individuals. The centers of re-discovery were lay/clerical circles of believers, religious confraternities, orders restored after the devastation of the Revolution, university faculties, and groups gathering round those journals and newspapers that seemed to spring up everywhere in the course of the nineteenth century. Catholic Spain, which despite the mighty—but somewhat brief—assault against the Baroque, had still managed to retain much of its spirit, and was not missing from this widespread endeavor.

Nevertheless, the most powerful forces in the outside world were to remain dedicated to the anti-Catholic naturalist spirit. Moreover, their fellow traveling "Reform Catholic" allies, while temporarily forced by a union of the Papacy with the nineteenth century "Baroque" revival movement to go underground, by no means disappeared. Both of these forces, together, aided by accidental political circumstances, were strong enough to thwart the revivalist attempt at Vatican One to deal with the *lacunae* of the ecclesiological problem through a doctrinally rich and much detailed definition of the "Constitution" of the Mystical Body obviously aimed at the project of "transforming all things in Christ." This projected succeeded only in defining Papal Infallibility—out of context—and in a manner that was to have serious consequences in creating the exaggerated Ultramontanism of the late nineteenth and twentieth centuries.

Militant Catholics, both cleric and lay, dedicated to the need to gain a sound doctrinal foundation in order to conduct an effective pastoral labor for transformation of all things in Christ, did yeoman service in a myriad of ways in the years after the First Vatican Council. They succeeded in developing still further and in a number of respects still more brilliantly what is, once again, not merely Baroque Culture but the full Catholic Tradition. Sad to say, inevitable personal failings and internal battles regarding how to accomplish this task also continued unabated.

Unfortunately, the solidity of the alliance of outside naturalist forces with internal proponents of a "non-doctrinal" Catholicism, immeasurably strengthened due to the unexpected addition to this federation of the Papacy itself—a Papacy that could count on obedience to an exaggerated estimation of papal infallibility and authority—proved capable, from the 1960s onwards, of having a Second Vatican Council separate "the pastoral" from the "doctrinal" once more. The consequences have been as palpable as they were inevitable: the redefinition of what is "Catholic" under the pressure of whatever the strongest "will" in any given place may be. These "wills" have proven to be "legion," quite diverse, but all purely secular and ever more unrecognizable as having anything whatsoever to do with the Roman Faith. Alas, after sixty years of influence, wherever such "wills" dominate, their definition of what is Catholic has become "customary."

But what is "customary" is not what is true. What is customary in a purely naturalist form cannot take the stubborn, sinfully marred, but nevertheless God-created and Christ-redeemed "stuff" of life and lead men into a glorious Roman piazza where things earthly and divine are united. It cannot build stairways to heaven, since heaven has been denied its central role as guide to the architects necessary for this task. Such staircases require the "Baroque" spirit; the Catholic spirit; the spirit that Spain did so much to revive in the sixteenth century; the spirit that *Verbo* contributes to maintaining still today.

26
The Day the Music Died[†]

ULRICH ZWINGLI (1484–1531), THE LEADER of the Protestant Reformation in Zurich, faithfully echoed his German predecessor, Martin Luther (1483–1546), in his expression of utter contempt for the Sacrifice of the Mass and the liturgy that solemnly—and joyfully—emphasized its reality. During Holy Week of 1525, when he felt that his influence over the governing City Council in Zurich had sufficiently matured, Zwingli demanded the abolition of the Mass as "blasphemous idolatry." On Wednesday, April 12, the Council voted by a bare majority to gave him the prohibition that he wished.

Demonstrating the fact that this action was the coup of an ideological oligarchy, "the last Mass was celebrated before a great crowd of citizens 'who wanted to have the Holy Sacrament administered to them according to the old custom, as before.'" The voice of the people revealed that "something that was still entirely alive was abolished by official decree." From henceforward, services were to be focused purely upon the written "words" of Scripture stripped from contact with the living Word of God and the loving adornment traditionally given to His worship by a natural world that He had created and redeemed.

> There was no community singing. Quite otherwise than Luther, the musically gifted Zwingli gave no psalms and hymns to those of his church. The organs remained silent. With the singsong of the Latin choral chant, which no one understood, what pertained to music entirely disappeared.[1]

Yes, it is true that Luther, the founding father of the Protestant Reformation, unlike Zwingli, very much disapproved of the iconoclasm represented by "the day the music died" in Zurich. But

---

† First published in *The Angelus*, November–December, 2021.

---

1 Hubert Jedin and John Dolan, eds., *A History of the Church, vol. 4, Reformation and Counter Reformation*, trans. Anselm Biggs and Peter W. Becker (New York: The Crossroad Publishing Company, 1982), 168.

this was only because he also—unlike the more rational Swiss reformer—willfully refused to accept the full logic of his own basic principle of the total depravity of mankind after Original Sin. Zwingli embraced that logic and ran with it, beginning the process by means of which the destruction of the liturgy centered on the Word made flesh unraveled the entire "liturgical" life of Christendom as a whole. This process eventually replaced a diverse, vibrant Christian community that was making its pilgrimage to eternity while singing the song of the "harmony of the spheres" with a drab collection of the living dead, chanting its enslavement to fallen nature in flat, cacophonous, monotonous words without any meaningful context or melody at all, on a journey to nowhere; words shoved down the throats of the bulk of the community in question by the strongest and most willful minority in its midst, and slavishly accepted by it.

Those following Zwingli took their place on this toneless and purposeless plod quite swiftly; others, following Luther and similar "conservative revolutionaries" like him, did so only gradually, as the dike waters they had unleashed overcame their attempts to use their fingers to hold them back. Both groups would have to pass through the still more convoluted but ultimately perfectly logical development of their message provided by the naturalist Enlightenment, itself advancing towards hell in similarly radical and moderate forms. In short, the "day the music died" in Zurich was a prophetic warning to the whole polyphonic chorus of a once charming Christendom of what it was that commitment to the anti-natural Protestant message and its *unnaturally* "natural-ist" Enlightenment progeny would ultimately inevitably mean: silencing the *schola* and its song.

I think that the best way that I can succinctly introduce the full tragedy of this muzzling of the music of life is with reference to Dietrich von Hildebrand's book on *Liturgy and Personality*. In this work—which I highly recommend for arguments against a multitude of evils—Professor von Hildebrand points to the basic difference and consequence of a liturgy that is Christocentric and one that seeks to take its guidance from the worshipper rather than from the God who is worshipped.

A Christocentric liturgy emphasizes that we, as sinners, are only saved and perfected through membership in the Body of Jesus

Christ, whose flesh and blood we literally eat and drink under the communal authority of the Church, His mystical continuation on earth until the end of time. A worshipper-focused liturgy, rather than being primarily receptive to the corrective community and grace that comes "from above, from the Father of Lights," looks first and foremost to the perceived "needs" of human beings for guidance as to how to shape it. The former, learning of mankind's true necessities by focusing on the teaching of its Creator and Redeemer, knows that this blesses all earthly tools as God-given, but then purges them of their fallen sinful characteristics before happily using them in worship, in an ordered hierarchy of values, each in its proper place, all "for the greater glory of God." The latter, even if concocted by well-meaning people, inevitably responds to the flawed, confused, and narrow desires of sinful men—especially its authors—who cannot accurately know what they require for their own betterment, confirming them in their blindness and encouraging them to "perfect" their dogmatic and moral slumber rather than awakening them to God's divinizing grace.

Traditional Christendom as a whole was Christocentric in nature. Following the model given by the Savior and His Mystical Body, which taught that the human person reached perfection through membership in a *supernatural* community, Catholic Christian civilization spontaneously organized individual activity on the earthly level through *natural* communities, ranging from families through to schools, guilds, militant lay crusading and religious "orders," cities, and states. It understood from the supreme communal model that life in community makes us aware of insights, merits, and, perhaps most importantly, flaws in our thinking and behavior.

Moreover, wave after wave of different monastic influences over the development of Christendom gave to all of its component communal elements a liturgical character as well. Monks dedicated to the hours of prayer drilled in the teaching that everyone was on an earthly pilgrimage to eternal life through Christ. They stimulated bishops, popes, and Doctors of the Church to encourage the use of all of the physical tools of nature created and redeemed by a good God to reach that safe port, and to do so in the many distinct ways offered to different individuals in their manifold natural conditions and in fulfillment of their varied natural responsibilities. In consequence, each community had its particular customs, symbols, feasts, patron saints, and place in the pilgrimage to God through Christ. Each sang its own special song, danced, and made merry in its own unique but clearly Catholic way. Each admitted—even if, alas, it did not necessarily always match its behavior to its beliefs—that it needed the grace that came from the highest of liturgies—that of the Eucharist; of Holy Mass—to ensure that is own melody, movements, and merriment fit into the proper hierarchy of values guaranteeing the harmony of the spheres.

Catholic Christendom could thus be said to have viewed the universe as an Unfinished Symphony. It called an orchestra together under the vaulted hall of the heavens, and explained to the musicians that a composer had given them parts of a magnificent piece that He had prepared, in order to test their ability to play it. It noted that the entire symphony would be given to them only after successful performance of the first movement. The musicians worked hard, though some fell by the wayside. They began to polish their instruments, put on their finest clothing, and walk with confidence and quiet pride as they realized the quality of the music with which they are dealing. They waited for the day that they would be given the rest of the piece with humility and with joy. They knew that they could finish the Unfinished Symphony.

In Zurich, on "the day the music died," the baffled citizens of that still Catholic city had played out for them a "prelude" to what was inevitably to come with the consequences of acceptance of the doctrine of total depravity: a prohibition of the completion of the Unfinished Symphony and the silencing of the sounds of the harmony of the spheres. This outcome was unavoidable regardless of the fact that Luther, the actual founder of Protestantism, did not himself "personally"—and quite illogically—particularly desire the dreadful hush that would ensue.

For what the pillar doctrine of the Protestant Revolution teaches is that nothing wrought by man and nature can please a God reduced to righteous anger due to the betrayal accomplished by Original Sin. No community, beginning with that of a supposedly "Mystical Body of Christ" now identified as the "Whore of Babylon," and ultimately continuing to include that of the State, the school, the guild, and the family can be of any value to the wretched, valueless individual, who is driven back to begging for the mercy of the angry God alone to enter His realm; no community, and no Catholic "good work" making use of all the tools of an originally good natural world, corrected of its sins and become thereby so very many valuable steps on an earthly stairway leading to heaven. And all this was drilled in by a liturgy of "words" preached by the charismatic oligarchs leading the Revolution, not to a real congregation, but to a basically inchoate mob of cowed "individuals" who needed to be told that each and every one of them and each and every one of their actions was contemptible and could not be otherwise.

"Thud" is the only musical tone that can accompany the pastoral approach that the doctrine of total depravity entails. But to make matters worse, that "thud" did not maintain the charismatic oligarchs in their commitment to unite atomistic individuals in the construction of a new social "pen" composed of terrified sinners. Instead, and quite ironically, what it actually did was to breed ideologues preaching the replacement of the real society and authority of complex Catholic Christendom, composed of many communities working to perfect their members, with a jungle-like pseudo-civilization in which all of the unredeemed sins of fallen individual men *misusing* nature somehow become untouchable "needs" which must perforce be satisfied.

This is not the time or place for us to show how the liturgy of Zurich on the day the music died drastically changed from one focused on answering the "needs" of a depraved people by abandoning the confection of the Sacrament and the eating of the Body and Blood of Christ, and preaching the absurdity of the attempt to correct the flaws of God's good natural world so as to use all of its elements as a stairway to heaven; how it changed to a message that would have seemed grotesque to the initial Protestant revolutionaries themselves. But change it did. Losing its Christocentric focus, the liturgy of "modernity," moving from Zurich Protestantism to the Enlightenment and, finally, to the madness of our own End Time, came to preach with fine-sounding, disconnected, undefined "words" the importance of satisfying the "needs" of men subject to natural passions no longer viewed as depraved but obvious, and built into the machine of the universe. This liturgy is "preached" today, in exactly the same manner, by the "religious" authorities of Progressive Church, Press, State, and of all the emasculated communities manipulated by them alike.

The "thud" of the "music" accompanying such a sick liturgy is the sound of the slamming of our minds and hearts into the flesh of a Creation that now wants to know nothing whatsoever of its sinful rejection of God's original plan for it, or what it is that it can know and do to lift itself out of the pathetic, parochial, debasing, and blinding consequences of the Fall. "Restore all things in fallen nature" could readily serve as the official motto of the preaching "liturgy" of our time. And the "mercy" offered by the ecclesiastical authorities under these circumstances comes at the expense of dumping a thick, wet blanket over all of nature's healthy characteristics and tendencies—whose cultivation is treated as though it were an arrogant reproach to the poor suffering vices they would uncharitably help to repress.

Rather than end by offering one of the many contemporary examples of the debasement of the glorious liturgical-minded world of Catholic Christendom due to the consequences coming from the teaching of "the day the music died," I would ask you to consider one closer to the initial destruction at the hands of the naturalist, Enlightenment, revolutionary heirs of the original Protestant heresiarchs. Listen to J. J. Norwich's account of the enslavement—ending in tragic self-enslavement—of a people to a liturgy of meaningless words guaranteed by rejection of the Christocentric liturgy focused on the full message of the Word Incarnate celebrated in Venice in 1797 soon after its takeover by Napoleon:

> It was Sunday, 4 June—Whit Sunday, a day which in former years the Venetians had been accustomed to celebrate with all the pomp and parade appropriate to one of the great feasts of the Church. But this year, 1797, was different. Shocked and stunned to find their city occupied by foreign troops for the first time in its thousand years of history, the people were in no mood for rejoicing. Nevertheless, General Louis Baraguey d'Hilliers, the French commander, had decided that some form of celebration would be desirable, if only to give a much-needed boost to local morale. He had discussed the form it should take with the leaders of the Provisional Municipality, in whom, under his own watchful eye, the supreme political power of the new Republic was now entrusted; and plans had been accordingly drawn up for a *Festa Nazionale*, at which the citizens were

to be given their first full-scale public opportunity to salute their 'Democracy' and the resonant revolutionary principles that inspired it.

Those who, prompted more by curiosity than by enthusiasm, made their way to the Piazza that Sunday morning had grown accustomed to the 'Tree of Liberty'—that huge wooden pole, surmounted by the symbolic scarlet Phrygian cap which bore more than a passing resemblance to the ducal *corno*—rising incongruously from its centre. This they now found to have been supplemented by three large tribunes, ranged along the north, south and west sides. The western one, which was intended for the sixty members of the Municipality, carried the inscription LIBERTY IS PRESERVED BY OBEDIENCE TO THE LAW; the other two, destined for the French and other less distinguished Italian authorities, respectively proclaimed that DAWNING LIBERTY IS PROTECTED BY FORCE OF ARMS and ESTABLISHED LIBERTY LEADS TO UNIVERSAL PEACE. The Piazzetta was similarly bedecked, with a banner in praise of Bonaparte stretched between the two columns by the Molo, one of which was draped in black in memory of those brave Frenchmen who had perished victims of the Venetian aristocracy....

After Baraguey d'Hilliers and the Municipality had taken their places, the bands began to play—there were four of them, disposed at intervals around the Piazza, comprising a total of well over 300 musicians—and the procession began. First came a group of Italian soldiers, followed by two small children carrying lighted torches and another banner with the words GROW UP, HOPE OF THE FATHERLAND. Behind them marched a betrothed couple (DEMOCRATIC FECUNDITY) and finally an aged pair staggering under the weight of agricultural implements, bearing words 'referring to their advanced age, at which time liberty was instituted'.

The procession over, the President of the Municipality advanced to the Tree of Liberty, where, after a brief ceremony in the Basilica, he proceeded to the most dramatic business of the day: the symbolic burning of a *corno* and other emblems of ducal dignity (all obligingly provided for the purpose by Lodovico Manin [the last doge] himself) and a copy of the Golden Book [of Venetian aristocrats]. He and his fellow-*municipalisti*, together with the General and the senior members of his staff, then led off the dancing round the Liberty Tree, while the guns fired repeated salutes, the church bells rang and the bands played *La Carmagnole*. The celebrations ended with a gala performance of opera at the Fenice Theatre, completed less than five years before.

This was the level to which Venice had sunk within a month of the Republic's end—the level of tasteless allegory and those empty, flatulent slogans so beloved of totalitarian governments of today: a demoralization so complete as to allow her citizens, many of whom had been crying '*Viva San Marco!*' beneath the windows of the Great Council as it met for the last time, to stand by and applaud while all their proud past was symbolically consigned to the flames.[2]

Long live "the music of the harmony the spheres" and the liturgy of the Holy Mass that faces God in its prayer encouraging the completion of the Unfinished Symphony! Down with the "thud" of the liturgy of Modernity!

2   John Julius Norwich, *A History of Venice* (New York: Alfred A. Knopf, 1982), 632–633.

ABOUT THE AUTHOR

John C. Rao obtained his doctorate in Modern European History from Oxford University in 1977. He worked in 1978–1979 as Eastern Director of the Intercollegiate Studies Institute in Bryn Mawr, PA, and was Associate Professor of European History at St. John's University in New York City from 1979 to 2021. Dr. Rao is also director of the Roman Forum, a Catholic cultural organization founded by the late Professor Dietrich von Hildebrand in 1968. He writes for numerous French, German, Spanish and Italian journals. Perhaps the most important of his works are *Americanism and the Collapse of the Church in the United States* (Roman Forum Press, 1995), *Black Legends and the Light of the World* (Remnant Press, 2012), *Removing the Blindfold* (Angelus Press, 2014), a discussion of Catholics rediscovering their own heritage in the post-French revolutionary era, and *A Centenary Meditation on a Quest for "Purification" Gone Mad* (Arouca Press, 2019). He has also written a companion volume to his collected works, *The Unrepentant Catholic's Cautionary Calendar* (Arouca Press, 2022).